THE ACCIDENTAL PLAYGROUND

THE ACCIDENTAL PLAYGROUND

PLAYGROUND

BROOKLYN WATERFRONT NARRATIVES OF THE UNDESIGNED AND UNPLANNED

DANIEL CAMPO

EMPIRE STATE EDITIONS   AN IMPRINT OF **FORDHAM UNIVERSITY PRESS** | **NEW YORK** | **2013**

Fordham University Press has no responsibility for the persistence or accuracy of URLs for external or third-party Internet websites referred to in this publication and does not guarantee that any content on such websites is, or will remain, accurate or appropriate.

Fordham University Press also publishes its books in a variety of electronic formats. Some content that appears in print may not be available in electronic books.

Library of Congress Cataloging-in-Publication Data

Campo, Daniel.
 The accidental playground : Brooklyn waterfront narratives of the undesigned and unplanned / Daniel Campo.
    pages cm
 Summary: "With its detail, depth, compassion and vision Campo's work makes an invaluable contribution to the growing literature on the unplanned and the undesigned spaces and activities in cities today. Highly illustrated and artfully researched, the book will draw readers into a unique space in one of New York City's most popular boroughs" — Provided by publisher.
 Includes bibliographical references and index.
 ISBN 978-0-8232-5186-5 (pbk.)
 1. Recreation—New York (State)—Brooklyn. 2. Communities—New York (State)—Brooklyn. 3. Waste lands—New York (State)—Brooklyn—Recreational use. 4. Waterfronts—New York (State)—Brooklyn—Recreational use. 5. Brooklyn Eastern District Terminal. I. Title.
 HT281.C36 2013
 307.09747'23—dc23
                        2013016262

Printed in the United States of America
15 14 13   5 4 3 2 1
First edition

In loving memory of my mother, Seena Campo,

and for my father, Vincent Campo

CONTENTS

Greenpoint and Williamsburg. (Map by Megan Griffith and Daniel Campo, 2013.)

THE ACCIDENTAL PLAYGROUND

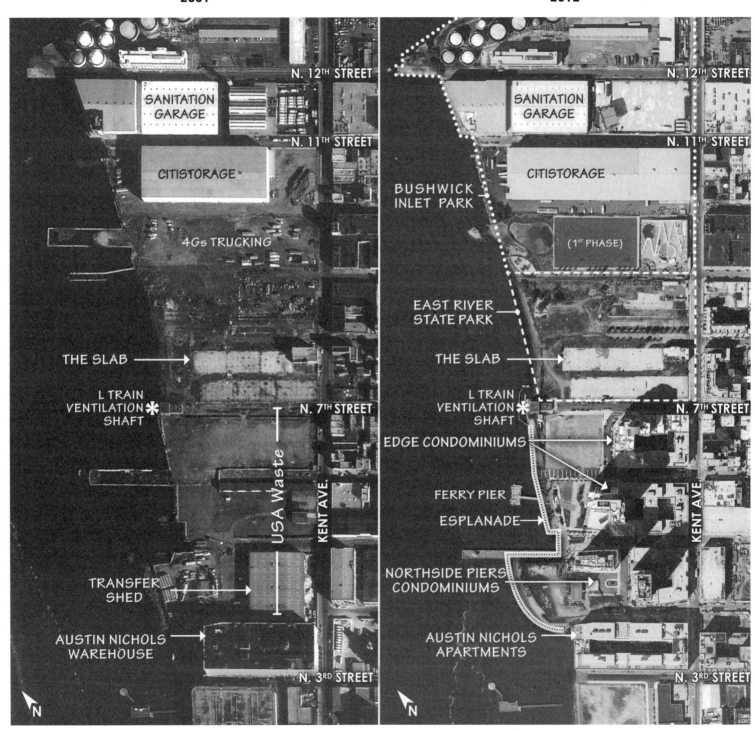

2001

2012

N. 12TH STREET

SANITATION GARAGE

N. 11TH STREET

CITISTORAGE

4Gs TRUCKING

THE SLAB

L TRAIN VENTILATION SHAFT ✳

N. 7TH STREET

USA Waste

KENT AVE.

TRANSFER SHED

AUSTIN NICHOLS WAREHOUSE

N. 3RD STREET

N

N. 12TH STREET

SANITATION GARAGE

N. 11TH STREET

CITISTORAGE

BUSHWICK INLET PARK

(1ST PHASE)

EAST RIVER STATE PARK

THE SLAB

L TRAIN VENTILATION SHAFT ✳

N. 7TH STREET

EDGE CONDOMINIUMS

FERRY PIER

ESPLANADE

NORTHSIDE PIERS CONDOMINIUMS

KENT AVE.

AUSTIN NICHOLS APARTMENTS

N. 3RD STREET

N

The former Brooklyn Eastern District Terminal and Northside waterfront. (Graphic by Megan Griffith using Google Earth satellite images.)

PROLOGUE

ON JUNE 13, 2000, New York Governor George Pataki announced that the state had agreed to purchase seven acres of waterfront property in the Williamsburg section of Brooklyn, where it would build New York's 160th state park. With its stunning views of midtown Manhattan, the property was part of a vacant waterfront railroad yard on Williamsburg's Northside known as the Brooklyn Eastern District Terminal or BEDT. Closed in 1983, the yard was for more than a century where freight cars were pulled off of and pushed onto barges, connecting Williamsburg factories, refineries, and warehouses with similar terminals on the New Jersey side of the harbor. With its tracks pulled up, freight houses demolished, and finger piers falling rapidly into the river, the decaying terminal was ripe for reclaiming. "By converting this underused site into a recreational opportunity for the community," the governor proclaimed, "we are taking one more step toward re-connecting residents and visitors with one of New York State's most important waterfront resources."[1]

BEDT was long thought of as an ideal site for a park in a neighborhood starved for parks and waterfront access. Two years earlier, at the urging of Brooklyn State Assemblyman Joseph Lentol and a coalition of local advocacy groups, the governor had placed the terminal on the property acquisition list of the state's Open Space Conservation Plan, which would make it eligible for purchase using the Environmental Protection Fund, a bond referendum approved by the voters of New York state in 1996. The governor had allocated $10 million from the fund for the terminal's redevelopment, but purchase alone would cost $8.3 million, setting a record for a state parks land purchase on a per-acre basis and leaving little money for the planning, design, and construction of the park itself. But the governor had a solution. Behind the scenes, the Trust for Public Land, a national land conservancy group, had been working for two years with officials from the state Office of Parks, Recreation and Historic Preservation and Williamsburg advocates to identify a partner who could serve to defray the development costs and act as co-steward of the site. The Trust had connected these parties with New York University, which desperately sought a place to build practice and competition sports fields for its NCAA athletic teams. The north edge of the institution's sprawling Manhattan campus was just three stops and a short walk to the waterfront via the L train subway, which ran underneath the edge of the future park en route to its first stop in Brooklyn at Bedford Avenue. NYU would pay for most of the development costs and maintain and staff the park in exchange for sharing the planned sports facilities with local community groups.

For the long-aggrieved residents of Williamsburg and adjacent Greenpoint, the announcement of the purchase was, in spite of the compromise of their having to share the future park with the university, a momentous occasion. For more than a decade, residents in these neighborhoods had fought to reclaim their waterfront from a variety of interests, including industrial landowners, speculators, and city agencies. Bordered by water on three sides, Community District #1 (comprising Williamsburg and Greenpoint) had only one official waterfront park, which was less than an acre in size. And while most public streets terminated at the waterfront, the ends of these rights-of-way had been mostly appropriated by adjacent property owners and businesses, denying residents of all but a glimpse of the water, often from hundreds of feet inland.

The irony of being denied access to the water was downright cruel. The decline of shipping and waterfront industries beginning in the mid–twentieth century had robbed these working-class neighborhoods of jobs and wealth. But even after industry had left, residents found that their waterfront was often less accessible than before, with port properties being gobbled up by waste transfer stations, recycling and scrap yards, truck terminals and warehouses, parking lots and equipment storage yards, gas-powered electric generating stations, and speculators who sat on several large vacant and lightly used properties. These uses added to the waterfront's existing petroleum, gas, and chemical terminals, a massive sewage treatment plant, a multi-block lumber yard, and the waterfront's sole remaining large-scale manufacturing facility, the Amstar (or Domino) Sugar Refinery, about one-half mile south of the planned park site. (Greenpoint's Newtown Creek waterfront was also the site of a 17-million-gallon underground oil spill, discovered in 1978, more than eight million gallons of which were still believed to be underground by 2007.[2]) Much like the dearth of waterfront access and recreation sites, the district also lacked traditional inland parks. By 2000, advocates had calculated that the district had only 0.57 acres of parks per 1,000 residents, ranking 48th out of the city's 59 community districts, and represented less than a third of the park space–to–population ratio of Brooklyn as a whole.[3]

Williamsburg residents had long dreamed of a waterfront park at the terminal. Many had participated over the preceding decade in planning meetings and workshops dedicated to reimagining the water's edge and establishing a larger vision that would guide its eventual redevelopment. Those exercises informed several plans, including a 1990 New York City Parks Council report, the 1995 Hunter College planning studio report (to which I was one of several contributors), and the neighborhood's 1998 community-based waterfront plan, written by local advocates with technical assistance from the city's Department of City Planning (approved by the City Planning Commission in 2001).[4] While the plans all envisioned waterfront parks for part or all of the terminal site (and at other points along the district's waterfront), implementation of these recommendations remained unrealized. At the same time that residents and advocacy groups were working on plans to reclaim the water's edge, more powerful actors were advancing a very different vision for this same waterfront. In 1987, New Jersey–based Nekboh Recycling began operating a waste transfer station on the southernmost block of the sprawling twenty-two-acre BEDT property. Seemingly immune to the growing neighborhood opposition, the company applied for additional permits and expanded its operation across a larger portion of the terminal.

By 1996, the resident activists had all but defeated Nekboh, whose president had run afoul of the law in multiple ways. But after its Kent Avenue station was shut down, the operation was quickly assumed by USA Waste of Houston, Texas, which, like Nekboh before it, wanted to enlarge the transfer station and expand the types of waste it could handle. USA Waste's expansion plan was backed by a powerful coalition of interests that by 1996 included Mayor Rudolph Giuliani, who saw the former rail yard as an ideal place to create a massive garbage processing facility. As part of the mayor's commitment to close Fresh Kills Landfill in Staten Island, the terminal was to be a one of only a few large transfer points for solid waste for the entire city. Accordingly, BEDT was to receive more than 5,300 tons a day of residential and commercial waste, which would be compacted and consolidated on site before being sent from the waterfront to out-of-state landfills by a combination of truck, barge, and rail. Vociferous neighborhood opposition ultimately played a significant role in the defeat of the mayor's plan for the Williamsburg waterfront, enabling the state's park plan to move forward.

While local residents, advocates, and their elected leaders rejoiced in June 2000 in the news of the planned property purchase, few at that moment or in the months ahead could have predicted that it would take the state another seven years before the waterfront park opened. Nor could they have predicted that the final park design would feature neither the sports fields nor the public promenade the governor had promised. Seven years later, state officials opted for a "soft opening" of the delayed waterfront park, which did not yet have a name. On the Saturday morning of Memorial Day weekend 2007, the park was opened without ceremony and without local dignitaries on hand. Most of the dozens of visitors on that first day had found out about the new park by serendipitously walking past the open gates. Even local elected officials and the neighborhood organizations that had been working with the state on the park's development found out only a few days earlier, when they received a faxed announcement.

One could excuse State Parks for forgoing the fanfare and obligatory first-day ribbon-cutting for the opening of what would eventually be given the name East River State Park, or ERSP.[5] While the views could not be beat, the seven-acre park was actually more of a park-in-progress—nearly bare of the trees, plantings, lawns, paved paths, benches, and play areas typically found in urban parks. In the eyes of some locals, over the course of seven years State Parks had done little more than clear the future park its trash and debris and install an iron fence around the perimeter of the property. (Local dissatisfaction only grew over the course of the park's first year, when the gate in that fence seemed closed more than it was open.) In the nine years since the terminal had been placed on the acquisition list in 1998, State Parks had indeed had a bumpy time developing ERSP. The park's development was compromised by a relatively stingy development budget of less than $2 million, a state budget freeze and staffing issues, the failed partnership with NYU, and State Parks' inaction as it waited to hear which city would be selected as the site of the 2012 Olympic Games, which was announced by the International Olympic Committee in 2005. (New York's ultimately unsuccessful bid envisioned the terminal enlarged with additional property purchases as the Olympic Aquatics Center and beach volleyball venue.) Additionally, on the eve of its long-anticipated opening, a week of severe rainstorms in June 2006 ruined the fledgling grass cover and landscaping, setting back the park's actual opening by nearly one year.

This was also State Parks' first foray into the Greenpoint and Williamsburg area of Brooklyn. Project staff in New York City and at its headquarters in Albany were largely unprepared for the challenges of development in one of the city's most contentious community districts. While well intentioned, their top-down project management style did not endear them to many of the locals, whose experience with environmental and development issues left them with a healthy sense of distrust of government agents. Many of the residents who were involved in the planning of the park had also spent a decade working on the city-sponsored community blueprint for their waterfront and thus expected a more collaborative approach to public development projects.[6]

While not all local residents were happy with the results, these missteps, delays, and unfortunate circumstances forced State Parks to be more resourceful with the limited resources available to them. The novel park they created at the terminal did not transform the existing waterfront as much as clean it up and smooth out its rough edges. It made use of remaining building foundations and retaining walls with only modest shaping of the landscape. It was an "in place" park whose most prominent feature, aside from the Manhattan views, were two long, gently sloping concrete foundations upon which warehouses once stood, and the accidental beach that stretched the length of the site. The smooth concrete surfaces of these "slabs," as they were called by locals and State Parks, were ideal for any number of events, activities, and programs. ERSP's beach was the product of decades of erosion and neglect of the concrete seawall. Undergirding the concrete and much of the ground inland were wood beams that were being eaten away by marine borers, the crustaceans and worms that have flourished in the East River as it has become cleaner over the past several decades. This not very stable beach also came studded with rocks, concrete chunks, bricks, debris, and the aforementioned wood beams (all of which had been used as fill during the nineteenth and twentieth centuries) and occasional landed objects of flotsam. In spite of State Parks' efforts to slow erosion and keep the beach clear, these materials keep reappearing as the shore gradually recedes. Nature was reasserting itself, slowly claiming ever-greater portions of the shore whose preindustrial extent was well inland from where it is in 2013 (and even farther from where it was twenty years earlier), and incrementally revealing layers of New York's long-buried past. Watching this process could be considered part of the charm of this unusual park, but many locals are less than happy as Williamsburg's only sizable and fully public waterfront park slowly shrinks in size.

The long struggle of Williamsburg residents to reclaim their waterfront from trash haulers, government agents, and developers who wanted to build multiplex cinemas, big-box stores, a large power plant, or residential high-rises and then build a park to serve multiple and sometimes conflicting constituencies on this same swath of the East River is a compelling story. It's filled with underdog heroes and seemingly omnipotent villains, successes and failures, opportune alliances and difficult compromises forged out of limited opportunities, and it balances critical losses of foresight with making the most of accidental circumstance. There are surely lessons here for planners, architects, advocates, developers, elected leaders, and public policy experts. But this is only part of the story of the Williamsburg waterfront and the redevelopment of BEDT. There is another part of this story—the untold history of this same waterfront over the same years. It is a radically different tale—one that might easily be forgotten as the waterfront continues to evolve and Williamsburg residents and organizations refocus their advocacy around gentrification, displacement, and affordability rather than trash and environmental hazards.

Around the same time that New York state began to contemplate the purchase of the terminal, I too became interested in this unique waterfront site. In 1999 and 2000, elected officials and their appointees met with the Trust for Public Land and NYU and negotiated with the property's owner, who only a year earlier had purchased the four-block north portion of BEDT for less than the cost he would eventually charge the state for half of that property. When Governor Pataki announced the purchase of the park site in June 2000 (the actual purchase of the terminal by the Trust on behalf of the state did not occur until December; State Parks assumed title in January 2001), I was spending long afternoons with people at the terminal itself who cared little about what was going on in Albany or at City Hall. Rather than wait for the state to purchase BEDT and develop a formal park, they had taken to the waterfront in its raw form—garbage, weeds, and broken glass be damned—and created their own park experience.

In fact, BEDT had long been an unofficial neighborhood park. With its stunning westerly views of Manhattan, it was *the* place to watch the sunset or enjoy a picnic in the rough. It was "the Brooklyn Riviera," as some of the locals called it. Attracting dog walkers, picnickers, anglers, musicians and performers looking for practice space and audiences; the middle-aged men of the neighborhood who gathered to drink, barbecue, and shoot the breeze; the Polish immigrants who played cards over folding tables while drinking from large bottles of Polish beer; neighborhood teens with nothing much else to do; and those who came with their cameras to get *that* shot of the skyline, the terminal was well utilized on weekends, with visitors swelling to one hundred or more in the late afternoon. The daily visits of people walking their dogs or fishing, and the presence of a small number of people who lived in tents or shacks, ensured that there were almost always a few people there, even in cold weather.

Of course, those who did not know about it or were unwilling to explore the mostly industrial back streets adjacent to the North Brooklyn waterfront would have missed this informal park entirely. And many did, even some who lived nearby. The consensus was that the terminal was vacant and had been vacant since the railroad yard closed in 1983. Accordingly, city planners, property developers, and elected officials held that the terminal's value lay *only* in its potential for the future use rather than in its informal present use. Many of the locals thought of it as a marginal, derelict, and decaying site that attracted illegal or undesirable acts and actors. "It's an eyesore," one resident activist told me. "It's not safe." And in many respects she was correct. BEDT was a decaying relic, neither safe nor clean. It was not attractive and was nothing like a real city park. For some residents, it also provided a stark reminder of both the decline of the neighborhood and the city's unwillingness to do anything to improve it. Since the yard closed, these residents understood the uses of the terminal, both legal and illegal, as mostly about throwing things out or activities that would have been considered objectionable in more prominent locations: garbage transfer and sorting, equipment and vehicle storage, prostitution, illicit and IV drug use, chop shops for stolen vehicles, illegal dumping, vandalism, unlicensed parties, and homeless encampments. Even as these activities became less frequent over the course of the 1990s, many locals remained wary. The waterfront had potential, they claimed, but for now it was a garbage dump and a dangerous place where people did illegal things.

When I worked at the Brooklyn Office of the New York City Department of City Planning in the late 1990s, the terminal was "Subarea 7" of a larger zoning study the department had undertaken in support of the district's community-based planning efforts. The twenty-two subareas, many on or near the waterfront, were all underutilized tracts zoned for manufacturing. But unlike some of the other subareas, the department took no action on Subarea 7 during the 1990s. Rezoning would have been contradictory to Mayor Giuliani's vision of garbage transfer and thus required retention of the terminal's manufacturing zoning that allowed for waste-handling uses. But things would change with the election of Michael Bloomberg in 2001. The new mayor's approach to planning emphasized private-sector real estate development as not merely a tool for neighborhood revitalization and broader economic development but as a cure for most urban ills. Largely freed of the bad blood between local residents and the previous administration but also any commitment to honor the decade-in-the-making community plan that was approved by the City Council just a month after Bloomberg's election in 2001, the administration and its planning department (of which I was no longer a part) again re-envisioned the North Brooklyn waterfront. By 2003, this mostly vacant edge with its million-dollar views of Manhattan represented perhaps the best opportunity for dense, large-scale residential development on open tracts of land near the core of the city. In the adjacent Northside of Williamsburg, perhaps the hottest neighborhood in Brooklyn, development interest was already well stoked. All the waterfront needed was a zoning change to permit residential development.

When I left the department in September 1999 to pursue a doctorate in city planning at the University of Pennsylvania, I was freed of my employer's top-down, political-economy approach that called for redevelopment consistent with the "highest and best use" or exchange for political benefit.[7] I was also freed of the conventions of advocacy planning, which stressed process and mandated that the future use of the terminal be determined through shared decision making and include a wide array of local stakeholders.[8] While these theories were about the future, my evolving perspective focused on BEDT's more common and imperfect use in the present. With my feet firmly planted on the terminal, I was able to see past the vacancy depicted by property maps, satellite images, tax records, and site photos. Amid the ruins, garbage, and weeds, I discovered a vital and well-loved place, offering something unique to local residents and many who had traveled from much farther away.

The terminal was a place where people had seized the moment, appropriating space for a variety of uses, leisure-based and otherwise. It was an inadvertent experiment in anarchy created by the uncoordinated actions of many diverse and occasionally conflicting actors. By 2000, I began my own study of this waterfront and its people, attempting to understand why so many came here and what they were looking for on this vacant swath of the East River. I also wondered how a place like this could provide inspiration and guidance for formal urban design and development, the kind that we facilitated at the Department of City Planning. It seemed like a stretch, but surely even the most conventional of development processes could learn something from the vernacular. So this book is a result of these efforts—my time spent on the waterfront exploring this accidental playground and the people who appropriated and adapted it while others fought or planned for a more glorious, profitable, or equitable future for this same decaying edge. The chapters that follow tell the stories of some of the people who appropriated this waterfront in its last moments of dormancy, as it awaited a transformation consistent with the rapid physical and social changes occurring in New York at the dawn of the twenty-first century. These narratives offer a radically different vision for parks and public spaces in a crowded and highly contested metropolis, one that may inspire more enlightened practices in the design and development communities and provide ordinary urban residents with the hope that these practices will be more common and less accidental.

CHAPTER 1

DISCOVERING AND ENGAGING A VACATED WATERFRONT

FROM THE END OF THE PIER at North 6th Street, I looked back toward the landmass of Williamsburg, Brooklyn. A section below me was collapsed, forming an irregularly shaped chasm that stretched across the width of the pier. In a shallow puddle at the bottom of this depression lay a series of well-eroded wood beams in layers both along and perpendicular to the length of the pier—the wood cribbing that had provided the pier's foundation. Several of these beams had been dislodged from the supportive positions in which they were laid untold years earlier. A carpet of weeds covered those chunks of dirt and gravel that remained in place and formed the top of the pier, but it was only a matter of time before these sections would also collapse. Less than twenty years earlier this pier, like others to the north and south, supported strings of railroad cars and their freight, which were pulled by locomotives off of (or pushed onto) "car-floats"—specialized barges equipped with railroad tracks—that had been towed across the harbor. (Within two years, this pier would be impassable, just a few small sections of concrete surrounded by water.)

From the only somewhat sturdy part of the pier, its concrete edges, a line of four or five men cast their lines and tended their traps. This was a favored spot for fishing, particularly when striped bass or the blues were running, and the areas around the edges of the pier were reliable places for crabbing. By late afternoon when conditions were good,

BEDT's rotting finger piers were popular spots for fishing (2000).

I would see people on this pier and a similar one to the north with large buckets full of blue crabs, which were usually caught with a trap baited with a chicken neck or wing. Beyond the pier was the southern part of the former rail yard, now a tightly packed mass of garbage containers of varying shapes and sizes. Larger dumpsters sat in tight rows perpendicular to the shore with smaller containers piled inside of them, many standing upright on their smallest sides. Weeds had aggressively claimed every sliver of space in between these containers while also claiming their tops, many of which still contained construction and demolition debris taken from some long-ago building site. Covering much of two waterfront blocks, this dumpster landscape was owned by national garbage carting giant USA Waste, which operated a controversial transfer station on an adjacent block to the south. USA Waste's large corrugated metal transfer shed was idle at that time on a Saturday afternoon.

To the north was the one-story ventilation shaft of the L-train subway tunnel, and beyond that, more piers, some in worse condition than the one upon which I was standing. Between the ventilation shaft and the pier at the end of

DISCOVERING AND ENGAGING A VACATED WATERFRONT

North 10th Street stretched a beach and above it an open three-block expanse of the former rail yard. I could see people arrayed across this beach on this hot day in June 2000. I had in fact just come from this area, where dozens of people were enjoying a leisurely afternoon by the waterfront. With its views and somewhat sandy edge, some of the locals called this spot "the Brooklyn Riviera."

I carefully made my way back to shore, following the edge of the pier, hopping over a few gaps in the concrete, and annoying one of the people fishing when I gingerly stepped over him and his stuff. Once on solid land again, I walked along the seawall back toward the ventilation shaft along the line of dumpsters. This colorful landscape of trash containers—many of which were so beat up they themselves had become trash—looked like a sprawling, postindustrial jungle gym that invited exploration and physical exertion. Looking for an appropriate dumpster to scale, I was soon distracted by music and laughter and the smell of lighter fluid. I could see the top of a beach umbrella over a wall of large concrete blocks.

Finding a seam between the blocks and the dumpsters, I followed the music and entered a small, irregularly shaped clearing perhaps fifteen feet across at its widest point. And there they were: seven men of the neighborhood partying amid the grimy and rusting dumpsters, piles of worn truck tires, old scaffold frames, demolition debris, garbage, and weeds. Sitting around a barbecue on coolers, folding chairs, or piles of scrap, clutching beer cans and cigarettes, the men were engaged in loud conversation that competed with the volume of the music. A boom box had been placed inside a container that was turned on its side, which had the effect of directing the sound back toward the clearing. Two of the men had come by bicycle, and their shiny late-model bikes stood out against the rust and garbage around them. An occasional waft of rotting garbage blew over the clearing, but the men did not seem to mind.

Social space created amid the refuse and junk of USA Waste's portion of the terminal property (2000).

Only somewhat surprised by my sudden presence, they initially ignored me until I pulled forward the camera that was strapped across my chest. This prompted some profanity-laced questions and laughter. I quickly surmised that a few of these men were quite drunk, which perhaps accounted for the verbal indignities and rude gestures I was forced to endure. But the ribbing they gave me was not particularly mean-spirited, and talking to them for a while—even as a few shouted back at me and one another—I gained a bit of credibility, which enabled me to take a few photographs of them and their unlikely hangout. Given their level of inebriation, I may have been forgotten as soon as I left, but I would see and get to know a few of these men a little better over the next two years.

This was *their* little weekend spot on the waterfront. Relatively inaccessible and cloaked by the abundant waste around it, it functioned as an open air club house where they could relax, do whatever they wanted, and not worry about being hassled by the police. The owners of the property, USA Waste, one of the men said, knew of but cared little about their presence. Likewise, the men seemed unperturbed that their social space was on the grounds of an often smelly and noisy garbage transfer operation. And while they enjoyed the privacy, if they stood they could see over the concrete blocks and take in the Twin Towers, which at that moment took on a silvery hue against the white haze around them. The similar vista to the northeast offered a dramatic and unobstructed view of the Empire State Building.

Appropriated Space

These men were a part of the rich social tapestry that spread across a waterfront that others had deemed vacant. Like many residents from the adjacent Williamsburg and Greenpoint neighborhoods—as well as some from farther away—they had appropriated space on a site that was awaiting a transformation. Short on parks and possessing only one small waterfront park, these residents had grown tired of waiting for the city to do something. But rather than call their City Councilperson, the local community (planning) board, or the mayor, they simply took to the waterfront with their beach towels and blankets, folding chairs and card tables, picnic baskets and coolers, fishing rods and sports equipment, art projects and musical instruments, and their dogs. This waterfront—the former Brooklyn Eastern District Terminal (BEDT) marine railroad yard, with its concrete building foundations, track beds, rotting piers, and bits of leftover maritime or railroad infrastructure—was *their* park. Few if any were happy about having to share BEDT with an active waste transfer station, but they did it all the same and by 2000 had been doing so for a number of years. Some had been enjoying this spot since the yard had closed in 1983; a few, even earlier.

By the turn of the millennium, BEDT had evolved into a well-used and fairly safe do-it-yourself recreation site where local residents did the things people do when they go to parks. Like the officially designated, formally designed, and properly maintained waterfront parks throughout the city, it was a place where people went to relax, recreate, social-ize, enjoy the water and the views, occasionally make new friends, and take in and savor the spectacle of life. It served basic recreational needs of some but not all local residents—including a place to experience beauty, solitude, play, or the company of others—but was no mere substitute for a city park. People could and did do what they wanted, whether it was to swim in the river, have a barbecue, build a skatepark, practice loud music, play with fire, or create art out of found rubble. One regular visitor held his bachelor party here. It was a place without explicit rules: You did what you wanted, but with the understanding that others would do the same. So the same dynamic that enabled recreators to indulge in sunset picnics while sipping wine allowed home-less people to build and live in encampments less than one hundred feet away. It also allowed for drug use, sexually charged activity, aggressive panhandling, and a number of other illegal or uncivil acts. But the experience of most was peaceful. In 2000 and 2001, weekends brought hundreds of people to BEDT, and the sheer size of these crowds provided a strong disincentive for criminal, threatening, or uncivil behavior.

Much like the lack of explicit rules and security, BEDT offered recreators none of the design features, landscap-ing, or programs offered in city parks. It was "vernacular" in that there had been no professional planning, design, or maintenance.[1] Nothing was provided: no paths, benches,

For decades, rail fans visited the terminal to see the active workings of the transfer yard and one of the only U.S. railroads that still employed steam locomotives. (Photo courtesy of Philip Goldstein, ca. late 1950s.)

BEDT was among the most prominent of the many rail-marine freight transfer facilities that once lined New York's waterfront. (Photo by Matt Herson, 1976, courtesy of Thomas Flagg and Morning Sun Books..)

plantings, or nature trails; no baseball diamonds or basketball or tennis courts; no grassy lawns or meadows; no rebuilt recreation piers or waterside esplanades; no comfort stations. Also no movie nights, concert series, corporate sponsorships, or fundraising campaigns. And most of all, no security to provide for public safety. BEDT was also vernacular in that its physical condition or "design" was often created, modified, or shaped by the immediate ways people were using it at any given time.[2] Intuitively responding to the lack of constraint and the empowering dynamic of "make your own environment," many people engaged the landscape in a way that was impossible or prohibited elsewhere. They built, altered, and occupied the various leftover spaces of this waterfront to suit a variety of needs and whims: play spaces, social spaces, creative spaces, event spaces, practice spaces, meditative spaces, and spaces of exploration. But most of these appropriated environments lasted only as long as they were occupied; the next set of recreators would be just as free to reshape, rebuild, or destroy.

A History of Informal Recreation on a Historic Waterfront

Time, in both the cyclical and linear senses and in the context of both the immediate and longer term, shaped the experience of those who spent time on this waterfront. The terminal had, in fact, been an informal recreation site for many decades. Untold numbers of area children (and sometimes their parents) played around the edges of the yard and on its piers during its active days. Some even swam in the river. Aside from the neighborhood kids, it also attracted railroad enthusiasts from nearby and far away who came to see the workings of a railroad that traveled no greater distance than a half-mile. They came to watch tugboats bring car floats to these piers where freight-laden cars were pulled across the threshold by ancient-looking steam locomotives, before their cargoes were unloaded into the terminal's freight houses or the warehouses and factories just beyond the yard. Rail fans were particularly delighted with the locomotives, which were all steam-powered for more than a half-century after the introduction of diesel engines (until 1963), making it nearly the last railroad in the country to make this transition.[3]

The terminal was in fact a significant place in history, where in 1876, when it was known as "Palmer's Dock," Brooklyn's first "float bridge" was installed to facilitate the smooth transfer of freight cars to track-covered piers.[4] In the decades that followed, the construction of hundreds of these transfer bridges and railroad piers formed a "water belt line"—the network of freight facilities that lined the waterfronts of all five of the city's boroughs and the New Jersey side of the harbor.[5] The BEDT Railroad was also long owned by the sugar scions, the Havemeyer family, who built and operated the area's massive refineries that made Brooklyn the sugar refining capital of the United States for three-quarters of a century.[6] While the cargo rarely included sugar in its last decades, after 1964 most of the bulk flour in the region was delivered here, before its distribution to bakeries and macaroni factories across the New York area (the terminal also received regular shipments of coal, lumber, newsprint, and metal scrap).[7] The people who came to watch the railroad were preserving the collective memory of Brooklyn's working waterfront; their written accounts, photographs, train rosters and schedules, and related ephemera can now be found on rail fans' web sites.[8] (Enthusiasts have also preserved a few of BEDT's steam locomotives, which are now housed in railroad museums across the eastern United States.)

The working waterfront's long history figured prominently in the recreational endeavors of those who appropriated it. Almost two decades removed from the demise of the working yard, this history was still quietly present in building foundations, track beds, parts of cobblestone streets, sinking finger piers, and the eroded seawall. Without this

BEDT provided visitors with a plethora of historic materials and objects ideal for manipulation and play (2002).

bulkhead, historic layers of previously concealed landfill comprising wood, stone, bricks, and gravel were now exposed. Some enjoyed probing the exposed layers and bits of infrastructure, imagining what used to be. Others enjoyed the site in its current form and cared not about the past nor future. A few looked ahead to a time when there might be real ball fields, groves of trees, new recreation piers, and a marina. In their minds, the present state of the terminal was about making do.

While opinion was far from uniform, many who considered the future of this waterfront were wary of grand plans and those who might make them. They sensed that BEDT was unlikely to remain in a state of colonized "benign neglect." Few fully understood the waterfront's complicated redevelopment politics, but most were aware that decisions being made by some unknown entity or person would eventually put an end to the "found" conditions they were quietly enjoying. How could such a prime spot in a fashionable Brooklyn neighborhood with all of its incredible views still be undeveloped? They understood implicitly that theirs was a temporary experience, one that could end at any moment. "Enjoy it while you can," advised one visitor. Another said he enjoyed the terminal's "anarchic flavor" but was "surprised it has lasted as long as it has." This feeling of uncertainty and ephemerality and sense of the impending end provided exhilaration and encouraged recreators to savor their experiences.

Living in the Moment at the "Unpark"

A significant part of this waterfront experience was the element of surprise. Happenstance and variable conditions meant that few visits would be consistent and that surprises frequently awaited, though not all of them pleasing. At some moments, the terminal was full of people doing interesting or boisterous things; it felt like a big party.

At other moments, it was quiet or desolate. Some days visitors were surprised to find a fantastic art installation or a seemingly impromptu musical performance. But other days brought uncomfortable encounters with marginal people, broken glass, or rodents. On a few days, recreators were denied entry by police stationed at the foot of North 7th Street, which was for a while the terminal's most prominent entry point. Few needed explanation and usually none was offered. The mere sight of the police car from afar sent most recreators in another direction. BEDT also had a somewhat regular pattern of temporal rhythms, changing personality from day to night, weekday to weekend, warm weather to cold. While few lingered long after sundown, others found the darkness to be magical or liberating. Late on Friday and Saturday nights, the terminal occasionally attracted partiers who after several hours in the Northside's bars ambled down to the waterfront to view the illuminated skyline and, if it was warm, enjoy the breezes coming off the river.

The seemingly arbitrary nature of when BEDT was accessible and when it wasn't reinforced a sense of living in the moment and that this moment would pass very soon. This was particularly true in the immediate aftermath of September 11, 2001. The terminal—from which hundreds of people watched the towers burn and in the weeks that followed took in the smoky plume that rose into the sky from the World Trade Center site—quickly evolved into a place of sorrow, remembrance, and respect. The many candles, photographs, works of art, poems, and dedicated objects formed an informal shrine at the edge of the water, encouraging others to visit, remember, and place their own tributes. But within a few weeks, police stepped up patrols and stationed an around-the-clock officer at the end of North 7th Street, with the purpose of keeping people off the waterfront. No one was sure what the official reason was, and the police themselves would not say. Given the unease of the moment, many attributed it to the fear that a terrorist might gain access to and place a bomb within the L-train ventilation shaft. Even at the time, such threats felt unlikely to those who frequented the terminal, and many noted that the shaft itself could be guarded without denying people access to the waterfront. But soon this moment too would pass, and by mid-October people were gathering at the terminal as they seemingly always had.

Security measures taken during the years that followed lacked the atmospheric unease of the fall of 2001 but delivered a similar message that discouraged human activity on the waterfront. The most prominent of these occurred in 2002 when State Parks, owners of this part of the terminal, undertook what they described as a "site cleanup." This mostly entailed using bulldozers to obliterate the thick green landscape and human constructions that had accumulated over the preceding years. Little was actually cleaned up, and giant piles of cleared earth, brush, and scattered debris were simply left in place. These barren hills would soon sprout a new cycle of greenery, and people would indeed return as well. But events like these along with other efforts such as new gates and fencing that were added soon after were part of a longer cycle of give and take, with each attempt to discourage human use building upon the last and ratcheting up the severity of the message. So when people did return, they did so in dwindling numbers. Some had heeded these not-so-subtle messages. And those who did return had an implicit comfort with or appreciation for risk and uncertain conditions.

This joy of living in the moment was intertwined with any number of related emotions that brought people to the terminal. They liked the feeling of being in spaces in which their presence was prohibited or discouraged. It was edge space, secret space, wild space, lost space, found space, outlaw space—a place for trespassing, squatting, and other extralegal activities. It provided a sense of drama and excitement. BEDT was an "unpark," a few frequent visitors said. "People need to feel like they can have a little bit of an adventure, that they can do something that's kind of crazy," one explained. The setting also changed the nature of even common or safe activities, such as watching the sunset. Partaking in this end-of-the-day ritual at the terminal engendered an additional sense of satisfaction given that recreators frequently had to climb through a hole in a fence to do it.

(*Top*) Residents gathered at the terminal to watch the awful spectacle of the September 11, 2001, attacks. (Photo by Theo Coulombe, courtesy of the Trust for Public Land.) After September 11 (*bottom*), the water's edge became a place of collective remembrance and mourning (2001).

Edge conditions, variability, freedom, and the thrill of "breaking the rules" were not the only factors that brought people to BEDT. The raw and seemingly lawless atmosphere was often appealing for very practical reasons. People were seeking out a place to do things that could not be done (or could not easily be done) elsewhere, either by law or logistics, such as skateboarding, practicing the bagpipe, or creating environmental art. These recreational or creative niches were not being served (or adequately served) by traditional parks and public spaces. As one of the "spinners" told me, it was a "perfect place" to practice the fire arts because the abundant concrete surfaces meant little chance of anything catching on fire.

The terminal was also just a nice place to hang out and a good place for a picnic. Some but not all of this was a function of the lack of traditional picnic grounds in the area. The community district's largest recreation space, McCarren Park, was heavily used during the weekend and evenings, and much of its space was designed for active recreation. Even on its quietest days, there was little at McCarren that people would find picturesque. The terminal was quite scenic, though not in the traditional Olmstedian or "splendor of nature" sense. It was a different kind of scenery, one of great contrasts and spectacularity.

It's a "beautiful spot and very peaceful and it makes me feel good," explained a young woman who had come to watch the sunset with her husband, who carried their infant daughter in a sling. The "nonpark status allows us to drink a beer," her husband explained, as they both clutched their beer cans. "And by the way, I'll take my beer with me and put it into a garbage can rather than throw it in the underbrush," he added. Finding an appropriate location to drink a beer or a glass of wine outdoors in a parklike or scenic setting is a challenge for many city residents. New York's "open container laws"—like those of most American cities—prohibit drinking alcoholic beverages in most public spaces. This may not seem onerous to those who have a back yard, terrace, or deck, but many New Yorkers do not have this luxury. And even while enforcement is sometimes lax, drinking in city parks is mostly forbidden. At BEDT, the lack of security

With its sweeping westerly views of the Manhattan skyline, BEDT was a popular place to watch the sunset (2001).

The terminal was an ideal place for the practice of logistically challenging or loud arts (*top*). BEDT's accidental beach (*bottom*) provided both visitors and their dogs with a chance to get their feet wet (2001).

enabled people to indulge, and many did so. For the most part it was not a problem and led to few obvious conflicts.

Other practical concerns figured prominently into the implicit or explicit calculus of BEDT recreators, and not just those of unusual or unwieldy crafts or those seeking to enjoy a beer by the water. The dog walkers, some of the most frequent visitors to the terminal, came so that their dogs could run freely without a leash. For non–dog owners, the city's laws that require canines to be tethered to a leash in most public spaces most of the time make perfect sense. But some dog owners liken it to a form of oppression or cruelty. "Dogs were not meant to be on a leash," one owner declared. Another complained about receiving a $100 ticket for allowing her dog to run off-leash in Mc-Carren Park. Conditions at the terminal, she said, were "just a lot freer." Like other dog owners, she was not overly concerned about hazards like broken glass. The terminal was also where dogs could get into the water. Fetching sticks thrown from the shore, dogs did not seem to care in the least about the less-than-pristine conditions. They eagerly swam out and returned with the sticks in their mouths again and again and again.

Like many other activities, dog walking flourished at BEDT because it was both apart from and connected to the neighborhood in which the owners lived, and there was no enforcement of rules prohibiting it. So the dogs ran free

DISCOVERING AND ENGAGING A VACATED WATERFRONT

while their owners socialized, and their regular presence helped contribute to the perception that BEDT was safe and that it was *okay* to be there. The dog owners were, as a few noted, "pioneers" of the waterfront.

Vernacular Waterfront

Like the joy it brought the dogs, the contact with water was also important to a great number of human recreators. There were of course few other places to be close to the water nearby, even though the Greenpoint and Williamsburg neighborhoods are bordered by water on three sides. The lack of waterfront parks has always been a sore point for area residents, many of whom long viewed the terminal as a logical place for one. But in its more raw form, BEDT was the local beachfront and a point of entry to the water.

New York's ambitious waterfront revitalization program, launched in the early 1990s, had by 2000 resulted in a number of new parks and recreation spaces across all five boroughs.[9] There were new large waterfront parks (completed or under development) at Battery Park City and farther north along the Hudson River in Manhattan, and, just to the north of Greenpoint, a new state park on the "Queens West" waterfront. The city and state were also in the planning and property acquisition stage of the eighty-five-acre Brooklyn Bridge Park, a few miles to the south of the terminal. Even Red Hook, another working-class Brooklyn waterfront neighborhood, had the new Valentino Pier and Park. Its central feature was an impressively long concrete recreation pier that jutted out into Upper New York Bay, offering spectacular views of the Statue of Liberty, lower Manhattan, Governors Island, and the Verrazano Narrows Bridge. Residents sometimes viewed these other neighborhoods with envy and looked forward to the day when they too would have a new waterfront recreation site. But trading the informal "Brooklyn Riviera" for a proper waterfront park would come at a cost: New parks often allowed for only limited access to the water.

Paradoxically, the city's rivers and bays were becoming more *and* less accessible with many completed waterfront revitalization projects. New parks greatly increased the places where one could be at the water's edge, but few afforded recreators the opportunity to touch, play with, or be *in* the water.[10] Some of the new parks were built on sites where there had been informal access previously. And in places where making contact with the water was possible, prohibitions and security constrain potential activities. Aside from ocean and Long Island Sound beaches, the city's waterfront parks do not allow for getting into the water. Safety concerns and New York's traditional approach of building an esplanade along the water's edge put recreators above but out of contact with the water itself: no swimming, no diving, no wading, and no skipping rocks.[11]

BEDT was part of a larger network of vernacular waterfront sites, those places where disinvestment and failed plans left piers rotting, bulkheads crumbling, buildings open to vandals and squatters, and infrastructure disappearing, often being carted off and sold for scrap by enterprising or desperate thieves. Large empty areas immediately adjacent to the waterfront, sometimes hidden behind walls or inside warehouses, also allowed for dirty, noxious, or illegal activities. But these same decaying sites, when appropriated for recreation, often offered intimate contact with the water. Brooklyn until relatively recently had many of these spaces, but BEDT was among the most accessible and prominent, one of only a few that had survived into the twenty-first century in a largely unimproved state.[12] Recreators could still get their feet wet, take a swim, skip rocks, dive off a crumbling pier, launch a kayak, or enjoy the gentle lapping of the water against the shore. They could do it whenever they wanted, as the terminal was never closed (or officially open).

The human need for water goes well beyond the biological. My own study of the vernacular waterfront in New York is consistent with the experience in port cities in every continent, nation, and culture. It suggests that even in the densest or most ruinous of urban settings, people have a visceral need to be near and touch the water and will seek out these opportunities regardless of traditional aesthetic considerations. For some, crumbling urban docks are a reasonable substitute for a pristine beach or mountain stream. And for a few, swimming in the East River was the local equivalent of swimming at Coney Island, the Rockaways, or distant Long Island beaches. A few swam at BEDT, including a middle-aged man who regularly did "laps" between the piers. He said he could not take "all the chlorine and chemicals," crowds, rude behavior, and the great number of people who he believed urinated in city pools. By contrast, he noted, he was essentially swimming in ocean water because the East River is not actually a river but a tidal strait. While swimming here was more invigorating than in the pool, he conceded that the powerful currents made it suitable only for strong swimmers.

Engaging, Altering, and Redefining Urban Nature

Like the water, the other elemental aspects of our earthly condition—the sun, air, and ground, those that we sometimes perceive as lacking in dense urban settings—were in relative abundance at the terminal. People came to experience these elements even if their presence was largely accidental. The open sky, movable earth, and greenness combined with the presence of the water created a robust sense of "nature" and contributed to many "nature experiences." For some visitors it was the equivalent of what others experience in trips to the beach, the mountains, or in suburban back yards. One regular user called the terminal his "oasis" and said all the trees made him feel "human." Another proudly proclaimed that BEDT was evidence that "nature is coming back."

The waterfront also provided a visceral experience, allowing visitors to touch and alter nature without mediation from formal design, planning, maintenance, security, program, or rules. In the 1990s and early 2000s, the ruinous yet pliable conditions allowed some to engage nature in a way that was largely impossible in seemingly more "natural" places such as Central and Prospect parks. Absent the finely manicured and expensively maintained Olmstedian landscapes of these great urban refuges, people could ply the earth and get their hands dirty. This basic human impulse—to shape and reshape, to arrange and rearrange, to destroy and rebuild—is not fully appreciated by architects, planners, and those who build and control the public spaces of American cities. It is nature as action, engagement, and creation; and recreation as "re-creation." We implicitly rely on leisure time and activity to nurture this primordial impulse; it is why many enjoy planting and tending gardens in their spare time. With the exception of community gardens, most urban parks provide few opportunities for the sorts of experiences that appeal to this often-neglected human need.

The creative altering of the natural landscape at BEDT took many forms, including land art; installations and sculpture; humble rearrangement of found objects and junk; graffiti; and street art. Some of this activity was a product of availability: People did things here because they could. But the decaying conditions also excited imaginations and encouraged reclaimative acts and experiments. One artist noted that he chose the terminal for his environmentally themed installation because he thought it could "use a little love." Another noted that he liked its ruinous condition because it reminded him of his own mortality. Some find beauty inspiring; others are inspired by decay. BEDT offered both.

The democratic nature of the terminal also allowed anyone, not just those who were sponsored by a museum, gallery, or university program, to move the earth and place objects together in creative ways. Some sculpted with dirt, wood, concrete chunks, construction and demolition debris, and found objects; others used these same materials to build club houses, social spaces, and improvised play equipment. BEDT presented an infinite number of immediately realizable constructive possibilities. However, while you were free to create, others were equally free to destroy. Most creators understood that their works could be gone the next day and made the most of these conditions. Some even planned for or took satisfaction over the inevitable dismantling or destruction of their work.

The way people "used" BEDT also suggests a more inclusive but problematic aspect of "nature" and one frequently betrayed by how we plan or design for it. This environment was an impossible-to-untangle combination of human constructions and the immutable elements of the earth. It was both "natural" and "urban," and these boundaries were constantly shifting and mixing. At the same time that recreators had reclaimed a waterfront formerly the province of port commerce and industry, the water itself was also making a claim. With evolving water pollution standards mandated by the Clean Water Act and the disappearance of the polluting industries that once lined the shore, New York's waterways were making a remarkable comeback. By 2000 they were cleaner than they had been in at least a century. Officially sanctioned swimming at this location could not be far off, some believed. However, this cleaner water body and the marine boring organisms that were now thriving in it were eating pier and bulkhead foundations, eroding the shoreline and reclaiming areas that had long been landfill. The eroded shore at BEDT formed a well-enjoyed informal beach, but without significant and expensive human intervention the terminal was becoming more water and less park.

Other contradictions abounded. As previously noted, many came to fish, and those who did often ate their catch. But few were aware of or had any apparent concern for state Department of Health guidelines, which advised against eating many species of fish and marine life caught in this section of the Hudson River estuary. For varieties that were safe to eat at all, guidelines usually recommended limiting consumption to one serving a week. The bucketsful of crabs that people caught on the piers were one such species. As bottom feeders, crabs had potentially dangerous levels of PCBs, cadmium, and dioxin and were among those to be consumed infrequently and in limited quantities.[13] But for those of limited means, the crabs and fish they caught were an important source of sustenance and nutrition. For others, some of whom had traveled from other boroughs or the Long Island suburbs to crab off of the terminal's decaying piers, it was a delight to eat one's own freshly caught seafood. One local told me he knew the crabs were safe because he had eaten a big plate of them the night before. He laughed heartily and noted, "I'm still here today, aren't I?"

Additional "natural" aspects of the terminal included the ever-thickening successional landscape. It was intensely appreciated by many visitors, some of whom noted its restorative qualities. But this verdant brush and canopy was made up of largely the invasive species, including Japanese knotweed, fragmites, ailanthus, and purple loose strife,

People came to the North Brooklyn waterfront to escape, discover, reflect, and experience a range of contradictory environmental conditions (2001).

the kind that park managers at Prospect, Central, and other city parks had invested significant time and resources in eliminating. Invasives are persistent, and they crowd out native species. Yet here, these hearty and fast-growing plants provided lots of pleasing green under harsh conditions, and no planting, watering, or "weeding" was necessary. So the nature at BEDT was not that natural, at least not in the conventional sense or in the way parks are typically designed in American cities.[14] One frequent visitor called the terminal "naturally relaxing" but "untainted by everybody's idea of what a relaxing situation should be."

While not of traditional beauty, the terminal's temporary but evolving ecology did support a range of uses and appealed to a variety of people. It also offered space for those who were marginal or who felt marginalized in more structured or planned environments. For some it was a place of last resort. These included the undocumented workers and others who for a variety of reasons were living at BEDT. It also included some of the men I met amid the dumpsters that June. They were part of a larger group of working-class men, most born and raised in Greenpoint or Williamsburg, and a subset of whom were Vietnam veterans. These men came to the waterfront for many reasons: to read and reflect; to drink beer, smoke pot, and barbecue; to enjoy one another's company in relative peace and take in the breezes and the views. But they also came to escape the rapidly changing neighborhood of which they no longer felt fully a part.

Contradiction and "Other" Space

People came to BEDT to pursue both conventional and eclectic endeavors. Some experiences were intentional but others wholly accidental. It was a place for both those seeking action and those looking for peace. Some came for celebration, others out of desperation. But most were drawn to the waterfront for combinations of these multiple and often contradictory reasons. Even those who were unfamiliar with the concepts of juxtaposition and paradox appreciated the contrast of Brooklyn's rotting piers and crumbling seawall with the grandeur of the Manhattan skyline. There were also striking differences among the people who frequented the terminal. Well-heeled new residents of the neighborhood were easy to spot alongside the local working-class men, Polish families, scrappy skateboarders, or the undocumented workers living in the tents and shacks. Sometimes these groups would freely mix, share a conversation or a beer, or kick a soccer ball around; other times they would argue and shout, and in a few cases confrontations escalated into physical fights.

The pairing and intermingling of seemingly contradictory conditions were in large part not just what people happened to find or experience but what they intuitively sought: beauty and decay, the natural and the constructed, the indestructible and the destroyed. Opposing conditions were always side-by-side, shifting, blurring, and in dialogue with each other. BEDT was neither utopia nor dystopia but "heterotopia," a paradoxical combination of both of these imagined states. It was, as Foucault might have reasoned, "other" space.[15] The *Village Voice* recognized the terminal's otherness by awarding it "Best Vacant Lot" in its annual "Best of New York" issue, while identifying it only by vague address ("Kent Avenue between 8th and 11th Streets in Williamsburg").[16] Many regulars also understood the terminal as a unique and meaningful place but could not give it more than a generic name; it was just "the waterfront" or "the river" to them. Even those familiar with the history of this waterfront rarely made reference to the "Brooklyn Eastern District Terminal" or "BEDT."

Planning, Designing, and Governing Public Spaces?

People came to BEDT for many reasons: creation, recreation, relaxation, exploration, self-growth, social engagement, and release. Make your own environment at the water's edge; explore a potentially threatening but compelling place of past and present dimensions; touch the water and experience nature; ply the earth; be spontaneous; be free of social and legal conventions; experience wildness; and, most of all, enjoy the moment. Yet this "unpark" was not necessarily a park for everyone. Plenty of people would prefer the state park that is now on this same waterfront site. Nor does BEDT as it existed in the late 1990s and early 2000s present a simple alternative to the conventional design, development, and governance strategies for parks and public spaces. Many circumstances, some accidental, contributed to the evolution of this dynamic and (by 2000) fairly welcoming, anarchic leisure space, including the Giuliani administration's refusal to consider rezoning the waterfront to facilitate non-industrial uses. This allowed a potentially valuable waterfront property to remain in a state of benign neglect for a few more years. Eventually, actions by both state and city governments and development pressure kindled by the 2005 rezoning led to the demise of the "unpark."

The accidental playground that evolved at BEDT could not have been designed or planned for, and the evolution of similar experiences will likely be unforeseen. However, certain aspects can inform how we build and use public spaces and more broadly impact the allied design and development arts.

Public dissatisfaction with professionally designed and managed environments and the limitations in the ways they can be used or adapted has been growing. While an ever larger chorus of critics has bemoaned contemporary urban building practices, their clarion calls have not greatly affected professional development and governance.[17] At the same time, an array of urban residents in cities across the globe have simply bypassed traditional political mechanisms for reform and those trusted to build urban places. Like the appropriation of the North Brooklyn waterfront that I document, similarly spirited appropriations of urban space and DIY development practices have become increasingly common in North American and European cities. While yet to be embraced by environmental design professionals or by the urban political establishment, these practices are just beginning to be recognized by scholars and critics as an important component of the contemporary and fully modern city.

Documented case studies are growing: street art, art events in unlikely places, guerrilla gardening, urban exploration, critical-mass bike rides, unsanctioned memorials, street vending and night markets, social gathering and ritual in residual spaces, social occupation of parking spaces, provocative street theater, and traditional and emerging forms of political protests. The sheer multitude and variety of these uses occurring in a similarly novel array of appropriated settings occurring at different moments in cyclical time create a matrix in three dimensions that defies easy definition, categorization, or "typologies" (a favorite form of analysis among urban design scholars). Indeed scholars searching for common attributes have often defined such practices by noting what they are *not* rather than by their intrinsic qualities. These places are vital precisely because they stand in opposition to or subvert more dominant space-producing practices.

Scholarly explorations include Karen Franck and Quentin Stevens's examination of "loose space"—the great variety of urban activities often occurring in spaces whose primary function, if one exists at all, has been "loosened" for "leisure, entertainment, self expression or political expression, reflection and social interaction" and "exist outside the world of fixed functions and fixed schedules."[18] Jeffrey Hou's "insurgent public spaces" offer a similar range of activities in appropriated settings, which he argues challenge the "increasingly regulated, privatized and diminished forms of public space" and the "conventional, codified notion" of the production of space.[19] Margaret Crawford delves into the everyday routines of urban life. Her concept of "everyday space" (or, as a practice, "everyday urbanism") stands "in contrast to the carefully planned, officially designated, and often underused public spaces that can be found in most American cities."[20]

I refer to the "everyday" or "insurgent" leisure practices that occurred on the North Brooklyn waterfront and some of those described by my colleagues as "the undesigned" and "the unplanned." By this I mean spatial practices that are carried out absent professional design or planning, or those practices that subvert the intent of designers and planners or subvert the governance or established patterns of use of urban space. I often use "the undesigned" and "the unplanned" interchangeably as most of these practices lack *both* professional planning and professional design.

Whatever these practices are called, people engage in them for a range of reasons, only some of which are explored in this book. The practices often involve an intrinsic pleasure or satisfaction that cannot be gained by "going to the park." The unplanned also seems to appeal to or move us on a deeper or visceral level. As I have previously argued, they stimulate our imagination and excite our innate desire for exploration, play, surprise, and intimate interaction with

DISCOVERING AND ENGAGING A VACATED WATERFRONT

the physical and social worlds that draw upon all of our senses and instincts.[21] Driven by opportunities structured in time as much as in space, these practices are more tactical than strategic.[22] Additionally, the production of this "other" form of urban space or spatial experience, as many previous commentators have noted, is often dependent on the tactics of occupation, appropriation, resistance, and exploiting accident.[23]

Our knowledge of the undesigned and its pursuers continues to grow, but few have figured out how such vital practices can be sustained and intermingled with or adopted by professional urban development. The difference between the undesigned and professional planning and design came into clear relief during the 2011 occupations of downtown park and plaza spaces as part of Occupy Wall Street and the larger Occupy movement. Protesters reclaimed these spaces for collective political expression and dialogue—a "loosening" of public space long controlled by the interests of governments, public authorities, property owners, and banks and corporations long accustomed to pliant, nonpolitical constituent users. Creating a city within a city—but one that operated by an entirely different set of rules and expectations—these occupiers rekindled the seemingly lost connection between public space and democracy, collective action and resistance.[24] Their spirited appropriations also injected variety, fun, excitement, and a sense of unpredictability into the predictable, controlled, and well-maintained environment of lower Manhattan and other American downtowns and civic centers.

A decade earlier, the North Brooklyn waterfront provided a similarly dynamic forum, though one not quite as prominent or public. As a frequent visitor to the terminal observed, "I think there is something that urban planners are missing; we need a new kind of park." Surely our vast and knowledgeable systems for planning, designing, building, and governing urban spaces should attempt to capture, facilitate, or nurture at least some of the informal dynamic once found on the North Brooklyn waterfront.

This is not a "how to" book, and I offer few specific directives. It does, though, aim to begin this dialogue between the vernacular and planned, the designed and undesigned, the deliberate and accidental. As the narratives unfold in the chapters that follow and the larger story of BEDT is told, it will become apparent that State Parks officials and others involved in the planning of East River State Park (ERSP), while well intentioned, were ill equipped to deal with the unique place they inherited and ultimately destroyed. Perhaps it was inevitable: Conditions such as these are always temporary; it is the nature of cities. But we can do better with places that evolve organically without the heavy hands of professional planning, design, and urban development.

Undesigned and Unplanned Operating Methods

The stories of the many people who built or occupied space on the Williamsburg waterfront at the beginning of the millennium and earlier are from my own experiences spending time with them, mostly on the waterfront itself. My research methods were mostly unstructured and improvisational. Meetings with people I describe were often, though not always, serendipitous, and I did not usually work from a script of questions. Sometimes I videotaped conversations and activity; other times I just photographed or observed and took notes. In some instances, I just hung out with my "subjects" and shared experiences with them.[25] Thus at times my own perspective or recounting of the history, actions, or thoughts of others will seem woefully incomplete, inconsistent, or limited by subjectivity. This is the nature of this sort of research. I met and got to know people on their own terms, on what was really their own turf and under circumstance that often fell somewhere between the prohibited and the illegal.

I refer to the people I write about in the chapters that follow by the names they gave me unless told otherwise. Most simply shared their first names and thus references are on a first-name basis. For others whom I met in a professional or advocacy role or initially off the waterfront or those who wanted me to know or use both their first and surnames, I accordingly use both (and sometimes interchangeably). In respecting people's privacy, I have omitted those events or information they asked me not to share. In other instances, I used my judgment about what to leave out. Like the people of the waterfront whom you will come to know in the chapters that follow, I did my best to make the most of accidental circumstances while being flexible and knowing when to pack it in.

Finally about methods, I was only sometimes alone in the field. Aside from the new friends I made while there, I was often joined by my longtime friend Brian Dworkin and sometimes by my unflappable videographers, Dan Wallenstein and Brandon Beck. Their perspectives and experiences surely informed mine, and one day there will be a documentary film of this experience that will demonstrate the full quality of their contributions.

Narratives of the Unplanned

The subsequent chapters each tell a story of a constituency of the waterfront, following their narrative through time and space. These constituencies represent only a fraction of those who spent time at or had a stake in the North Brooklyn waterfront in the late 1990s and 2000s. There were surely many others, but these are the people and groups I came to know. Chapter 2 tells the story of the builders of Shantytown Skatepark, the most intensively used and dramatic of all vernacular constructions at BEDT. From its modest inception, Shantytown quickly became a local, then national, magnet for skateboarders and was celebrated by skateboarding magazines and web sites, bringing it a brief period of notoriety before its demolition by the state, which had assumed title to the terminal just as the popularity of the skatepark was rising. Chapter 3 tells the story of the resident performers of the Brooklyn waterfront, the Hungry March Band (HMB) and the fire spinners who used the same "Slab" of concrete as the skateboarders as a rehearsal and performance space. A self-described "public" marching band, HMB was (and still is) dedicated to playing in public spaces and inciting "in your face" encounters and renowned for performances in parades, protests, parties, and subway cars. The spinners were practitioners of the fire arts, a growing performance craft popularized in recent years by the Burning Man Festival in the Nevada desert and similar, smaller events throughout the world. Chapter 4 surveys the environmental art of this waterfront and documents the stories of a few of the artists who made this unlikely location their studio and gallery. Their creations made amid and of waste, in a variety of media and forms, were powerful gestures of reclamation that resonated with the inadvertent audiences who were fortunate to experience them.

Chapter 5 tells the story of the waterfront's most regular and longest-tenured constituency, a group of multiethnic working-class men who gathered to read, socialize, drink beer and barbecue, take in the breezes and views, and appreciate life. These men of the neighborhood, some of whom I met amid the dumpsters, were representative of the vanishing culture of the working waterfront and the working-class enclaves that Greenpoint and Williamsburg used to be. Often remaining at the terminal long after dark and throughout the cold weather months, their self-made clubhouses provided a comfortable social setting and an "escape" from their rapidly gentrifying neighborhood. Chapter 6 tells the story of those who lived on the waterfront: a group of mostly young, foreign-born men who worked as day laborers on nearby construction sites or as itinerant workers throughout the city. When not working they lived communally at the terminal and slept in shacks or self-rigged tents. Most were also undocumented immigrants, a status that greatly complicated their quest for work, housing, and a more permanent way of life.

Chapters 7 and 8 are less about on-the-ground insurgent occupation of space than those that precede them. They examine the recent history of this waterfront and politics of redevelopment largely from locally based perspectives. The former tells the story of the local activists who organized, then fought and defeated, the garbage haulers' and the city administration's plans to build a massive waste transfer facility at BEDT. It also chronicles their later struggle to plan for a formal waterfront park working within the context of a unique (but ultimately failed) public–private partnership with New York University. Chapter 8 examines the development of East River State Park partially from the perspective of its builder and owner, the New York State Office of Parks, Recreation and Historic Preservation while chronicling local conflicts over the park's design, use, and governance. Chapter 8 also considers the larger transformation of the Williamsburg waterfront into condominium towers, luxury loft conversions, and formal leisure spaces.

The conclusion, Chapter 9, considers the future of the undesigned and unplanned both at and away from the water's edge, in New York and elsewhere. It advocates for ways in which the vernacular can be better understood, appreciated, facilitated, and incited; noting what professional practices might learn from the unplanned and how ordinary people can harness these same forces to co-opt or subvert professional practices.

CHAPTER 2

THE RISE AND FALL OF SHANTYTOWN SKATEPARK

FROM THE STREET, BEDT might have seemed an unlikely venue for skateboarding, a sport dependent on continuous paved surfaces. But tucked behind the terminal's only remaining building were two long expanses of concrete, each slightly pitched toward the water. These were the one-time foundations of freight houses into which bulk materials were unloaded from rail cars that ran on flanking tracks. While concrete is the preferred medium for skateboarders, these surfaces were covered with so much garbage, debris, and weeds that they hardly suggested a potential skateboarder's paradise.[1] But in late 1999, neighborhood skaters organized a cleanup of the north "Slab," as it was known among them and others who frequented the terminal. Placing a few homemade ramps and improvised obstacles on this expanse, the skateboarders created a spot that was instantly popular. By the spring of 2000, the Slab was being skated continually throughout the daylight hours, seven days a week.

Standing at the top of Slab on a warm June 2000 afternoon, I took in this spectacle: Ten skaters were making their runs with the Manhattan skyline spread majestically across the background. This was no mere transgressive appropriation of urban space. While not a skateboarder, I understood that the Slab was a particularly compelling spot for a sport whose participants pride themselves in finding such places. By this time, the local skateboarders had already dubbed

Nevitt catches air off of the ramp he built. The smooth concrete of the Slab and homemade obstacles helped make Shantytown an instantly popular skatespot (2000).

the site "Shantytown"—inspired by the improvised shelters built by the men living at the terminal, some abutting the Slab. While the park's pioneers stuck to this name, others who soon followed had their own, including "Skankytown," "Skateland," and "the Lot," and some just called it the Slab.

As the summer progressed, the word spread, bringing more skateboarders to the waterfront. But Shantytown's popularity really took off that October, when the skaters constructed "the Volcano," the first of three concrete installations they built on the Slab. Instantly iconic, it catapulted this improvised skate venue to a brief period of fame on the national skateboarding scene. In spite of its success and perhaps because of it, this DIY construction did not last long. In July 2001, Shantytown met its demise when BEDT's new owner, the New York State Office of Parks, Recreation and Historic Preservation, bulldozed the skatepark, leaving piles of rubble where the Volcano and other installations once stood.

From its inception to demolition and beyond, I came to know some of the skateboarders who built and frequented Shantytown. I retell their story here and attempt to understand what made this park unique and particularly in tune with the skateboarding scene in the neighborhood and city, while assessing those aspects of Shantytown that might impact how we build and maintain a broader array of urban environments. Most of my time was spent with a core group of skateboarders, most of whom lived in North Brooklyn. They included Nevitt, a then–thirty-year-old scruffy veteran of the local skateboarding scene who lived just two blocks away. A metal worker by trade, Nevitt was preparing to open a skateboard shop that, once open, quickly evolved into a local hub for skateboarders just a few blocks from where Shantytown once stood. After a November 2001 State Parks–hosted community "walkthrough" of the terminal, which the skateboarders had attended to press their case to rebuild their skatepark, Nevitt told me the story of Shantytown's rise and fall. As he talked, four of his fellow pioneers (Dean, Bob, Roger, and Denise) intently listened, added their own recollections and thoughts, and laughed at Nevitt's frequent anecdotes about the scene that evolved around the park's use.

THE RISE AND FALL OF SHANTYTOWN SKATEPARK

A year and a half later, I spent an evening talking skateboarding with Steve Rodriguez, a veteran New York City skater and founder of the 5Boro skate team and company, at his Manhattan apartment. While never a local of the neighborhood, Steve regularly skated Shantytown, which he called "the Lot" or "the Brooklyn Lot," with a prominent crew that included some of the best-known skateboarders in the city. My conversations with many other Shantytown protagonists also inform this chapter. Additionally, I draw upon my own observations of the action on the Slab and a review of the trove of published and Internet content concerning skateboarding in New York and elsewhere.

Shantytown Inspirations and Antecedents: Co-opted Space and Conflicts

While there were many skateboarders in North Brooklyn and no dedicated skating venue, Shantytown was born less out of need than opportunism. Local skaters, like those across the city, were continually looking for surfaces and obstacles that might provide novel or interesting rides. These places were not hard to find during the 1990s. Greenpoint's and Williamsburg's vast inventory of abandoned or lightly used industrial properties, vacant buildings, paved lots, and sleepy back streets provided a veritable cornucopia of skating environments. As other residents bemoaned the area's relentless hardscape and lack of green, the skaters thrived, finding it conducive to "street skating"—skateboarding in appropriated urban space. The philosophy of street skating is that *any* part of an urban environment—a street, sidewalk, ramp, embankment, staircase, ledge, railing, loading dock, parking lot, or Jersey barrier—can become a skatespot, even if only for a short period before it reverts to its intended or more common use.[2] Skatespots are found in and out of the limelight, and street skaters find themselves at home in both dense and desolate locales. Times Square provides a buzz for many skateboarders—the Internet is filled with video depictions of daredevil maneuvers amid the cars, cabs, trucks, and pedestrian hubbub of New York's iconic crossroads—but so too does a rarely used staircase or ledge far from other activity or people. Urban skateboarders are rarely impeded by inconvenience or apparent danger, and skating marginal, out of the way, or abandoned spaces is in their minds a form of reclamation. As Nevitt observed,

> That's really the spirit of skateboarding: looking at something that the rest of the community would toss away or throw away—or think is unsafe or garbage—and ridin' it; getting your skateboard on it and ridin' it.

Skatespots often have a counterintuitive logic to them; many seemingly unlikely urban spaces are often those that appeal the most to skateboarders, and frequently because they are unlikely or challenging. Word of mouth travels quickly among skateboarders in and beyond their immediate cities (and did so even in the days before the Internet), and those skatespots that are repeatedly appropriated evolve into destinations and attract skaters in ever larger numbers. New York has had many such famous spots, including Washington Square, Union Square, the fountain containing the Unisphere in Flushing Meadows–Corona Park in Queens, a place called the "Deathbowl" in the Bronx, and an untold number of modernist office plazas in Manhattan. Many, though, are short-lived, as they evolve with skateboard use into sites of contestation and are eventually reclaimed by property owners, developers, city government, and improvement districts—in New York and elsewhere.[3]

Shantytown skaters made several references to a somewhat similar skatespot known as the "Brooklyn Banks." Later, I learned that the Banks, which is actually in Manhattan, is an isolated plaza underneath and between two approaches to the Brooklyn Bridge. Where the plaza meets one of the approaches, it curves up into the supporting wall, forming an ideal if unintended skateable bank. The plaza is also inclined, which helps skaters gain momentum as they propel themselves onto the abutting wall and other "found" obstacles. The Banks is legendary and known to skateboarders all over the world. The spot has been celebrated by skateboard magazines, books, videos, and web sites and has provided inspiration for the digital terrain of a Tony Hawk–designed video game. For sites such as the Banks, skaters reserve the title "skateboarding mecca." While the term is frequently invoked, there are few universally accepted meccas. Steve Rodriguez called the Banks one of the "Big Four" of the 1990s, with the others being LOVE Park in Philadelphia; "Pulaski" underneath the highway of that name in Washington, D.C.; and the Embarcadero in San Francisco.[4]

Closed in 2010 to accommodate a four-year reconstruction project of bridge approaches, the Banks has followed a somewhat typical pattern of spatial conflict for skatespots, with on-again, off-again periods of closure enforced by New York City police whose headquarters are just down the street.[5] Because the Banks was deemed a potentially sensitive area that might be of value to terrorists intent on destroying the iconic bridge above, this conflict was particularly acute in the years immediately after September 11, 2001. But by 2005, these conflicts had eased somewhat as the Parks Department, Department of Transportation, and the police adopted a more accommodating approach to governing this space. Steve, a veteran of the Banks, served as an intermediary and advocate for the larger community of its skateboarders. He worked with city officials to resolve conflicts and negotiated a

THE RISE AND FALL OF SHANTYTOWN SKATEPARK

skateboard-friendly compromise when a redesign and beautification plan threatened to end skateboarding at this hallowed site.[6]

Like Steve, many of Shantytown's regular skaters also frequented the Banks, so comparisons between the two spaces were natural. While Shantytown was lacking both the ready-to-skate terrain and the more central location of the Banks, after the Volcano was built some believed that Shantytown was destined for the same sort of mecca-like status. This feeling was reinforced when the park found its way into the skateboarding magazines, videos, and web sites. Manny, a frequent Shantytowner in his early teens, rattled off a list of professional skateboarders who had skated their self-built park. "This was going to be a real famous spot!" he proclaimed.

Because Shantytown's terrain was constructed as opposed to merely found, many also compared it to two other notable skater-built parks: Burnside Park in Portland, Oregon, and FDR Skatepark in Philadelphia.[7] Built in the 1990s in otherwise underutilized space underneath a bridge approach and a highway viaduct, respectively, both of these parks featured concrete constructions woven into the existing fabric of hardscape. Initially constructed without permission or without full permission (FDR), these parks have evolved with use and notoriety over several years to gain legitimacy or tolerance from the public authorities that own the underlying land, an achievement that seemed to bolster the cause of Shantytown in the minds of its creators.[8] These parks continue to be used, and in the time since Shantytown's demolition, several other DIY skate venues have been built in American cities, including Seattle, St. Louis, and Houston.[9]

Building Shantytown

No one told us what to do; we knew what we wanted and that's just what we did. —Dean

Shantytown was constructed collectively by many individuals in an ad hoc fashion without professional plans, designs, funding, or assistance. Bypassing the Parks Department, elected officials, and local development and advocacy organizations, Shantytown's builders opted for another politic, one that favored sweat equity over fundraising, and immediate action over community discussion. "There was no money and it wasn't planned out, it sort of happened naturally," Nevitt explained. It was also not built in one continuous period; rather, it *evolved* over time with many starts and stops, intertwined with immediate and intensive use of the park's "incomplete" terrain. So Shantytown grew in size, capacity, and sophistication as its constituency of users grew.

Nevitt said that the impetus to create Shantytown partially evolved out of the demise of other local skate environments. These included an abandoned warehouse the skaters used during the late 1990s, the interior of which was gutted by a fire and which was subsequently torn down by its owners or the city. With the warehouse gone, the skaters took to nearby streets. Using sheet metal and wood, Nevitt built a modest ramp and set it out on North 8th Street. The ramp worked well, and soon other neighborhood skaters joined him and his roommate, Jerry, for long sessions in which they placed it in a variety of local spots. But with frequent use and mastery, the ramp began to give them a better-than-expected ride, tossing them farther out and "a little too close to the neighbors' brand new, shiny SUVs," Nevitt said.

Thinking about alternatives that would provide challenges and variety and be conflict-free, they took their ramp to the Slab. Nevitt and Jerry had already skated a spot at the terminal where an angled piece of concrete formed an interesting obstacle. But to create a decent-sized skating venue would be a more ambitious undertaking. After enlisting the help of other neighborhood skaters, they spent a weekend sweeping away all of the broken glass and debris on one of the two concrete warehouse foundations. They placed Nevitt's ramp and an old metal file cabinet in the middle of the cleared expanse, and the Slab was ready for skating. "Everybody just came down," Nevitt recalled, noting the park's immediate popularity. "And we just used to have super fun times with two little—tiny little—beat-up ramps."

As 2000 wore on and the word continued to spread, skaters from beyond the immediate neighborhoods began to descend upon this waterfront skatespot. To meet this growing demand and make the park more interesting, various skaters added to the growing circuit of obstacles. These were mostly just found objects or simple homemade constructions. (Later they would also create a small sitting area from discarded furniture.) Up to a dozen of these obstacles were often spread across the Slab in various configurations, left out all the time for anyone to skate or reconfigure. With the park's popularity growing, in the fall the skaters constructed the park's first permanent obstacle, the Volcano, a cylinder-on-a-cone installation that reached a height of nearly five feet and had a diameter at its base of ten feet.

The Volcano was Dean's idea. At thirty-six, he was one of the older members of the scene, a two-decade veteran of New York skateboarding and a longtime area resident. During a long skating session on the Slab, he was suddenly struck with a vision of a flat-topped conical structure. Nevitt laughed as he described Dean's vision as "just like *Close Encounters*," alluding to the flat-topped mound that haunts Richard Dreyfuss throughout the 1977 film *Close Encounters of the Third Kind.*[10] Other skaters did not take Dean seriously at first, but soon they found themselves collecting wood, bricks, paving stones, and other debris, piling it into a large mound on the upper portion of the Slab.

The process of building the Volcano unfolded over several weeks, all while skateboarding continued around the growing pile of collected materials. Dean described it as a community project to which everyone pitched in, including "ten or fifteen little kids [who carried] as much rocks as they could to help pile it up." After they collected enough debris and arranged the pile into a symmetrical shape, growing progressively narrower toward its flat top, the skaters pooled their money to buy several batches of dry concrete mix. According to Bob, then a twenty-six-year-old member of this group, it took several successive weekend trips to Home Depot, where they purchased large sacks of mix and five-gallon buckets. "It got to be a weekend ritual," he recalled. Initially underestimating just how much concrete the Volcano would require, they had to make more trips to Home Depot, each time unsure if each trip would be the last.

Even though no one in the group had any masonry experience, they did all concrete work by hand. Using buckets of water carried up from the river, they mixed each batch with wooden sticks and then carefully applied and contoured the wet concrete to the mound of collected debris. It was a crude but ultimately effective process. When the Volcano was complete, it had taken "20,000 pounds of concrete," Bob estimated. While their construction techniques were

(*Left*) The concrete applied to the Volcano was still setting when three of its builders (*from left*, Jerry, Dean, and Chris) posed for this photo (2000). (*Right*) Jerry takes a test run on the Volcano (2000).

relatively primitive, the skaters enjoyed the process and took pride in the communal aspect of their labor. The fact that so many people had participated in the construction engendered a creative spirit that would continue after the Volcano was completed.

Having not been to BEDT in over a month, I serendipitously found myself there on that late October afternoon when they completed the Volcano. The last application of concrete had been meticulously applied and smoothed just an hour earlier. Dean, Jerry, and Chris were there to clean up and keep people off their still-setting creation. From the steeper part of its upper cone, its slope gently lessened as it spread toward the ground, meeting the Slab at a long, low angle. Slightly longer and larger on its north face, the Slab had a modest asymmetry that did not take away from its artfulness or from its usability. When the concrete seemed dry, they each did a few test runs. Able to get up and down the face of this construction smoothly, they deemed their creation a success. But the test runs had left some light streaks in a few places, so they roped off the Volcano using the buckets and wood for additional drying and planned to return an hour later. Nevitt, who had already left the Slab by the time I arrived that afternoon, later described their philosophy:

> Not that we really knew anything about building anything out of concrete—but we had the determination to get it done. Whether or not it was built correctly or solid or not—the main point is that it was rideable.

More skaters descended upon Shantytown as word of the Volcano spread. They came throughout the day and evening, on weekdays and weekends, and in good weather and bad. On many afternoons, twenty or more could be found skating the Volcano and temporary ramps and taking in the scene. BMX bikers also found the park compelling and vied for time with their skating counterparts, which was sometimes cause for mild conflicts. Roger, a teenager and frequent Shantytowner, said the crowds came because the Volcano was "an original." Not a single skatepark anywhere featured a similarly shaped obstacle, he claimed.

As Shantytown flourished, so too did the accidental park in which it was located. The skateboarders were acutely aware of the larger scene. Skating frequently entailed sharing the Slab with others, including those who sunbathed, socialized, or were just hanging out. On Sunday afternoons, they shared it with Hungry March Band, whose practice sessions made use of the lower end of the Slab (Chapter 3). And the homeless men whose shanties were built along its edge carried on much of their daily lives on this same concrete expanse (Chapter 6). They also shared the space with occasional art installations or events (Chapter 4).

While the skaters mostly kept to themselves, they appreciated BEDT's larger social dynamic. The public nature of street skating and the city's great density make New York street skaters comfortable with people around them. But Shantytown was different; here they shared limited terrain with a variety of others, most of whom they did not know. Operating beyond the conventions of the city's public spaces, they also shared an outsider status, and thus the skateboarders were inclined to accommodate others. Nevitt felt that the Slab's growing popularity for skateboarding and other activities incited a counterintuitive dynamic. Instead of feeling more crowded or competitive, he claimed, the scene "got better and better" as more people used the space. The band, artists, the dog walkers and random strangers all played a role in keeping the scene cool. "It [was] just a great place to hang out," he said.

Photo and video shoots were frequent occurrences at Shantytown. (Photo courtesy of Steve Rodriguez, 2000.)

Other Shantytowners viewed the Slab's (and the larger terminal's) evolving social landscape similarly. As Jocko Weyland reflected in his *Thrasher* tribute to the park after its demise,

> The impromptu skatepark was reason to go there, but it was the atmosphere that made it really special. It was an antidote to the sterility and organization of society in general, a place to get away from rules and order. The reports of people getting arrested and impending doom created an ephemeral quality that made you savor the moment. Added to that was the ebb and flow of humanity's splendor in all its varied guises: the punk rock marching band practicing in the distance, pretty girls walking

their dogs, old men curiously watching, Puerto Rican teenagers smoking pot, and Japanese tourists with their video cameras.[11]

Steve Rodriguez noted that successful urban skatespots were places in which skaters could not only skate but also socialize and watch. "To see and be seen" was "vital" to the activity, and spectators, even those who were not skating, were an important part of the experience.[12] This social aspect was missing at many dedicated skateboard parks. Steve lamented that the greatest flaws in the recent redesigns of cherished New York skatespots, including the Brooklyn Banks and Union Square, were less the loss of terrain and more the loss of comfortable space for spectators and socialization. By contrast, Shantytown was not located at a natural crossroads of urban humanity, but it did facilitate some of this social aspect. It was good urban theater, with nonstop action, real-life characters, great scenery, and occasional conflicts.

As word continued to spread, the skatepark began attracting people from well beyond the city. Skateboarders are legendary for their road trips, and the Internet is filled with blog entries, photos, and videos of these board-in-hand pilgrimages. Those visiting New York added Shantytown to their list of must-stops, along with more established sites such as the Brooklyn Banks and Washington Square Park. Among the many visitors were "professionals" often from California, who came with their crews to stage photo and video shoots. As Nevitt described,

> Before you know it, it's in the big international skate videos, it's in all the big international skate magazines and you know the companies out in L.A. fly out their pros and the photographers for the weekend, fly them out here to take pictures and then fly them back—it sorta became that kinda scene.

Shantytown under various names was also featured several times in skateboarding magazines and on their Internet sites.[13] At that time, before the widespread advent of social networking and photo and video sharing web sites, this was among the principal ways that skateboarders learned of new spots beyond their immediate area. Having one's local skatespot written up or photographed in *Transworld* or *Thrasher* was also a prestigious milestone and source of pride, even if it meant that your site was now "discovered" and you had to share it with ever more people. While some of the older skaters were wary of the attention the park was receiving, others, including Nevitt, did not seem particularly concerned and in fact took particular satisfaction in Shantytown's growing notoriety. The younger skaters also basked in this glory; it was something special to see the skateboarding greats of magazines and videos suddenly appear at their local spot. Later it would be equally thrilling to see photos from these sessions in print or on prominent web sites.[14]

The Volcano-plus-skyline juxtaposition was so visually compelling that Shantytown itself was appropriated several times for photography shoots that did not involve skateboarding. Nevitt recalled one particularly outlandish incident, when they arrived on a cold morning only to find a lightly dressed model posed atop the Volcano. They waited as the photographer and attending assistants deliberately worked through a series of shots, aided by the portable light fixtures set up around the model. As their patience began to wear thin, the skaters attempted to nudge the crew off the Slab with some forceful attitude. "We tried to shake 'em down for some dough," Nevitt said, laughing. "We didn't get anything out of them. We went easy on them but you had that all the time."

While Shantytown's quick rise to fame was a source of pride for the park's builders, they maintained that it was still a relaxed venue that served the needs of the locals, a place where skaters of any skill level could enjoy themselves and feel at home. The pioneers were very concerned about building and maintaining this communal vibe. Bob became a bit choked up as he reflected upon this social dynamic a few months after the park had been destroyed:

> This scene out here was like better than most scenes across the country, just because it was just thrown together. There were no real cliques of skaters down here. It was like little kids with twenty-year-old skateboards, who had never been on a skateboard before; and fathers, forty-year-old dudes, that hadn't skated in fifteen or twenty years. They just came down and it was awesome—people having barbecues down here, drinking beers. . . . It was beyond just a skatepark; it was a total family vibe.

By building the Volcano, the local skateboarders had made some claim approximating ownership, but the Slab remained open to other skaters and available for other activities, particularly the lower end, which had no permanent skateboard installations. Even before the Volcano was built, another group had begun work on a different obstacle. By summer 2000, a slender six-foot length of cinderblocks neatly piled to a height of three feet stood uncompleted along the south edge of the Slab about sixty feet from where the Volcano would rise. Even after the Volcano was constructed and drawing crowds, this obstacle remained unrealized. In late 2000 or early 2001, another group, led by a local skater named Andrew, transformed this unfinished project into the park's second permanent installation: a quarter-pipe,

The builders of Shantytown's second permanent obstacle, a quarter-pipe, improved upon the construction process of the Volcano. Their refined techniques included the use of power tools, forms, improvised rebar, and ready-to-use wet batch concrete. (Photo by Steve Rodriguez, 2001.)

long a classic element of skateparks and backyard skateboarder constructions. A few of the builders of the Volcano were involved but this time played supporting roles to a group that included several well-known New York skaters, including the filmmakers Buddy Nichols and Rick Charnoski, writer Jocko Weyland, and Dave Mims, co-owner of Autumn Skateboard Shop in Manhattan. Steve Rodriguez was also involved, though his participation in the actual construction was limited as a result of an injury he was then nursing. He provided me with an account of the quarter-pipe's design and construction and shared photographs he took of the event. Nevitt and Dean (who was also involved in its construction) also recounted their experiences.

The construction process had many similarities to that of the Volcano, but rather than merely repeat the methods and steps, the quarter-pipe's builders drew upon "lessons learned" from that earlier effort and their vast experience skating it. They incorporated several refinements to the building process. While the concrete of the Volcano was applied over the course of several weekends, the masonry for the quarter-pipe took shape in a single evening. Instead of the more expensive, time-consuming, and labor-intensive process of using dry concrete mix and mixing by hand with river water, they paid a local cement company to drop a batch of wet concrete that was ready to mold. The concrete was "slag"—left over from a completed job—which enabled the skaters to get an additional discount, as wet concrete has a very limited shelf life even in a mixing truck.

Working from a motorized trough that kept the concrete moving, the skaters poured and molded the concrete over a cinderblock and brick core that was reinforced by metal bar. Closer to the bottom the skaters had created a series of shallow, debris-filled terraces onto which the concrete would be poured. The builders also used a jackhammer to cut a long, shallow groove into the surface of the Slab so that the poured concrete could smoothly meet it. This better anchored the quarter-pipe to the Slab and prevented potential chipping of its thinnest section, which had been a problem with the Volcano. While the curved face of the quarter-pipe was mostly molded by hand, the skaters also used plywood forms to hold the poured concrete in place. Nevitt compared the construction of the quarter-pipe with that of its predecessor:

> This was done with just a bit more knowledge of concrete structures than we had [in building the Volcano]. It met with the concrete Slab really nice and it was a really smooth transition. So if you got up high enough to catch a ride on it, you were king of the world. That was the best feeling in the world.

In addition to the savings reaped from using batch concrete, the builders took advantage of the popularity of the Volcano and were able to collect donations from a larger pool of skaters, thus reducing the cost to each individual contributor. All of these innovations helped make construction easier *and* create a more durable obstacle when completed.

Shantytown skater-builders continued to build on their construction experiences and leverage the park's growing constituency, in funding the third permanent installation, another quarter-pipe on the opposite edge of the Slab. They found sponsors who were willing to pay for the materials, including Emerica (a skateboard apparel company) and Dave Mim's skateboard shop. Consistent with the first two jumps, the labor was a collective, all-volunteer effort. Reflecting upon the role of the sponsors, Dean noted,

> They knew [Shantytown] could be torn down at any moment—but they were interested in the kinda vibe that we had going on down here.

The third obstacle embodied in many respects the "growth of constituency" and "learning to build" evolutions that characterized the development of Shantytown. These vernacular builders were perfecting their craft, and this quarter-pipe had the greatest degree of uniformity and smoothness. Its more gentle curvature and long, sloping edges would make it skateable for even the most inexperienced skaters, while serving as a nice complement to the Volcano, just a few feet away. Working with Emerica, the local skateboarders organized a community event in which the obstacle would be finished. I found a picture of the event on the Internet depicting neighborhood kids proudly posing around the still-setting concrete installation. This second quarter-pipe "had the biggest conglomeration of help, the whole gambit of what had gone on down here," Dean said. Unfortunately, it was destroyed, along with the rest of Shantytown, less than two days after its completion.

Shantytown's construction over time allowed a constituency to grow with it. Given the humble resources of Shantytown's pioneers, it would have been impossible to create a park of its eventual extent—in terms of size, permanence, and popularity—following standard development paradigms. Building on their initial successes in a way that incorporated the ideas, labor, and experiences of many user-builders with no formal hierarchical structure allowed them to continue and refine the collective building processes they had initiated with the creation of the Volcano. Construction, like every other aspect of the development process, was never quite finished, as piles of debris that would form both quarter-pipes sat for months before receiving their outer shells of concrete. No matter, though—Shantytowners were less interested in the aesthetics of completion than being able to skate and having the satisfaction of "doing-it-yourself."

Designing Shantytown

Everything was sorta designed, sorta accidental—no one has this one overall plan where everything was going to go—we just started plopping things down and it just sorta worked itself out. —Nevitt

Shantytown was not explicitly "designed" in a conventional or comprehensive sense. Yet Shantytown's builders did implicitly follow a design process that began with the placement of portable ramps and found objects and through intensive use evolved with the incremental construction of three permanent obstacles. The success of the park's layout was tied to the fact that it was conceived of, designed by, and built by its eventual users—and built in increments, giving them time to ride and evaluate existing elements before adding new ones. This collective, incremental design process yielded a well-designed park.

In contrast to professional practices, which separate this process into distinct phases of planning, design, construction, and, finally, when it is complete, use, the Shantytown building collective followed no similarly rigid proscription and were not guided by a vision of a final design. Without this ordering in time, each of these phases occurred in dynamic fashion—stretched, intermingled, and essentially never completed—enabling the park's building collective to capitalize upon feedback received during any of these phases to improve the others. Because the process was ad hoc, innovations could come from anyone at any time. This created more design possibilities as the park began to take shape, as opposed to most professional practices, which are oriented toward completed and perfected design.

While visually dramatic, the terrain of Shantytown was suitable for skaters of all ages and skill levels (2001).

The design for Shantytown also evolved out of the need for economy and the intimate knowledge of the constraints of the site on which it was located. Developing the park in this manner, the building collective was able to create a skate venue that served a great range of needs and incorporated many innovations not found in conventional parks. The most prominent of these innovations included efficient design that made the most of a small site, terrain that was suitable for skaters of all ages and skill levels, arrangement of the park's principal obstacles that enabled a greater number of skaters to use it at one time, and a design that was more in keeping with the "street skating" ethos of the East Coast. I discuss each of these aspects in greater detail in what follows.

Unlike many professionally developed skate parks, Shantytown had terrain that was suitable for all ages and skill levels. In fact, it achieved this with no specialized areas or segregation in time or space by skill level, unlike a ski slope with beginner, intermediate, and expert trails. The same elements that served the experts also served the novices. As Nevitt described,

> It was extremely challenging for really experienced skateboarders yet safe for little kids to ride, in that little kids couldn't do anything that was beyond their capabilities and get hurt. They couldn't just roll out into something that they had no idea what they were doing—they had to push off on flat ground and if you didn't have the strength, you wouldn't be able to do something that would get you hurt.

Both Nevitt and Steve compared the design of Shantytown with those of conventional skateparks. The bowl-like contours of many skateparks were inspired by serpentine shapes of the empty southern California swimming pools where skateboarding came of age in the 1960s and 1970s.[15] To construct these parks, the ground is hollowed out and lined with concrete to create bowls, curves, and undulating terrain. Shantytown's elements in contrast were necessarily built upward starting from the concrete base of the Slab. Thus, skaters began their runs from the *bottom* of the park's obstacles, forcing them to use their own strength to climb them. The slightly pitched surface of the Slab helped build acceleration, but still the ability to climb the Volcano or one of the quarter-pipes was mostly dependent on the skater's strength and agility. In contrast, novices cannot handle much of the terrain of conventional parks, where runs begin from the *top* of a bowl from which skaters are swiftly propelled downward by the force of gravity. The walls of the Volcano got progressively steeper toward its top; thus, experts would be sufficiently challenged to make it to the top and perform a "grind," an "ollie," or other maneuver. But younger or less-skilled skaters were usually able to go only part of the way up, turn, and go back down. In the case of a wipeout, these skaters would come off their skateboards with little force behind them and often managed to stay on their feet.

Like the Volcano, obstacles two and three were designed to be challenging to accomplished skaters while allowing novice skaters to also use them without high risk of injury. The second quarter-pipe with its gently sloping edges would have been particularly friendly for beginners, while the first quarter-pipe was more challenging. Bob described the first quarter-pipe as "steep, tight and sketchy, and hard to ride." Nevitt agreed but added,

> If you really didn't have the experience you couldn't really go crazy on it and hurt yourself. It's sorta hard to explain to people at the Parks [Department]. . . . Sometimes things that are more difficult to ride are actually safer than objects that are easier to ride because kids can do something that they can't quite do and barrel into it and realize they got themselves into a lot of trouble when it's too late.

The bottom-up design features that essentially made Shantytown a skatepark for all skill levels also made it a park that could be used by more people at once by facilitating a greater flow of skaters through its circuit of obstacles. As Steve explained to me, in conventional parks, starting from the edge (or top) of the bowl, skaters plunge into the center (or lowest point) of the bowl. Most bowls can be used only one at a time. A skater who "drops" into a bowl precludes the possibility of anyone else's doing the same (to do otherwise is contrary to skateboarding etiquette and increases the risk of injury via collision). Skaters generally watch and wait patiently along the edge for the person in the bowl to finish his or her run. If a skater wipes out—a frequent occurrence—those waiting will have to endure an additional delay while the skater picks him- or herself up off the ground, retrieves the skateboard, and climbs out of the bowl. In contrast to the way bowls concentrate motion bringing skaters inward, Shantytown's bottom-up obstacles dispersed skaters, propelling them away from the jump and allowing the next skater to follow in rapid succession. Shantytown skaters rarely had to wait long for their runs, as even wipeouts usually sent the errant skater quickly back down the obstacle and his or her skateboard off to the periphery.

Considering the issue of capacity, the natural comparison to Shantytown at the time was the Millennium Skatepark at Owl's Head Park in Bay Ridge, Brooklyn. This new city-built and -operated park, which the skaters referred to as simply "Owl's Head," was not particularly convenient to those who lived in Greenpoint or Williamsburg—an hour's subway ride away—but most had skated there. As Shantytown was destroyed around the same time that this official park was opened, the timing raised suspicion among skaters that these actions were related (this was unlikely, as they were undertaken by the state and the city, respectively). When completed, Owl's Head was the only officially sanctioned skatepark in the entire borough of Brooklyn (population 2.4 million in 2000) and thus was crowded from the moment it opened.

Shantytowners complained that the park's terrain, which was essentially a series of bowls and hollowed contours, created long waits and limited opportunities for runs. Steve was particularly dissatisfied with the park. When it was being planned, he had worked with the city Parks Department on its design. Partially inspired by the terrain of the Brooklyn Banks, he envisioned a park that included both contours and more hard-edged obstacles that mimic the streets, staircases, ledges, and railings of urban spaces. He was surprised when the Parks Department dropped his more *urban* design concept in favor of a more conventional layout of bowls and curved surfaces, in keeping with a more suburban, West Coast style of skateboarding, inspired by the fluid curves of surfing and refined in empty backyard swimming pools.

Like most skateboarders I spoke with both at and away from Shantytown, Steve preferred the East Coast style of street skating that came of age in the 1980s and early 1990s on the streets and hard-edged public spaces of cities like New York, Philadelphia, and Washington, D.C. While Shantytown was not purely street skating in the sense that it was removed from the normal hubbub of the city streets, it pushed skaters toward one challenging jump or maneuver per an obstacle, which if the skater was skilled enough could be combined with a subsequent move on another obstacle. Where successful runs in a bowl involve a long series of up-and-down or back-and-forth segments, the event-like quality of each run or maneuver on the Slab was similar to what many enjoyed in skating urban plazas and on staircases, or made use of other adapted elements of the streetscape. The general grittiness of BEDT, with its graffiti, garbage, and characters, was also more in keeping with the ethos of skating on the street.

Shantytown's incremental design process also allowed its builders to make decisions concerning the location of new obstacles based on their experience skating existing park elements. The resulting design ensured that all three concrete installations formed a coherent dialogue with one another and their site. Strategically placed portable ramps and found objects could customize, enhance, or creatively disturb this dialogue, facilitating a larger set of possibilities for compelling use. In professional building practices, parks are conceived of, designed, and then constructed in succession and according to plan—allowing users little opportunity to provide iterative feedback that could potentially lead to adjustments or wholesale changes to the design.

The conception and design process for the quarter-pipes helped the skaters to overcome a constraint inherent in the site. The Slab was a 400- by 88-foot concrete platform that is anywhere from two to five feet above the surrounding ground. Given that it was many times longer (east–west) than wide (north–south), wherever they placed the Volcano it would be in fairly close proximity to one of the Slab's longer edges. As a result, many skaters could safely come off the Volcano only in two directions, while for others, momentum gained in descent represented a lost opportunity to transition to and climb another obstacle. The second quarter-pipe was to address this condition on the north side of the Slab, where the Volcano was little more than ten feet from this edge. Bob described the rationale of its placement:

> You couldn't ride most [of the Volcano]. . . . You couldn't get an approach to it, so we figured if we make a wall over here there would be more flow, more lines throughout the park. So we can use the backside of the Volcano instead of jumping off right away because you're going to go off the edge. Just build another ramp there—we can come off the Volcano and have something else to turn around on.

Relatively close to the northeast corner of the Slab, the second quarter-pipe was also harmonious with the established pattern of skating at the park—the existing "lines and flow." While skaters moved through the circuit of permanent and movable objects in any order and direction, the general pattern of use often began from the northeast corner, where skaters often waited in queue to make their runs. This pattern was facilitated by the Slab's slight pitch toward the water, from east to west. From this spot, skaters could now exploit various combinations of the three obstacles in smooth succession, starting with either the Volcano or the second quarter-pipe, whose western edge had a sloping lip to facilitate these transitions.

Conventional design practices may have also been able to understand the constraints of the Slab and how to maximize utility within those limitations, prior to construction. There are also examples of professional skatepark design processes that actively engage skateboarders in the design process and share decisions with them.[16] But the development of Shantytown was more purely user-driven, allowing its designer-builder-users to react to a range of challenges and opportunities, both foreseen and unforeseen. Unfolding over time, it allowed them to craft a park that fit the idiosyncrasies of the site and their needs as the users of their constructions, as they too evolved.

Managing Shantytown

The art of skateboarding is inherently in conflict with authority.—Jocko Weyland[17]

Management or governance would seem antithetical to skateboarding, an individual sport that requires no specialized environment or equipment other than a skateboard. The nature of street skating, in particular, is co-option, and skateboarders create their own terrain, rules, challenges, sense of competition, and achievements. Yet as Shantytown evolved it betrayed this sense of opportunistic appropriation of found space, exhibiting a degree of permanence and intensive use that exceeded most other anarchic activities at the terminal, which were more purely "in the moment" or required limited construction. Could this park continue to survive and grow without a system to govern its use, maintain its terrain, and, when necessary, mediate among participants (and nonparticipants) in a way that would ensure fair and enjoyable access for all? Could it do so without betraying the renegade spirit of the sport and the larger "no rules" ethos of BEDT?

These contradictions perhaps doomed Shantytown from the moment the Volcano was finished. Its rapid evolution from informal to formal, temporary to permanent, from a local to national skatespot, and the unexpected and swift

The incremental placement of the second and third permanent obstacles expanded the park's "lines and flow" and helped maximize its relatively limited terrain (2001).

destruction after did not give the skateboarders a real opportunity to consider governance or build a dialogue beyond their own constituency—not with State Parks, which owned the terminal; other regular users; or local waterfront advocacy groups. Yet Shantytown's ad hoc management system (if it could even be called that) did work for a little while, and it is worth deconstructing it to understand how it might inform the governance of a wider array of urban spaces. The implicit management of Shantytown evolved from two aspects of its construction and use. First, it was built by its users who maintained and watched over the park, frequently acting as de facto owners. Second, constant use reinforced the stewardship of the pioneers, providing a self-organizing form of management wherein expectations and the watchful eyes of other skaters greatly reduced opportunities for destructive or antisocial behavior.

With a heightened sense of responsibility, the park's builder-users dealt with most aspects associated with park management: keeping the area clean, repairing park "equipment" when needed, discouraging disorderly or destructive behavior, mediating disputes, and maintaining good relationships with non-skating recreators. They did it all without written rules or assigned roles. Before the skaters cleaned it up, the Slab was mostly a weed-strewn patch of concrete covered with broken bottles, rusting metal, and piles of debris. While Shantytown stood, I rarely saw a piece of trash, even though there were no trash cans or collections (though the margins below the Slab were often heavily strewn with garbage). Many skaters came only with their skateboards, generated little waste, and usually picked up after themselves. Nevitt explained that when they began construction of the Volcano,

people had a lot more respect for the area, because it wasn't something that you just happen upon and it was there. It was something that all the kids in the neighborhood eventually had a hand in, and

THE RISE AND FALL OF SHANTYTOWN SKATEPARK

as a result no one really littered, no one was breaking bottles anymore—and people would go out of their way not to start fights or get loud. Everyone was real respectful to this [neighboring] landlord, because it wasn't something that someone gave to you—it was something that everybody spent their own time, money, and effort in building.

This physical and social investment went a long way toward keeping the scene cool, even as the use of the park rapidly increased. Nevitt thought that publicly funded skateparks did not engender the same ethic because those who use it "didn't put any money or time into it." Even dealing with the homeless or occasional IV-drug users, the skaters tried to get along with their neighbors in such a way that would ensure the survival of their construction, while showing respect for others with whom they shared the terminal. The homeless men, mostly day laborers who when they were not working spent much of their time on and around the Slab and slept just feet away, were generally nonthreatening. They too did not appreciate destructive behavior. As Nevitt noted,

we sorta looked out for them and they'd look out for us—like a little community in that way. We respected their space and where they live and they respected us. We kept an eye on the place and we kept an eye [on] where they lived too. So if kids were throwing rocks, we'd stop them; we'd tell them not to.

Aware that their claim to the Slab was tenuous, the skateboarders viewed their own personal investment in Shantytown as being tied to a larger sense of community and facilitating equitable use. Part of this investment entailed defusing tensions before they had a chance to turn into something more serious. Nevitt could remember only one potentially serious incident. It involved four nonskateboarding older teenagers who had been harassing people across BEDT, including a man teaching his son how to ride a bike. He noted that these "kids" were belligerent and drunk, and at least one showed signs of being "dusted" (on cocaine, PCP, or other hard drugs). When their aggressive behavior began to interfere with the activity of those who were skating, it appeared that a fight might be in offing. The twenty skateboarders on the Slab greatly outnumbered the four kids, but instead of getting baited into an altercation, Shantytowners kept cool and restrained those among them who were more apt to strike back. Nevitt said they were able to get the troublemakers to leave before anything got serious. As he described,

Because it's something we all built and we put all of our time, money and effort into it—no one's going to let it go to waste over a stupid fight or [let] kids out there doing drugs or anything like that. We can't risk allowing anything like that here. . . . Otherwise this whole place gets taken away from us.

Complementing the sense of ownership among its builders and frequent users was a self-organizing policing mechanism that required no special actions or roles. Much like the safety of city streets and sidewalks of Jane Jacobs's New York, governance was a product of use, and most users played a role.[18] With Shantytown in almost continuous use, there were few opportunities for destructive behavior and a strong incentive toward civility. Most skaters appreciated that this was not just another park and understood that even without rules, they needed to control themselves and accommodate others. Those who did not feel the need to be civil could be reminded by others, and thus the ad hoc system of order usually worked.

While the watchful eyes and presence of its builders and users generally kept Shantytown well maintained and the vibe cool, these mechanisms also benefited from an ethic of self-reliance that often characterizes skateboarding. The mantra of "skate at your own risk" is akin to a gospel among skaters, and I frequently heard this and similar slogans from Shantytowners. Even as they disputed stereotypical depictions of skateboarders as outcasts, outlaws, or reckless thrill seekers, they also talked about their sport in terms of freedom and individuality, and not being bound by the same hierarchical patterns of rules that govern other sports. "Skateboarding is really not a sport," Nevitt insisted. Jocko Weyland felt similarly, noting that "there is an irrepressible act of freedom in skateboarding." It's a "solitary sport that engenders intense camaraderie" but has "no coaches, no rules, no one telling you what to do," he argued, calling it "a physical activity that really isn't a sport but definitely a way of life."[19]

Many skateboarders embrace this sort of individuality and believe that conventions governing their conduct come informally from their peers and experience. The "way of life" Weyland refers to also includes the assumption of risk and the responsibility to deal with potential injuries on one's own. It requires skateboarders to shake off injuries quickly and live with the pain that may accompany them and resolve conflicts without seeking mediation or authority. This makes injuries at skate spots *individual* concerns rather than *collective* or public ones and often forces adversarial parties to work out their conflicts expeditiously, face to face.

While the skaters felt that Shantytown functioned well without outside supervision, most of my discussions with them occurred after it was destroyed. Thus, they were willing to consider more hierarchical forms of management if a new park could be built at BEDT, accepting that official public skateparks could not quite duplicate the "no rules" atmosphere of street spots. Yet they still believed that the management of public parks in New York greatly exceeded what was necessary and again drew upon their experiences at Owl's Head to illustrate.

Nevitt, Dean, and Bob were generally satisfied with the terrain of Owl's Head—which had also won the endorsement of *Thrasher* magazine—but they complained about a range of other issues.[20] They felt that the park suffered from too much supervision and a host of lengthy rules. Skateboarders had to sign a waiver before skating; if they were under eighteen they would need a waiver signed by their parents and had to wear a helmet and kneepads. The fence surrounding the park ensured that the area was only for skateboarding (and rollerblading and BMX bicycling), keeping potential spectators far from the action. The lengthy waiver or "Participant Agreement, Agreement to Indemnify, and Risk Acknowledgement" had a full page of single-spaced clauses requiring skaters to "voluntary release, forever discharge, agree to indemnify and hold harmless" the Parks Department and the city.[21] It also required skaters to "certify" that they had "adequate insurance to cover any injury or damage [they] may suffer or cause while participating" or agree to "bear the costs of such injury or damage" and have "no medical or physical conditions" that could interfere with safety or else "assume and bear risk" created by such conditions. Below this particular clause was a line on which the skater was to write the name of his or her insurance company and policy or group number.

Reading, agreeing to, and signing such documents do have a tendency to take the joy out of a spontaneous recreation experience, but Shantytown skaters were even more concerned about very pragmatic issues such as operating hours. The park did not open until 1:00 P.M. in the spring and fall and 10:00 A.M. in July and August. As Nevitt noted,

> You can't skate when it starts raining, you can't skate when it gets dark, it stops in November; you can't skate until noon or whatever because they don't want kids playing hooky and skipping school. But if kids are gonna play hooky, they're gonna play hooky—if you ain't skating in a skatepark, you're skating in the street where there's traffic, so you might as well have the park open all hours of the day.

Skateboarding is often popularly imagined as a sport appealing mostly to teenagers, but the majority of those who skated at BEDT and a large portion of those in New York City are well beyond school age. The ability to skate at night and into the winter was also important to the skaters. Owl's Head closed at 8:00 P.M. and closed entirely from November

1 to April 1. Like dedicated participants of other urban sports played outdoors, including basketball, cycling, and jogging, skateboarders do not simply stop when the weather gets cold.

Even when Owl's Head was open, Dean felt, the limited hours of operation, numerous rules, and terrain that limited skaters to one-at-a-time in the bowls made for a "tense atmosphere" in which skaters were mostly concerned about "getting in the their runs" before the park closed. *Thrasher* advised, "Go early before it gets crowded" and noted the competition for time and space between skaters and bikers.[22] In contrast, the more relaxed atmosphere at Shantytown allowed skaters to take their time and socialize. Nevitt felt that the impatience of more experienced skaters at Owl's Head intimidated younger skaters. He said that it was unheard of for a veteran to take the time to guide a young skater through a new move, something that happened frequently at Shantytown.

Owl's Head was a specialized facility designed for a very limited number of activities reinforced by management policy that ensured specialization. Shantytown by contrast was more of a general-use space where skaters (and spectators) came to skate, socialize, and engage in other pursuits. The skateboarders praised the unsupervised and self-regulated environments at the user-built parks in Portland and Philadelphia and the conventionally built Millennium Skatepark in Denver, which operated twenty-four hours a day, seven days a week without supervision. Yet this notion of self-regulation and self-risk was at odds with the assumed perspective of State Parks. While Jim Moogan, the state official who was directing the development of the park planned for BEDT, consistently refused to discuss the demolition of Shantytown, an informal consensus among those who attended the community planning meetings in 2001 and 2002 was that the state took this action because of liability and insurance concerns.

My own thoughts about the safety and security in unsupervised space were briefly shaken when Steve showed me video footage of a fight that occurred at Shantytown. Neither he nor any of the park's pioneers were involved, and he did not know who the combatants were or the circumstances as to why the fight started. The footage began too late to provide any larger sense of this context, and it was unclear which if any (or all) of the participants were skateboarders. As the sound of people yelling back and forth could be heard in the background, the two combatants quickly wrestled each other down to the concrete of the Slab. One gained a commanding position on top of the other, while others tried unsuccessfully to pull him off. Eventually they did succeed, but the guy at the bottom of the pile lay motionless as the video ends. Steve said that this person was ultimately okay, but seeing this video was unsettling and seemed to contradict Nevitt's assurances about safety and peace among participants.

Perhaps this altercation was the worst thing that ever happened at Shantytown, or maybe conflicts such as this were more frequent? Skatespots have always been Darwinian in nature. Some approximation of "survival of the fittest" ruled the Brooklyn Banks for many years, and the Internet is filled with stories of fights and menacing or abusive behavior at this spot.[23] The hazing of newcomers was commonplace and often included "board jackings" (coerced borrowing without return of skateboard) and other forms of theft and intimidation. Some of these stories are fondly remembered as skateboarders have a tendency to bask in the machismo of their own tales of survival of these acts and eventual acceptance among their tougher peers. But the wanton atmosphere that was prevalent at the Banks was also a reflection of the more lawless time of the 1980s and early 1990s, when the streets and public spaces of New York were generally less safe and crime was more frequent.

Even in tougher neighborhoods like Williamsburg, the streets and appropriated spaces like BEDT were much safer by the turn of the millennium than previously.[24] Physical fights at the terminal were relatively rare, but because there are no real records of such instances, it is difficult to say just how much so. Fights occur wherever there are people, and there may be thousands of similar altercations across the city in any given year. They are often more of a reflection of the people involved than the setting in which it occurs. When there is an altercation in Central Park—even a particularly violent one—no one suggests that the park or any part of it be closed. Still, I can't help but think that this sort of incident, however infrequent, is precisely the thing that state officials feared and, while likely having no knowledge of this particular altercation, why they deemed the park's demolition as necessary.

The state's hesitation in embracing a new skatepark at BEDT, much less an unsupervised park, perhaps also shed some light on why there were so few built in New York City in the 1990s through the mid-2000s, even though the number of skateboarders had greatly increased throughout this period. Iain Borden attributes the closure of many U.S. and U.K. skateparks in the late 1970s and early 1980s to concerns about safety and "large insurance premiums" in spite of "impressive safety records."[25] These concerns were likely a factor in New York City, where in 2001 there were only six public skateparks (five operated by the city and one operated by the state).

The idea that skateboarding is a "self-risk" sport has been codified in some states, including California, Oregon, Maryland, and Nevada. While regulations vary, these states generally consider skateboarding (like skiing and rock climbing) a "hazardous activity" and those who participate in it do so at their own risk.[26] Parks in these states can be unsupervised, which actually lowers the potential liability for injury claims. In fact, municipal liability experts have reasoned that sensible policies treat skateparks like basketball courts, which are generally unsupervised, noting that "free play" without supervision limits municipal risk.[27] Over the past decade New York City has begun to embrace self-risk, building new skateparks that are left unsupervised, as will be discussed later in this chapter. Still it would be hard to mistake the atmosphere of these public facilities for that of Shantytown.

Destroying Shantytown

On a July 23, 2001, posting to their Internet site, *Transworld Skateboarding* noted that their agents had arrived at Shantytown one afternoon to do a photo shoot, only to find agents from *SLAP* and *Skateboarder* working on their own productons. They noted,

> The unprecedented attention to this tiny renegade concrete volcano triggered awareness in the minds of the powers that be. Now that New York University owns the land, it is said [they] want to shut it down. [28]

While their facts were not entirely straight (the owner of the property was New York state; New York University was the state's development partner), their warning proved prescient as a State Parks–hired demolition crew began taking down the park within days of the posting. Without consultation or warning, heavy construction equipment brought down the concrete obstacles of the park, ending the Shantytown experiment one year and a half after it began, and only nine months after the completion of the Volcano.

At first, no one was quite sure who was responsible. Someone said he had called "the city" and they said they had nothing to do with the demolition or knew who was responsible. Many then naturally thought the responsible party was the owner of the three-story building that projected into the terminal and abutted the skatepark—the "in-holding" property, as State Parks officials called it. Illegally renting the building out to residential tenants, the owner, some thought, had been prompted to take action on land that he did not own in response to complaints about the noise generated by the skateboarders.[29] This remained the prevailing theory until an October public meeting in which Jim Moogan, State Parks' project manager, hastily acknowledged that his agency had indeed demolished the park, though without providing a definitive rationale for having done so.

The destruction of Shantytown was a tremendous blow to its pioneers and frequent users. I learned about it on a hot Saturday, a few days after it had occurred. In the aftermath of its demolition, Shantytowners built a small memorial out the rubble of the Volcano and the quarter-pipes. It was just a simple pile of concrete chunks and rocks, but this too was too much for State Parks. I arrived on the scene just as the bulldozer had cleared these vestiges of remembrance. As the bulldozer left, I found three teary-eyed teenage skaters—Manny, Roger, and Denise—sitting on the Slab, still trying to make sense of the destruction before them. They expressed sadness, anger, and confusion. While I heard the story of what happened from Denise and Manny, Roger was the most upset and visibly shaken:

I love this place—I love this place more than any place in the world—and they fucked it up! Fuck them!

The park's destruction, even months later, brought an emotional response from Roger and the others with whom I spoke:

Roger: This is my second home. I met most of my friends down here, and my friends are like my family—when it got knocked down, I lost my family right there.

Dean: That was one of the saddest days I ever had. I really think a lot of other people feel the same way.

Bob: I cried, man, I really cried, like I lost a pet or good friend. It wasn't just because [of] all the work we put into it—it was just like the destruction of our lives. . . . Every time I skated down here it was like, man, I'm going to be hanging out with my closest friends and doing what I love to do.

At the November 2001 BEDT walkthrough, Denise, one of the few females who regularly skated Shantytown, wore a hooded sweatshirt emblazoned with "BROOKLYN" above an image of the Volcano. She noted that the younger skaters were now on the streets, which generated complaints and calls to the police from neighbors. "It's just a mess," she said. Nevitt, a very positive and forward-thinking person by nature, was also still feeling the pain of this loss. Along the edge of the Slab, he found the metal ramp he had built and that had served as the catalyst for Shantytown. He recalled all of the joyous times they had had with this little ramp. It had been bent and flattened beyond repair. Pointing out the marks created by the teeth of the bulldozer, he noted,

> This was just one thing that when they tore this place down [that] just added insult to injury, is that the guy obviously came down with his bulldozer, dug it right in the ramp, squashed it, then pushed it off the edge. That wasn't necessary; that wasn't right. We could have taken that away. But now it is sort of an inanimate martyr for Shantytown.

The skateboarding magazines also lamented the destruction of Shantytown. Writing in *Thrasher*, Jocko Weyland mourned its passing but noted that "skatespots come and go" and "even seemingly everlasting concrete can't survive the inevitable."[30] As more people used the park more often and for more hours, individual ethic and responsibility—the principal way in which the space was managed and controlled—were probably overwhelmed by the sheer volume of use. Shantytown was in a sense a victim of its own success. Intensive use and the notoriety of the park perhaps prompted State Parks to take action in accordance with state law to stop what it deemed a potentially dangerous situation.[31]

After Shantytown

In October 2001, I received a mass e-mail message from Denise with the subject line "HELP SAVE OUR SHANTYTOWN!" imploring attendance at a public meeting hosted by State Parks. Unlike most of the other constituent users discussed in this book, the skateboarders embraced the planning process for the waterfront park. They strongly believed that a skatepark was good for the neighborhood and thought that, if their voices were loud enough, state officials would allow them to rebuild Shantytown.

While the original was gone, some had started working on a new Volcano, a few feet from where the old one once stood. On a sunny October afternoon, I found Dean alone, carefully adding chunks of broken concrete and debris onto this ever-growing pile. The installation was taking a familiar shape and was close to reaching the height of its predecessor. He told me with considerable pride that the new Volcano was being built out of the rubble of the original as well as

THE RISE AND FALL OF SHANTYTOWN SKATEPARK

the two destroyed quarter-pipes, and that it would be even larger than the first. The skateboarders had hoped that this new Volcano could be incorporated into the design of the state park—or at least be sanctioned as a legitimate interim use. Though this mound stood for many months, it was never finished. At one of the community meetings the following spring, a skater told me that they were not going to invest any more time or money in the skatepark unless they received assurance that it would not be destroyed, at least not until construction on the new park began. The mound was cleared in the summer of 2002, as part of the initial cleanup that also destroyed the terminal's other vernacular creations, topographical features, and plant life.[32]

The skateboarders also expressed a willingness to work with State Parks and local stakeholders and their development partner, NYU. On the day of the community walkthrough, Nevitt proposed a skatepark designed and constructed by hand by neighborhood residents, much like the one that State Parks had demolished a few months earlier. He reasoned that a new skater-built park at BEDT would have many positive aspects for the neighborhood and the city.

For local skateboarders, the summer of 2001 was to be known for three demolitions. The destruction of Shantytown in late July was bracketed by the spectacular (and fully planned) demolition of two massive gas tanks on the nearby Newtown Creek earlier that month and the fall of the World Trade Center on September 11.[33] From my conversations with the skaters that November, it was clear that, as with many New Yorkers, the destruction of the Twin Towers still weighed heavily upon them. Some local skateboarders were among the crowd of residents who watched the awful spectacle of September 11 from BEDT. The skateboarders made several references to the destruction of the World Trade Center and seemed to view the destruction of their own little piece of the city as symbolically coupled with this much larger tragedy. In fact, they believed that rebuilding the skatepark would be a small but important step in the physical and psychological rebuilding of the city. As Nevitt described,

> Just like the dark day that September 11th was—when this place got bulldozed . . . it was just, like shocking, a really sorta senseless blow—it really knocked the wind out of ya. It was a real dark day. [We] would like to set [the construction process] up in such a way so kids can—everyone in the community can—come and get their hands dirty rebuilding a piece of New York. It's one of those healing process sort of things.

While Nevitt preached working within the system and reaching out to other stakeholders, Dean remained more skeptical, noting his displeasure with the "big boring conversation" that was already unfolding. He said he was willing to participate in the planning process but was concerned that they might wind up with a "rinky-dink" skatepark or nothing at all. Bob said that state officials needed to let them "take control" or the park might be an expensive waste of money that no one would want to skate. Yet Dean, Bob, and other skaters did attend the three community planning meetings the following spring.

While these meetings are chronicled in detail in Chapter 7, it is important to note that the skateboarders showed up in large numbers and were prepared to work with other stakeholders, even as BEDT's other informal constituencies did not participate. At the second of these meetings, the twenty skateboarders in attendance, most with skateboards in hand, discovered that the state was no longer considering a skatepark as part of its plan. However, Jim Moogan promised the skaters that the state would work with the city's Parks Department to build a skatepark at a nearby city-owned location. He would not say where that location was or provide any other pertinent details. Disappointed, the skaters sat quietly and participated infrequently through the rest of the meeting. After it ended, a few of the skateboarders again pressed their case with Moogan, who assured them of the sincerity of the state's commitment. At the conclusion of the third meeting, attended by only a few skateboarders, Nevitt, Denise, and Denise's mother (who had been present at all of the meetings) took up their case with State Parks representative Warren Holliday (Moogan had moved on to another job), who had driven down from Albany for this forum. However, Holliday could reaffirm only the state's general commitment to assisting the

Dean rebuilds the Volcano using the rubble of their destroyed skatepark and other debris. This new Volcano would never be completed (2001).

THE RISE AND FALL OF SHANTYTOWN SKATEPARK

city in building a skatepark in the area (but not at BEDT). By 2004, the issue of the skatepark had been taken up by the Friends of BEDT Park and other local open space advocates, who pressured the city to include it in the redesign of the McCarren Park Pool. By 2010, the city's Parks Department completed the area's first public skatepark at the pool site.

The modest skatepark at McCarren was hardly a replacement for Shantytown, and by the time it was completed Shantytown builders had long moved on to a series of other spaces. Some skated the bowl inside Nevitt's KCDC skateshop on North 11th Street. They also skated the streets around KCDC. Even with new residential developments and loft conversions, there was less skateboarding conflict than one might imagine. Space in many of the area's trademark industrial buildings had been leased to art, design, workshop, or new media tenants, who were more likely to tolerate the presence of skateboarders.

By late 2003, many former Shantytown skateboarders could also be found less than a mile up the waterfront in a large, mostly vacant warehouse in the Greenpoint Terminal Market complex. Previously known as the American Manufacturing Company, in the early twentieth century this was the fourth-largest private employer in the city. Within its twenty-plus buildings, which sprawled across the waterfront and inland blocks connected by a network of bridges, the company produced rope, jute, and other maritime and shipbuilding products.[34] As part of a guerrilla marketing campaign entitled "Ouch!" to reach cool, risk-taking twenty- and thirty-somethings, McNeil Pharmaceuticals, makers of Tylenol, gave a grant to Dave Mims and his group to design and build the 2,500-square-foot birchwood skateboarding bowl inside the warehouse.[35] Unlike at Shantytown, the use of this space, alternatively called the "Autumn Bowl" after the name of Dave's Manhattan skateshop or "Tylenol Bowl" after its funders, was controlled through membership, and access was limited to those who had a key. While the bowl was not really a secret (there are many videos of it on the Internet), members were generally wary of attention. The arrangement was legal, though, and through member dues Dave paid the owner of the complex monthly rent.

The warehouse in which the Autumn Bowl was located survived a massive fire in May 2006 that destroyed many of the buildings of the Greenpoint Terminal Market complex.[36] But responding to rent increases and a lack of willingness among key holders to pay higher dues, Dave Mims closed the Autumn Bowl in 2010.[37] The warehouse space that once held the bowl is now a concert venue.[38] As the entire property was rezoned for residential use in 2005, this concert space may also be short-lived.

Learning from Shantytown?

Since my time with the skateboarders of the Brooklyn waterfront, New York City has built several new skateparks, bringing the number in the city to thirteen, more than double the amount of 2001.[39] These facilities include the skatepark that was part of the renovation of the McCarren Park Pool in Greenpoint. While demand continues to grow, the city has also begun to embrace the concept of self-risk, with some of the newer parks being unsupervised. Additionally, led by Parks Commissioner Adrian Benepe (who stepped down in 2012 to take an executive position with the Trust for Public Land), the city has shown a willingness to work with skaters in designing new parks. This includes a skatepark in Flushing Meadows–Corona Park that contains elements modeled after the Brooklyn Banks and several other famed New York City skatespots. Benepe was also willing to discuss, consider, and compromise when conflicts occurred in spaces controlled by the Parks Department, such as the Brooklyn Banks.

The 2010 closure of the Banks has facilitated recollections of its more glorious past and conjecture about its future among many skateboarders. The Parks Department's plan is to reopen the Banks after the bridge renovations are complete, in 2014.[40] But Steve Rodriguez and others feel that this storied spot was never really the same after September 11. The renovation and 2005 compromise he brokered with city officials that brought skateboarding back to the Banks came at a steep price in terms of lost terrain and atmosphere.[41] Some skaters also believe that even if it is reopened it will be in a diminished form. Is this just nostalgia for the old days? Perhaps, but formal recognition and a seat as a stakeholder in political deliberations come with a price, rendering "outlaw" experiences much less so.

As the Banks shows, legitimacy does cost such a place some of its beyond-the-rules feel. In cities like New York, regularization of informal spaces into the conventional and contentious geography of the city also means dealing with messy land-use politics, assumptions of responsibility, and the necessity of working with other stakeholders, including those who are seemingly external to the events on the ground. Even DIY skateparks, such as Burnside in Portland and FDR Park in Philadelphia, which have survived more than a decade and retain some of their outsider spirit, are still tenuous places. While attaining some legitimacy, they have not fully blossomed into the all-welcoming, "family vibe" skatepark that North Brooklyn skaters envisioned for Shantytown.

Yet the story of Shantytown shows the potential of DIY design, construction, and governance in public space. It demonstrates that less is often more: less structure, less planning, less professional involvement, fewer rules and regulations, and less money. It shows that when given the opportunity to engage in place making, nonprofessionals can aptly see to their own needs and desires, and sometimes spectacularly so. Shantytown also engendered a communal spirit and sense of local pride among neighborhood youth and young adults and added to the distinctive social geography of Greenpoint–Williamsburg as an area for urban counterculture and creativity. Its hands-on development also provided an opportunity for personal growth and learning that would not be present in even the best-designed professional skateparks or in a more typical community-based but professionally built project. Shantytown's builder-users learned the requirements of not only concrete construction but also of social dynamics—how to cooperate with others and deal with conflict, leverage personal investments, and make the most of limited communal resources and talents.

On a broader level, Shantytown demonstrates the value of the present city, not some grander, more perfectly imagined or equitable metropolis of the future. It was not so much that the skaters valued a site that others had found lacking but rather that they valued it in its *present* and highly imperfect state. While others saw BEDT as an opportunity to boldly reimagine the waterfront, the skateboarders valued it for immediate use. Any larger sense of grandness, reclamation, and physical expansion grew from use itself. This represents an inversion of State Parks' initial approach to the terminal and the city's larger vision of the waterfront as a well-planned necklace of green anchored by housing and leisure spaces that formed the basis of its rezoning initiative passed in 2005.[42] But the demise of Shantytown also demonstrates the limits of the vernacular. With increasing popularity, investment, sophistication, reputation, and geographic extent, informal uses formalize. Following this arc of formality, the DIY creation either becomes more like conventional urban space or cannot survive.

Shantytown was denied a chance to evolve toward conventionality, its builders denied the opportunity to be part of any meaningful deliberations about the future of the waterfront. The deal between New York state and New York University that later unraveled was at the time widely praised and popular with many neighborhood residents and their local representatives.[43] As will be discussed in Chapter 7, the partnership was hailed as a pragmatic way to stretch public investment while providing a fitting reward for those residents who had long fought to reclaim their waterfront. Shantytown was, by contrast, never about making a deal; its politics was on the ground. While the Slab still stands, few involved in the planning of what would become East River State Park ever recognized the unique contribution of the vernacular builders, who made Shantytown, for a short time, a skateboarding mecca.

CHAPTER 3

MARCH AND BURN

Practice, Performance, and Leisure without a Plan

THE SKATEBOARDERS WERE NOT the only creative constituency that made regular use of the Slab. The dynamic conditions of this building foundation—expansiveness, relative flatness, and a lack of obstructions—also lent itself to a number of other practices, performances, and events. Many of these activities occurred on an ad hoc basis, and practitioners appropriated as much concrete as they needed. But the waterfront did have its "resident" performers—a punk rock marching band and a troupe of fire performers—who exploited the lack of rules and supervision, and BEDT's relative remoteness, to serially remake this platform into a semi-public rehearsal venue every Sunday. Noise and fire prohibitions—either by rule or expectation—usually kept these performers out of traditional public spaces, while a lack of money or status kept them from obtaining commercial or institutional studio time. The terminal, by contrast, provided them with a convenient practice site that was free and always available, and no one would care how loud or fiery they got.

These eclectic performers were not driven merely by a desire to find cost-free, out-of-the-way space; their spirit and the anarchic flavor of their respective crafts were greatly sympathetic to the conditions they found at the water's edge. They added to the unlikely carnival that unfolded every weekend and made the experience of their mostly inadvertent audiences all the richer. About the band in particular, one regular visitor called their performances the "soundtrack" of the waterfront.

This chapter documents the waterfront narratives of these performance groups: the Hungry March Band and the fire spinners. As their stories will show, the Slab provided them with a dynamic platform where they could practice, perform, experiment, and be inspired by unique physical and social conditions around them. Their weekly appropriations helped foster the waterfront's creative milieu and contributed to Williamsburg's emerging reputation as a hub for arts and counterculture. BEDT's anarchic conditions also enabled interesting synergies that blurred traditional distinctions between performers and their audiences and performance, practice, and play. These narratives suggest more fluid conceptions of not just "arts and leisure" but how we define, plan, and manage leisure spaces in a creative and unpredictable city.

The two "performance crafts" documented here are also part of larger movements centered on alternative cultures—a millennial blend of disparate folk traditions, DIY ethics, and creative hedonism—that are becoming a more

The Hungry March Band provided the "soundtrack" of Sunday afternoons on the Williamsburg waterfront (2001).

prominent aspect of American city life. Rejecting the arts, entertainment, and media generated and controlled by ever larger global corporate conglomerates, these practitioners desire to be producers rather than just consumers of cultural experiences, and to be members of a community built around locally generated arts. The Brooklyn neighborhoods of Williamsburg, Greenpoint, and, increasingly, Bushwick have been a haven for DIY practices over the past two decades—and these groups helped propel this local scene.

The Hungry March Band and fire spinners are also part of a longer tradition of urban street performance. Like the city's more traditional buskers—the cellist on the corner, a troubadour with an acoustic guitar on a subway mezzanine, and even break dancers in Washington Square Park—these artists are part of a greatly expanded vernacular of "playing in public" in New York and other big cities. Over several decades the number and variety of these artists have increased: Mariachi bands, circus arts, situational theater, dance, performance art, and instant happenings generated by electronic media are now as common as pop, jazz, or classical music. All of these practitioners incite a form of urban triangulation, creating encounters that are some combination of density, creativity, and happenstance.[1] Reaffirming something essential about city life, they have the power to surprise even the most jaded of New Yorkers or provide cause for the invocation of that cliché "only in New York," even if it is not entirely true. But impromptu street performances are often the end product of a larger arc that involves hours of practice, composition, coordinated rehearsal, and looser play. So the narratives of these groups and their waterfront sessions are also, in part, a story of the city we do not often see, an underbelly of twenty-first-century cultural production.

March and Play: The Soundtrack of the Unplanned

> We March! We Move! Unthwarted by electricity or space confines, we are in your face and on the street. We are the music of the People. We are a parade, a party, a blazing entity of flesh, blood, brass, steel and wood. — Hungry March Band web site

Few musical ensembles are so thoroughly synonymous with New York City's underground scene as the Hungry March Band. Over the past fifteen years they have established themselves as *the* band that will play anywhere and everywhere, at any time and under all circumstances. Dedicated to "in your face" encounters with mostly unsuspecting

Appropriating the Slab for their weekly practices helped HMB develop into a brash and versatile ensemble. Sasha (*far right*) describes the band's sound as a "big soup of influences" (2001).

audiences, they are a "public" marching band and frequently take to the streets with their instruments, whether they have been invited to do so or not. Once dubbed "Best Anarchist Parade Group" by the *Village Voice* (among its many media accolades), HMB gave performances on the streets, sidewalks, and subways of the city that are legendary.[2] The band is large, loud, and unafraid to be heard, even if its presence leads to confrontation with police or arrest, which has happened a few times.

The Hungry March Band is not what you would typically find during halftime of a college football game. Rarely found in the stadium and with parades making up only a small portion of their performances, this band inhabits a broader milieu and embraces a greater spectrum of possibilities. Likewise, their principal purpose has not evolved to support the team, honor soldiers and public servants, or provide musical accompaniment to yearly holiday ritual. They may indeed do these sorts of gigs, but the band is really more about making music, mischief, and the most of a good time.

Their music also diverges from standard marching band fare. Playing mostly originals composed by individual band members, HMB incorporates a veritable kaleidoscope of source materials and inspirations, drawing upon the rich mix of sounds heard on the streets of the city. Sasha Sumner, a saxophonist with the band since 1998 and video editor and adjunct college instructor by day, described their music as "a big soup of influences and different styles," noting its appropriation of Balkan, Latin, Klezmer, New Orleans jazz, Caribbean, Afrobeat, Bhangra, and European brass. Some have also compared the group to Sun Ra's Arkestra, the revolutionary free jazz band. Their music is also part of the emerging "Gypsy Punk" movement, a New York City–grown hybrid genre that the *New York Times* described as "mingling the passionate rage of Punk with the theatricality of traditional Gypsy music."[3]

When I first met the group, HMB had approximately twenty musicians and a few performers, which included someone who carried the band's distinctive "ear plus crossed knife and fork" color guard. During the early 2000s they grew larger, and for some special events, Sasha said, they "customized" personnel to include more than fifty musicians, dancers, baton twirlers, and others. In the late 2000s, though, the band became smaller and their playing style became tighter. While still marching, members now often refer to their group as a "brass band," which reflects its somewhat reduced size and more refined sound. At the same time, the group embraces its roots as a marching band and relishes its role in bringing this tradition back to the fore and popularizing it with young people.

HMB has inspired the formation of other marching bands, and ex-members have gone on to form their own eclectic ensembles, including the Rude Mechanical Orchestra, which has established itself as its own New York countercultural institution.[4] HMB compositions are also infiltrating the standard marching band repertoire, Sasha says. She found an Internet video of a Michigan high school marching band playing their song "Bumper to Bumper" and noted others like this. Additionally, the band enjoys sympathy with ensembles in countries like Germany, France, and Italy, where there is a long tradition of local brass or marching bands that play in seasonal celebrations and festivals scattered across the countryside. Touring these areas and playing the festival circuit themselves, HMB has found that local groups are already familiar with their music. Without plan or prompting, they often play along when the band strikes up a song.

No venue has proved too large or small, no event too eclectic or conventional. HMB has played block parties and festivals; rallies, protests, and fundraisers; loft parties and guerrilla art happenings; birthdays, weddings, and funerals; and all varieties of parades and public celebrations. They have played on rooftops and in basements; at Lincoln Center, Madison Square Garden, and a cardiologists' convention in Washington; on the Staten Island Ferry and in the Mardis Gras parade in New Orleans. Nearer to BEDT, they have often provided background music to New York City Marathon runners as they make their way up Bedford Avenue. Through the sheer volume and variety of events they have played, HMB has become emblematic of the city's larger millennial underground of music, entertainment, and nightlife while evolving into ambassadors for the city's creative scene through their travels both nationally and abroad and their recordings. When the band plays, people know that New York's unique performance scene is still thriving and that gentrification has not swept away audacious street-level arts.

But countercultural fame and international renown gets the band only so far, and their lack of organizational affiliation, while surely liberating, has come at a price. Without a university athletic field at their disposal or an auditorium or gymnasium when the weather is poor, where can HMB practice? Over the past few years they have often rented time in a variety of indoor spaces (the most recent of which being a performance loft in the Dumbo area of Brooklyn), but finding space and time has been a constant struggle. For a while BEDT was their rehearsal spot, and they practiced there most Sunday afternoons from 1997 until 2003. It was in the middle of this period that I got know the band. Over the course of several of these Sunday sessions, I hung out with the group. I sometimes shot video and took many photographs, but rarely did I have a serious conversation or formal interview with them; it was just not their way.

One of my first intimate HMB experiences came on a chilly late October afternoon. I found Doug and Toto—a drummer and a cornet player, respectively—patiently waiting for the others to show up at their spot near the southwest corner of the Slab. I waited with them. Toto said the others would be there soon, but a half hour passed and still no one had showed. I asked if they were sure that the others were coming; had the session had been canceled? Toto reassured me—this was their regular practice gig; it had definitely not been canceled. The band had been practicing here every Sunday almost since its inception more than three years earlier. By 2000, coming down to the waterfront on Sundays was not something that needed to be scheduled; it was second nature, and band members came each week out of habit. As it grew later, the wind picked up and Toto, who was already wearing several layers of clothes and a ski cap, sought refuge underneath a Mexican blanket; Doug soon joined her. "I'm sure some of them will be here soon," she said, a little less sure. After an hour, they too began to wonder, and Toto got on her cell phone and made a few calls. No one had canceled practice—rarely did someone take it upon him- or herself to make decisions for the entire group—but individual members they spoke to were not going to show for a variety of reasons. "I guess no one is coming so we're not practicing this afternoon," Doug told me matter-of-factly. He said to come back on the following Sunday.

This was the normal course of affairs for the band, and Doug and Toto had long come to expect this sort of inconsistency from their mates. In the middle of a rehearsal the following October, Sasha described some of the challenges they had in getting members out to both practices and gigs. While the band had twenty members back then, typical attendance on Sundays was often closer to a dozen at that time. Performances were even more problematic. "We haven't been a full group for a while and we have been playing a lot of shows," she said. "Whoever can make it, makes it." For a show they played the night before, a Brooklyn loft party, they'd had only twelve. "We just played our greatest hits," she explained, adding that they were fortunate that their sound was enhanced by the band's commanding perch on a mezzanine above the party floor.

As Toto reminded me later that fall, HMB was no one's day job, and members often had to balance gigs against their work schedules. Many of those in the band (then and now) earned a living in creative industries—music, film and video, and Internet media—and often taught these subjects at colleges, community workshops, and elsewhere. Others members, past and present, were educators in other subjects, construction workers, writers, and massage therapists; one member who recently left the band is a cardiologist. Late-night gigs were not very conducive to maintaining a conventional work schedule. Some of the more musically inclined had other competing (and paying) gigs that sometimes kept them from making it to a show, while others had to balance attending a performance that might not start until after midnight with personal obligations and, for a few, with family time. Four or five members of the group were unemployed, Sasha said at the time. While this did not keep them from coming to practice or a show, it may have dampened their enthusiasm for rehearsals.

One afternoon before practice, Scott, a sousaphone player, attempted to tell me the story of the band's origin and early history. While he talked, six or seven other band members were hanging out; some ate bagged lunches and others warmed up on their instruments. They listened and occasionally added their own acerbic comments. The band was formed in 1997 to march and play at Brooklyn's annual celebration of counterculture and grand freak show, the Mermaid Parade in Coney Island. Its name refers to its "hunger" for authentic musical and urban experiences and is a play on the adage "Will play for food!" which the band has done many times. Beginning with just a few people from the neighborhood, it was more of a concept than a musically adept ensemble. The person who dreamed up the band and its name, Dreiky, quit the group soon after its formation. While neither Scott nor the others present at that moment were original HMB members, many had an opinion about why Dreiky had left the band. Someone said she was a "control freak" and did not get along with the others. Toto tried to clarify. "No, she had the concept, the idea, but there just wasn't enough people to make it work."

When the band had formed, its members mostly lived in the Greenpoint and Williamsburg neighborhoods, and a few more lived in the East Village a short subway ride away. (By 2012, their membership was more scattered across the entire city.) They tried practicing at nearby McCarren Park, but it was too crowded and they found the activity around them distracting. "It sort of seemed like a free concert," Toto explained. Living locally, band members knew about the waterfront and the people's park dynamic that unfolded there on weekends. At an earlier rehearsal, Theresa, a drummer and founding member who long served as the band's publicist and webmaster, said, "Timmy wanted to come down here, so we just came down."

Timmy (*with cigarette*) attempts to lead the band through the rehearsal (2001).

Of original members, only three were left by fall 2001: Theresa; Timmy, who played snare drum with an attached cymbal; and Sara, the band's baton twirler. With his muttonchop sideburns and old-fashioned cap, Timmy, perhaps thirty years old at that time, often played with a cigarette hanging out of his mouth. His sense of vintage flair and somewhat gruff demeanor transcended his more diminutive size. He was never interested in talking and often seemed annoyed with my presence, which he thought distracted the band from rehearsal. He was probably right on a few occasions, but many band members were given to distractions and if not me it might have been something else.

Another original member, a bit like Timmy in temperament but more outgoing, was Gam, the band's mercurial trombonist. In his early thirties, he too he had a certain timeless charm to him, no doubt enhanced by his tendency to wear vintage-style caps and sleeveless undershirts. A local kid from the neighborhood, he was well familiar with the waterfront. I would often see him at BEDT with or without the band. After his initial suspicion of me subsided, he became quite garrulous and talked authoritatively about the social lore of the waterfront and neighborhood. One afternoon we discussed the social lore of the terminal, and he began many of his sentences with "Do you remember when . . . ?" "Do you remember when there were raves in the warehouses here?" I had indeed remembered the physical landscape to which he referred but had not attended any of the raves in the 1990s that several other people had also recalled. Never interested in talking about the band, later that summer he was absent from several rehearsal sessions. By the early fall he had dropped out of the group, though neither he nor any of his former band mates were willing to say why. From its modest beginning, BEDT was a good fit for the band and an excellent place for them to grow, eventually becoming the bigger, brasher, and more musically savvy ensemble they are today. Nobody seemed to mind their loud and sometimes raucous presence on the large, sloping platform, which the band, like almost everyone else, called the Slab. Sometimes when it rained they would practice in another co-opted neighborhood waste space, underneath the Brooklyn–Queens Expressway. When it was too cold they practiced in someone's loft or basement, or not at all. Even as the area gentrified, there were still large studio, event, or live-work spaces available to them in Williamsburg or Greenpoint loft buildings that could serve as practice or performance venues. But BEDT was their principal rehearsal site, and their sound and identity evolved from their Sundays spent on the waterfront. "It kind of gelled once we got down here; the band wasn't really together before that," Theresa explained. "Once we came down here—on Sundays—this [became] like our church, our religion so to speak. This is a very spiritual place."

Gam (*left*) and Jay during a break in rehearsal. The band's sessions often unfolded over long afternoons that freely mixed practice with social time (2001).

What was it about the terminal that made it so ideal for HMB? "It's a free space, it's got a nice view, and it's available—and it's in the neighborhood," Doug said. In assent, a few of the others who were sitting around him repeated, "And it's in the neighborhood!" Toto noted that "there's very little hassle . . . that is why we like to hang and continue to come back," John, a trombone player, said, "It's a vibe. It's the most conducive practice space." And "nobody bothers us," he added.

Proximity, cost-free anytime access, views, and the lack of hassles were all important to individual members, but as an ensemble the setting also fit the tenor of their music: loud, free-spirited, unpredictable, and occasionally angry. Their sessions had an anarchic quality—in method and song—and the volume, volatility, and festiveness of their sound helped create the soundscape that would color other leisure experiences occurring across the waterfront. But those qualities of the terminal that were particularly advantageous to the band were time-based, suiting its idiosyncratic rehearsal routine, which blended practice with play and often unfolded over long afternoons. Without designated areas or constraints of schedule, they rehearsed, performed, and partied, in no particular order and often all at once. Rolling into and out of sessions, they moved freely between practicing and hanging out, ensemble and uncoordinated play, and played for as little or as long as they wanted.

On a typical Sunday, members collected themselves near the southwest corner of the Slab, often around 2:00 P.M. (No one would tell me the "official" start time for rehearsals, and after a while I began to think that it was whatever time that afternoon people showed up.) Those who arrived early (or on time) were not bothered by the lack of an immediate quorum with which to practice, and this waiting became a sort of social time. As a critical mass formed, some picked up their instruments and warmed up individually or in groups of two or three. As different members noodled on their instruments, being joined and left by others without apparent plan or consent, some of their mates, seemingly oblivious, continued to socialize. At some point and often without explicit cues, the entire contingent came together to begin formal rehearsal. But getting to this moment could often take a while, and sometimes it never really happened.

The end of rehearsals followed a similar pattern, though in reverse sequence. The music often devolved slowly, becoming more chaotic as more people broke off from the group to do their own thing, musical or otherwise. Sometimes the music just petered out, and by the time the last band member had stopped playing the others were well into "after-practice" beer-in-hand socializing or getting ready to light the barbecue. This was particularly true during good weather, and the Slab's physical dimension and lack of social constraints accommodated these quick transitions to or from playing soccer or football and barbecues and parties. The looseness of these sessions was surely a reflection of the band's idiosyncratic character, and most members knew to expect this sort of mild anarchy on Sundays. About the quality of rehearsal, John noted, "Sometimes it was marvelous and sometimes it was crap," not sounding particularly bothered by the group's lack of consistency. At times, though, some members were clearly frustrated with their mates who were seemingly determined to play solo or socialize.

Rehearsing the theme song from "The Muppet Show" in mid-October, a relatively rare non-original played by the band, provided a taste of this dynamic. Brandon and I watched and rolled videotape as Timmy tried to get the group together after what seemed like an unexpected break. "Okay, listen up! Let's do this song," he shouted, straining to be heard over the cacophony of talking and random sounds. "Let's do this song!" He repeated as his frustration continued to build. "Enough talking, let's do this song!" The band went through several starts and stops but did not have it together. Trying to get the various parts to harmonize, Timmy offered instructions to individual members and barked out the beats he expected. To demonstrate the proper tone and cadence, he sang a line from the song: "Why don't we get things started?" He approached different members and repeated the line, and they sang it back him, attempting to match the requested octave and accentuations. "And with all the highs and all the lows!" he added. They did it a few more times. Twenty minutes later their final version was perhaps not at the level of harmony that Timmy had expected, but it did contain the appropriate amount of oomph and well entertained those of us listening and watching on.

As practice was breaking up, Sasha tried to better explain how these sessions usually worked. As we talked, Emily, another saxophonist, tried to corral her nine-year-old son, Sam, who usually attended the rehearsals with her, often banging a drum as they practiced or sneaking some notes in on the sousaphone while it lay unoccupied on the ground. Sasha, a tall woman with long, streaked hair who wore a vintage dark coat with stripes sewn onto the sleeves (perhaps this was a genuine marching band coat?) and a similarly vintage cap, said the group had a "musical director" only for recording sessions, and there was no similarly designated role for practices. Different band members would sometimes attempt to guide the group, as I had watched Timmy do on that afternoon. As she described,

> If there was one leader, then that leader would say, "Hey, let's all do this." And everyone would do it. But we don't have one leader, so we're not going to just sit here or stop playing a song because some people don't want to do it. . . . To accomplish something, it ends up taking a long time. But that's the nature of a large group like this one—because people want to have fun.

I thought the session was over, but Theresa and Samantha, the band's cymbal player, came over and smiled at us. "I think we're gonna play one more song, special for you guys now, 'Asphalt Tango,'" Theresa announced. "It's a really good song!" Samantha added. And with that they launched into a furious version of this Gypsy Punk number, a signature song of their early years.

The anarchy of space and sound—the waterfront and the Hungry March Band—went hand-in-hand and made for some lively if not always productive afternoons. "It was a lot of partying," Sasha recalled when I caught up with her several years later. It was the band's golden era and a time when rehearsals were inseparable from social pursuits, sometimes stretching over several hours punctuated by many starts and stops. Even when the band was "on," these sessions often devolved into long, semi-structured jams in one key, she explained. (I too remembered and did enjoy these improvisational journeys, which were a prominent if not completely intended feature of these rehearsals.) She noted that there were few remaining band members from this period (less than a third of its 2011 members), and most had never experienced one of these waterfront rehearsals. Both the terminal and the larger scene that it facilitated are now part of the memory and lore of the band: the crazy place where the band found its signature style and swagger.

These rehearsals also coincided with and fueled the band's wilder and crazier antics, including their unsanctioned performances on the subway and street encounters, including an infamous East Village parade on Good Friday, when a profusion of fireworks led to a float's catching on fire and the eventual arrest of five band members. (They were released without charges.) On another occasion, the police chased band members from a pavilion in a Bronx park in which they were playing. All escaped, except for Timmy, who was arrested (and released without charges the next morning). "We used to crash loft parties—just show up and start playing," Sasha said. She missed these sorts of musical adventures but recognized that they were no longer possible; band members were "more mature" now and their complicated lives with partners, children, and careers effectively prohibited their old modes of practice and play:

> Gradually we have become much more refined, more professional. We still party and get down—but when we rehearse, we have to make good use of this time. You're paying for two or three hours, so you better be focused, otherwise you're just throwing your money away.

The band, like other regular visitors, understood that their rehearsal site was temporary, and even as they anticipated its eventual closure they continued to draw inspiration from it. Their self-titled first album, released in 2001 (now entitled "Hungry March Band Official Bootleg"), featured a few songs recorded at the terminal—including "I Cover the Waterfront" and "Sweet Water." About the former, the CD liner notes state that it was "recorded on a windy, wintry day at our beautiful abandoned waterfront rehearsal space." About "Sweet Water," the notes say it was a shortened version of a song written for an Italian art film that featured scenes of the band marching around the waterfront and makes mention of the "banjos and wind up alarms" that were used in its recording. The group's second album, "On the Waterfront," recorded live in a Williamsburg loft space in 2003, was both a celebration of their practice site and a lament of its impending loss. As described by the band's web site:

> "On the Waterfront" is dedicated to the endangered slice of home turf carved out of the embattled vacant lot we fondly refer to as The Peoples Park, in Williamsburg, Brooklyn. The East River site is currently surrounded by fencing, locked up awaiting its fate. This vanishing wildness has been the location of the HMB's weekly rehearsals for 5 years and has also hosted demolished cars, fishermen, public art, virulent urban plant life, homeless immigrants, [and] skateboarders and has been an oasis for this vital NYC neighborhood.[5]

Many BEDT recreators experienced their setting intimately and developed a bond with the landscape, because they had shaped it in some way. The band, while not literally changing the form of the ground like the skateboarders or land artists (discussed in the next chapter), shaped it with their occupation and use. The great frequency and regularity of their sessions reinforced their connection to the landscape. And as with other constituents of the waterfront, the band's physical presence—along with their great volume—helped establish BEDT as a safe and inviting place to spend an afternoon. People naturally gravitate toward music, and band members understood their role as an anchor for the larger scene. They were a social band, not always outwardly friendly but usually appreciative of those who enjoyed their sounds. One regular visitor summed up the feelings of many when he said that it was nice to have what amounted to a free concert there every week.

The site was "just remote enough," a band member explained, so that *some* but not too many people could find and enjoy the music. As the band played—particularly in the summer when the site was completely overgrown—it was not easily seen from Kent Avenue. But their sound must have enticed more than a few to venture onto the waterfront in search of the music and its makers. Most had come to the site not so much to hear the band but rather to do those things that, like the band, they could not do or easily do elsewhere. Others came simply to take in the larger atmosphere of which the band was an essential part on Sundays.

Burn and Play: The Unplanned Spectacle of the Williamsburg Waterfront after Dark

"Yo, I'm from Brooklyn!" "Is there any fire in Brooklyn?" "Are you kidding me?!" —Greg, a 1337 Collective member

During those years when the Hungry March Band reigned over the lower part of the Slab on Sunday afternoons, another creative constituency laid claim to the same patch of concrete in the relative quiet and darkness of Sunday nights. Illuminated only by the light atop the L train ventilation shaft, the ambient glow of the Manhattan skyline, an occasional flashlight, and their own flaming balls, the fire spinners serially remade the Slab a few hours after the band had left.

The spinners came to the waterfront each Sunday to "play with fire," as they liked to say. They produced their own personal pyrotechnics using mostly homemade equipment, which prominently included Kevlar or "Poi" balls that were attached to one end of a chain with a looped handle attached to the other end. These balls were doused in kerosene moments before performance (spinners always bring a supply of this or a similar fuel to practices), ignited, and then spun or manipulated around their bodies. The practice of spinning was adapted from the rituals of the Māori, an indigenous people of New Zealand (Poi means "ball" in the Māori language), and the spinners also made use of other homemade flaming props, such as staffs, batons, and harnesses. Like the many thousands of fellow "burners," as they are sometimes known, they are practitioners of the "fire arts," which also includes fire eating and breathing and lighting various body parts aflame. Major performances frequently incorporate more advanced pyrotechnics and the burning of specially made art objects. These events most prominently include Burning Man, the celebration of alternative culture and temporary utopia created in the Nevada desert each August, which many of the waterfront spinners had attended. Noting its connection to the rising popularity of their craft, one spinner shared an estimate of 800,000 recreational practitioners worldwide, a number that has surely increased in the decade since. The fire arts are also strongly connected to a circus tradition, and burners often incorporate various acrobatics, body contortions, and feats of strength, agility, balance, or pain into their routines, employing props like blindfolds, straitjackets, or a bed of nails.[6]

The spinners came to the Slab on Sunday nights to play with fire (2002).

I spent a few evenings with the spinners of BEDT in fall 2001 and spring 2002. These sessions were essentially open to anyone, including those who were relatively new to fire or were unknown by the regulars. At that time the popularity of these sessions was beginning to take hold, with as many as twenty-five spinners attending. I came to know a few of the spinners well. One was Splinter, a tall man in his early or mid-thirties, who like many of the group always wore a bandana around his head to protect his long hair from burning. An audiovisual engineer and producer by day (like the band members, many of the spinners had jobs or a background in film, video, and creative media industries), he was among the most regular attendees and an enthusiastic ambassador to the fire arts, never shy to talk about his craft. Another was Erin, a nanny, substitute teacher, "pottery princess," and aspiring photographer who was in her mid-twenties. A petite woman whose septum was pierced with a thick bull ring, Erin, like many of the spinners, had a

The fire arts have evolved from a combination of Māorin ritual and circus arts. Here Gear (aka Doug) spins blindfolded (2002).

healthy sense of humor and was given to occasional bursts of outrage as she described the group's experiences on the waterfront.

Splinter estimated that over the past year these sessions had been attended by thirty-five "regulars" and roughly eighty people total, including those who had come only once. That fall some of the regulars had formed the 1337 Collective, "an industrial performing artists' collective focused on producing, choreographing, and performing with fire and light."[7] Erin offered her own explanation in a dramatically hushed voice: "We're like a band, but with fire—and no instruments!" While Collective membership was about twenty, these sessions frequently drew burners unaffiliated with the group who had learned about them through word of mouth or Internet postings. Members were mostly in their twenties and thirties and an equal number of men and women. Aside from those who were involved with creative media, members included a diesel mechanic, a molecular biologist, a chemistry teacher, and a massage therapist. Several of the regulars lived nearby or in the East Village and Lower East Side; others were from the city's other boroughs, the New York suburbs, and New Jersey.

The sessions that I attended turned out a modest ten to fifteen participants, most of whom were 1337 members. The Collective was gaining notoriety by performing at a series of parties in underground but well-known Brooklyn art spaces, including Rubulad in Williamsburg and the Lunatarium in Dumbo. Their upcoming re-creation of Dante's *Inferno* at the 12-Turn-13 Loft in Brooklyn had earned them a prominent endorsement from the *Village Voice*.[8] They had also performed at a number of more public outdoor spaces and administered a series of clinics in New York City parks. The group performed at Burning Man the previous year and smaller out-of-town events that Splinter called "regional burns." He noted the camaraderie among spinning troupes and said that most U.S. metropolitan areas have at least one such collective.

Visiting burners to these waterfront practice sessions—whether it was a city resident hoping to learn how to spin or an experienced burner who lived hundreds of miles away—fed the larger creative scene. The dialogue between regulars and visitors was fruitful, and sometimes visitors became regulars. As Splinter described,

> People from other places come into town, they meet somebody who knows someone who says "I know some people who do fire spinning." "Where do they do it?" "Oh, they're down at the waterfront." And they come down here and we've met a lot of people [that way]. . . . Like these guys from New Jersey—they've been trying to do fire spinning and get a circus thing together for a long time. And they heard about us and then came down here. They were amazing—and then all of sudden they were part of the group.

Erin spins on the Slab. (Photo by Adam Louie, 2002.)

Greg, an actor in his mid-twenties, had been attending these sessions for two years, almost as long as he had been spinning. We talked as he showed me a few of the moves he had mastered. During his freshman year at college he'd met someone who "turned [him] on to juggling and fire" and showed him a web site of a group in Australia that provided instructions for making spinning implements. Another member, Michael Saab (aka Dirt), told the *Times* that he had picked up the fire arts from a troupe of German street performers while traveling through Europe.[9] These stories were typical of burners.

While the 1337 Collective was less than a year old, some members had been spinning at BEDT for almost three years by 2002. No one was quite sure who first conceived of the Slab as an ideal fire venue, but some of the spinners were friends with members of the Hungry March Band (with whom they sometimes performed at events) and other Williamsburg performers.

> Splinter: People who lived out here and knew the area—and walked their dogs out here. . . I think Mike Conner [a regular dog walker and the person who staged his bachelor party at BEDT] has been down here a long time and he just knew about it; and I think the Hungry March Band was practicing out here, before we were doing fire here—and then when the "fire thing" happened in New York, it was like a shoo-in place to do it.

> Erin: We all hung out with this guy who knew a lot of spaces in Brooklyn, because this is where he was from. He's like, "It's a huge concrete slab—there ain't nothing going on down there—go down and burn some shit." And we're all like, "All right, let's go!"

The dynamic of a session with the fire spinners was similar to that of the band, usually a loose affair that mixed practice and party. At any given time, some of the group would be spinning while others were watching them, socializing or drinking beer. Certain members sometimes played percussion instruments while others were spinning. Crowds were minimal after nightfall at BEDT, but those who found themselves there for whatever reason were welcome to watch. It was a relaxed situation, one that they emphasized had few of the hassles or risks that might be expected in a more prominent or traditional public space. The social and communal aspects of their sessions easily blurred with the creative aspects. As Erin described,

> People just come down here and hang out and spin fire and teach each other shit. . . . We've been a part of this entire community of people who just met each other through learning stuff like spinning fire on sticks and on chains. It's been really nice—it's a good group of people.

Like the band, the spinners appreciated BEDT's unique mix of conventional and eclectic qualities. It was ideal, they said, because it provided *both* proximity and remoteness. It was close to where some of the group lived and just blocks from the Bedford Avenue L train station, making it readily accessible for those coming from Manhattan. Splinter also said he appreciated its location adjacent to a nocturnally oriented neighborhood where affordable late-night food choices were plentiful and praised the area's "vibrant arts scene." At the same time, it was still an "out of the way" place where few people ventured long after dark, leaving the group to practice without too many hassles. As he described,

> This area is pretty good for us because it's far enough away from residential stuff; it's got a beautiful view . . . it's near a subway. . . . And because the group's activities are generally contained to the concrete Slab, there's not really a chance that you'll be lighting the neighborhood on fire. It's almost impossible because we are so far away from anything that can be trouble—I mean you can't even make enough noise here to wake anyone else up, they live so far away.

Practicing on an open concrete platform minimized the possibility of a major fire, but it still carried the risk of bodily harm. Splinter was quick to emphasize that while their sessions were relaxed and informal, they placed a priority on safety and approached their craft with a high level of professionalism. They always had someone spotting while others performed, and they kept safety towels and water in close proximity. Touting their own self-safety record, he noted that they "never had a major burn—ever." Another spinner, Jan, expressed his feelings about safety just as he was igniting a strange and dangerous-looking harness. Fire spinning was "incredibly safe—if you know what you are doing," he said. Minor burns, however, did seem to occur with some frequency. I often heard spinners discuss or compare small burns they had suffered, particularly on their arms.

Dori's loud but unpanicked call for help immediately brings fellow spinners to the rescue. Ben (*center, facing forward*) helps her untangle her chains (2002).

One evening I had the opportunity to see their safety and emergency procedures in action. Five members were spread out across the Slab spinning while a few others watched on. When Dori accidentally got her two chains twisted in such a way as to leave her left arm pinned behind her back, balls still aflame, she was unable to untangle herself. She made a loud but unpanicked call for the "help squad," and quickly three other spinners carrying the towels came to her aid, and her balls were extinguished within seconds. She made it through the incident without even a minor burn, and the session continued as it had before.

In addition to the seeming remoteness and a physical layout that made the chance of unintended fire unlikely, the spinners found other aspects of BEDT appealing. They viewed the waterfront's decaying landscape as an *opportunity* rather than an *impediment* and relished their roles as agents of change. Their occupation and adoption of this abandoned site—a place that by the conventional standards of beauty and safety was suspect—provided them an additional sense of accomplishment:

> Erin: It's really an amazing space—it just has this energy to it. . . . It's really ugly and you know there's broken glass and shit growing and whatever. You just kind of ignore all that and it becomes this beautiful, wonderful place where amazing people find each other and hang out and learn shit that's just amazing and life changing.

> Splinter: This area is all beat up and nasty, and it doesn't look like you can do anything here—and it's the perfect place for us to come and hang out.

While the skateboarders altered the landscape in a physical and fairly permanent way, the spinners' more ephemeral transformations used the dimensions and qualities of the terminal as they found it. Like the band, their "building" was not so much physical as social and structured in the moment in which they were there. It was a temporary reclamation, but one that they felt offered lasting contributions to the larger social and creative dynamic of the waterfront and neighborhood.

Like HMB's, their relationship to the terminal was nurturing; the group grew in skill, maturity, and cohesiveness as their sessions on the Slab grew in number. In 2002, they were coalescing into a solid performance troupe, regularly developing new routines, choreographies, and feats. Collective members saw themselves as more than just people who "play with fire." As Splinter described,

> It started out really informally around here. Everyone just wanted to learn it and do the basic stuff. [Then] some people just wanted to do more organized stuff, more performing . . . so a couple of different groups have formed to do different sorts of practices and work on gymnastics and martial arts moves, and all of it integrating into some sort of performance that uses fire, that mainly has fire—but we've moved away from just doing fire to having a character or having a piece that you are working on.

Earlier that evening Splinter gave me a video he'd produced that showed the Collective's growing skill and cohesiveness as an ensemble. It featured troupe members performing alone and together at different spots at BEDT at night, set to the blasting sound of a well-known 1990s rap star. But many of their waterfront sessions were in preparation for larger multimedia performances to be held elsewhere.

Later in 2002, I had the opportunity to experience a 1337 performance spectacle at a Brooklyn loft party. The event was held in the cavernous interior space of a six-story industrial building that sat amid a run-down mix of vacant land, garages, smaller loft buildings, and dilapidated housing on an out-of-the-way street just north of Flushing Avenue, where Williamsburg meets Clinton Hill. Well removed from any subway station, this area was a bit of a backwater, one that had mostly resisted the gentrifying forces that were sweeping Williamsburg and other Brooklyn neighborhoods. Things were changing, though; the ultra-Orthodox Satmar Jewish community had been expanding in this direction from their traditional center in South Williamsburg. While I worked at the Department of City Planning in the late 1990s, rezoning this industrially zoned area to facilitate housing for the growing Satmar community was a high but controversial priority for the department's Brooklyn program.[10]

Buildings and properties in this area were being bought up by Orthodox developers and speculators in anticipation of this zoning change, which was passed by the Planning Commission in 2001.[11] A year later, though, the market was not strong enough to demolish some of these old buildings and redevelop the sites as housing, as had been done to the west in Williamsburg, or to renovate them fully for residential living. There was some irony here, as I thought about these Orthodox real estate entrepreneurs now renting unrenovated space to young creatives as studio, live-work, and event spaces, rather than providing apartments for Satmar families, the principal rationale for the rezoning. Some of these buildings would probably not pass muster with the city's stringent, sometimes ignored building and fire codes for such uses, and the parties were surely lacking proper permits.

As my friend Brian and I approached the building by car, it seemed like just another old factory building on a nondescript, decaying block. And then from the corner, the block was suddenly awash in what seemed like two dozen costumed performers spinning fire and acting as *dramatis personae*. Looking for a parking space, we slowly passed the building and were soon enveloped by the performers around us. With the car now fully stopped, the fire-wielding thespians peered through the windshield, gesturing with their flaming implements but then moved away and into the building. Later, up in the loft, amid the party's many revelers, 1337 Collective members danced and performed to house and techno music with assorted light effects. Video from the "Seven Deadly Sins," a performance art piece that had taken place on the subway en route to the party, was projected onto the walls. The subway drama featured a brief moment of nudity, as participants took off their clothes at the appropriate moment. But it was hard to see when that occurred as every time I looked up at the projected video, participants were costumed or wearing regular clothes.

This was one of many events at which the Collective performed, the moves for which had been worked out over several Sunday evenings at BEDT. Like the partygoers in the loft that evening, those who encountered their performances on the waterfront were often intrigued. While the number of potential spectators was greatly diminished by the time they arrived, those who happened to be at BEDT late enough often became enthusiastic spectators. About these inadvertent audiences, Erin noted:

> Generally people love it. They'll stop, they'll hang out; they'll ask us some questions; they want to know what's going on. You have some people who will get involved, some people might join a mailing list. Pretty much people are intrigued and want to see more.

Whereas the band was sometimes indifferent to outsiders and the skateboarders formed an even more insular community, many of the spinners possessed an earnest enthusiasm about their craft and felt good about sharing it with others. Splinter, who had a particularly infectious love of fire, said that they were "all into people coming down here and checking it out" and had few reservations about providing on-the-spot instruction for those who asked. He also talked about the camaraderie among the people he met on the waterfront. When I asked him about what the police thought of the fire arts, Splinter maintained his positive tone. He said they had been chased off the waterfront a few times but generally the police did not bother them. As he described,

> They show up and realize we are not a bunch of yahoos. They can't really say, "Go ahead," but they really don't want us to stop because they are interested in what we are doing too. . . . Generally, the cops would like to see this stuff happen and they're just as much interested as anyone else in someone playing with fire. . . . They're usually doing what they are told—which is usually a sucky job. . . . Talk to them for five minutes and they say, "Can we see it?"

Erin was less philosophical about these encounters with law enforcement. She had recently received a ticket for trespassing while at BEDT to do an art project. It was daytime and she was not there to spin, nor was anyone else. But such was the arbitrary nature of the law, and how and when it was enforced. She characterized the police as "mean" and said the officers she encountered were "talking such trash" as they handed out trespassing tickets. (Her ticket was eventually dismissed.)

Jen Colosuanno, a one-time Collective member who now lives in San Francisco, shared a similar perspective with me via e-mail in 2011. She said that what Splinter had alluded to was actually an incident that happened on the Queens waterfront. Collective members were caught off guard when the police suddenly appeared and threatened them with arrest. The situation was tense, but Splinter "talked them down," she said, and they were able to extricate themselves without tickets. Jen characterized the larger scene in the city during the early 2000s as "not fire arts friendly." This was particularly true in the years after September 11, when the police sometimes equated a recreatator's presence along the waterfront not merely with trespassing but potentially with intent to commit terrorism. They often let you know this in no uncertain terms, no matter how comical the situation may have seemed.

Of course, the spinners were proactive about avoiding interactions with the police and had an advantage over daytime users of BEDT. Activity on the Slab was cloaked from the street and difficult to detect from a car. Usually there after dark, they were able to see the lights of a police car traveling down North 7th Street toward the L train ventilation shaft and the terminal's main access point. Such a car would be less noticeable by day. Eroded cobblestone and large ruts and potholes forced police to drive slowly, often with high beams on. This usually gave the spinners ample time to extinguish their fires and music and dump open containers of beer or wine. Loath to chase would-be trespassers through the darkness, the police usually stayed in their squad cars unless they saw something they thought might be truly sinister or dangerous or had received a tip or complaint concerning illicit activity.

Creative Constituencies and Shared Space

The band and the spinners were well aware of the other constituencies that occupied the Slab and, accordingly, tried to accommodate others. They were also proactive about "maintenance" and left the terminal with whatever garbage they created, while also participating in periodic cleanups organized by Mike Conner. As the level of activity was considerably higher during the day, the band had a particular need to be in tune with the needs of other constituents. Even as they occupied space, their footprint was relatively minimal, expanding or contracting to fit the number of members who were present at any particular moment.

Until Shantytown was destroyed, the band shared concrete with the skateboarders, who were always present. But skateboarding was mostly concentrated around the Volcano in the upper third of the Slab, while the band usually gathered in the lowest third. In between there was room for transition, and this middle space was appropriated as needed by members of either group. As fellow pioneers, many skateboarders held the band in admiration—Sunday HMB rehearsals in fact, predated Shantytown—and enjoyed hearing the music while they skated. Band members felt likewise and credited the skaters for sweeping up the broken glass and debris, making the Slab more viable for everyone's activities. While the respective groups did not spend much time hanging out together, Doug often joked about forming a "people's park union" with the skateboarders and resident homeless. Mutual praise was generally the rule and I never witnessed or heard of a conflict between them, but there may have been occasional tension. Not long after the skatepark was demolished, a band member told me that he was happy it was gone and referred to the skateboarders as "dirtbags"—but his was surely a minority opinion.

The band also enjoyed a certain camaraderie with the homeless men whose shanties were on the edge of the Slab and who were almost always there on Sundays (Chapter 6). Carrying on their everyday lives amid the larger carnival of the terminal, these men were a sort of built-in audience. Band members were at ease around them and often shared food and beer; it was all part of keeping the scene cool. Similarly, these residents came to expect and enjoy the music; some even danced or hummed along as the band played. Often these men kicked a soccer ball around with band members or borrowed it while they rehearsed, playing with Emily's son, Sam, or whoever else happened to be around. Words were infrequently exchanged between the groups—some of the residents did not speak English; likewise, some band members had little or no knowledge of Spanish—but soccer is the sort of universal pursuit that needs little verbal coordination.

Aside from run-ins with the police, both the spinners and the band had experienced a few minor conflicts that were perhaps unavoidable given the divergent interests vying for time and space on the large but still finite concrete of the Slab. How were these conflicts resolved with no pre-established or universally recognized rules and no supervisory presence to mediate such disputes and take appropriate action when dangerous situations arose?

For the most part, members of the band and the spinners, like others, simply tried to avoid or defuse conflict. The band was such a fixture on the waterfront and so many people appreciated their music that few questioned their right to play. The most significant conflict anyone could recall was a time when they disturbed a man's meditation session. As was often the case, members had conflicting recollections, with Scott, Emily, and Doug each offering their own version of this incident. Emily said that the man had become quite agitated when the band did not immediately comply with his request for quiet. Trying to reason with him, she told him they would be practicing for only another half hour, but this made him even more incensed. Ultimately the band resumed play and the man was forced to endure the music.

I was present when a similar conflict unfolded between the fire spinners and a particular homeless man whom I could not see. Like the band, the spinners tended to be sympathetic toward these men whose shanties were often less than fifty feet from where they practiced. On this evening at approximately 11:30, about six spinners were performing while a few others looked on, one of them beating a conga drum. From his shanty, we heard the voice of an angry man:

> Please stop! You've got no right to disturb the peace! You've got nothing better to do with your time
> than to disturb mine? Please stop! And you got nobody playing a drum in your bedroom! You've got
> to realize that other people have rights too!

The voice was unfamiliar to me and was not one of the men whom I had come to know over the past year. Multiple spinners yelled back at him, one of whom shouted, "Majority rules!" and another, "Get a job!" He yelled at them again and they traded insults for another minute or two. Eventually, Splinter, always a peacemaker, went down to his shanty with an offering of beer, and whoever was playing the conga cut it back to an occasional soft tap while everyone reduced the volume of their conversations. We did not hear from the man again and the session ended before 12:30 A.M.

Both of these conflicts and their respective resolutions were indicative of the larger social order of the terminal. With no one officiating, it was up to the individual parties to resolve them directly. Similar to the meditator, I doubt the homeless man was happy with the accommodation and peace offering. Was his need for sleep and asserted right to quiet any greater than the spinners' right to practice and socialize in a setting where conventional codes of conduct do not apply? In a more purely public setting, like a neighborhood park, neither this man nor the spinners would be able to do what they were doing, or to do so without violating park rules or city law. These resolutions may not have seemed fair to either of the men who lost, but the conflicts were resolved without escalation or major incident. A sensibly and expediently resolved dispute does not necessarily imply fairness, which being relative to point of view can often be a fuzzy objective. All parties in these disputes surely thought they were right.

The alternative—outright prohibition of certain activities, loud music, open fires, and sleeping in public spaces among them—would not have served any of these constituencies except for the meditator. Not allowing the band to practice in particular would also have been a disservice to the many bystanders who enjoyed hearing them play. Similarly, neither HMB nor the spinners would have been well served by a scheduling or a "sign up" system employed to ensure fair use of the Slab. Such practices would have also precluded the possibility of more spontaneous or accidental uses. Not every public space should be treated like a tennis court or golf course, where reservations or tee times may be necessary.

Of course, prohibition of numerous activities, many quite innocuous or inoffensive, is a common strategy employed to attempt to limit conflicts (and liability) in parks in New York City, including East River State Park (ERSP; see Chapter 8). While conflict is sometimes avoided, overly proscriptive park governance—however well intentioned—can contribute to a fear of confrontation and can diminish our ability to understand and get along with others.[12] At ERSP, the Slab exists in physical dimension as it did a decade ago, but rules and security designed to ensure safety and fair play greatly constrain potential uses, including those that involve open fires or loud music.

Post–People's Park: Insurgent Performers and Community Planning

Splinter called BEDT "the perfect location for what we do" and could think of no alternative that would be as convenient or conducive. He and other spinners hoped that they could still practice at the terminal, even after it was transformed into a formal park. Thinking about how the waterfront brought people together, Splinter hoped that those planning the park had a spectacular or at least democratic vision for the site. He invoked the turn-of-the-twentieth-century planner-architect Daniel Burnham, who famously warned, "Make no little plans; they have no magic to stir men's blood." Burnham, who popularized and promoted the City Beautiful movement, is famous for staging the 1893 World's Columbian Exposition in Chicago's Jackson Park on Lake Michigan and, later, for creating the 1909 Plan for Chicago.[13] Splinter felt that the fire arts in public spaces were in a way a descendant of this grand spectacle on the lake and thus should be embraced by those who plan for the city. Yet he was doubtful that anyone involved in the BEDT park project had such a playful sense of possibility:

> The people who are planning something new for this space—I'm sure they have this wonderful idea, about bringing *their* community to this area . . . [to do] this sport or that sport. People doing planning are often really myopic. They have this one goal in mind, and they forget that there are all these other options for it. Doing fire performance is not a standard use of a place. I'm sure anyone who is doing a development doesn't say, "At night we are going to have people playing with fire."

As I hung out with the spinners in May and June 2002, the planning process was already unfolding (Chapter 7). Splinter was proven correct; at three community planning forums no one had mentioned fire performance, and it was clear that the park would not be open late at night, let alone for flammable arts. He asked me about the meetings. When I told him about the sports fields being planned, he became a bit more incensed:

> Part of the wonderful thing that goes on here is that random, weird acts of fun—skateboarding, fire performing, and marching bands—happen, and putting a fence around it and saying it's only for the ball field is great for the people who want to [play ball, but] . . . the waterfront should be for the

people and we should make sure it can be used for a lot of different uses. . . . It doesn't seem that the people who are planning have the whole community in mind. There's a big amount of community here already using [the waterfront] and using it for good stuff and bringing people together, and it would be a real shame if they went to the point of locking all those people out.

The fire spinners, like others, embraced BEDT's landscape of multiple uses and users and understood the Slab, in particular, as a nexus of activity, creativity, and happenstance—one that could not easily be replicated elsewhere. While none were participating in the planning process, the spinners hoped that those who did understood the Slab similarly and might act as advocates for the unplanned or unusual uses it had facilitated.

The band continued to practice at BEDT throughout 2002 and into 2003, even after many other informal users had been deterred by the "cleanup," the locking of the terminal's "official" gate, and increased patrols by city police, whose sometimes overzealous enforcement policy resulted in a trespassing ticket for anyone whom they encountered on the waterfront.[14] (Tickets were usually dismissed later but often required a trip to the court complex in lower Manhattan.) No one in the band was happy to lose their rehearsal site, but some seemed resigned to it. Theresa, however, was more combative. "We're entrenched," she told me. "And if they don't let us come down here then there is a real problem with the world!" Given the local notoriety of their waterfront sessions and their relatively long tenure, Theresa thought they might be "grandfathered in" and allowed to practice in the new park. She had attended one of the preliminary planning meetings and kept in touch with Neighbors Against Garbage (NAG), the group representing local interests in the planning of the park (Chapter 7). But none of the band members attended any of the three public design forums that were held in spring 2002. Even after the partnership with NYU collapsed, HMB did not actively pursue dialogue with State Parks or its representatives. The fire spinners were even more removed from these planning discussions.

After these meetings, some members of the Friends of BEDT Park (the local advocacy group that grew out of NAG and is now known as Friends of ERSP) were working to ensure that some of the site's more notable activities would be accommodated in the new park. But with neither the band's nor the spinners' explicit participation and assertion of their right to use the future park during these forums, nothing came of creating time and space for their practices. Their skepticism and ambivalence were something close to the rule among the constituencies that

Partygoers listening to members of the Hungry March Band perform on the Slab in 2001.

informally used this waterfront. And justifiably so: Never during any meeting or workshop did a state representative express enthusiasm for the informal activities that were occurring at BEDT and rarely acknowledged that they were occurring at all. It was also hard to imagine that State Parks (or NYU) would allow the band to occupy newly constructed "state of the art" ball fields for several hours in the middle of every Sunday.[15] And then there was the band's approach to mixing practice and social time. Doug, who is no longer with the band, pondered the possibility at that time: "We can play in a completed park, but we just can't drink or smoke pot, probably." It was a compromise they were not willing to fight for.

Later in 2003, the band had moved their Sunday afternoon sessions to Grand Ferry Park, one-half-mile south of BEDT. While more constrained in space, this one-acre landing at the end of Grand Street was similar to BEDT in that it was on the water, was relatively far from residences, and had a history of informal use that predates its official park designation and redesign by the City Parks Department (Chapter 5). Hemmed in by the then still-in-use

Domino Sugar Refinery to the south and petro-chemical tanks to the north, it seemed remote enough that its use by the band would not bother anyone.[16] But within months, other users complained to the City Parks Department and the police, and the band was barred from practicing there, thus ending their hungry and sometimes manic tenure on the Brooklyn waterfront.

The spinners also made alternative plans. By late 2002, their primary rehearsal space became the Lunatarium, the Dumbo party loft where they had frequently performed. Jen explained the novel agreement they made with the lease-holders for the loft. In exchange for performing there regularly on Friday and Saturday nights, they were allowed to practice free of charge on evenings when there was no other scheduled programming. While lacking a public, outdoor dynamic, the Lunatarium was in some respects like BEDT, with its share of eclectic events and parties that sometimes included the spinners or HMB, as well as the works of some of the artists discussed in the next chapter. The 1337 Collective was in fact part of its famed Burning Man "Decompression" parties thrown by Dumboluna and the Society for Experimental Arts and Learning (SEAL) collectives. But much like BEDT, its status as a club was never quite legal. Between 2002 and 2004, it was shut down on several occasions by city agents citing various building code and permit violations, and eventually its operators stopped trying to reopen the space.[17]

Unlike the band, which continues to play and be a vital contributor to New York's creative scene, the 1337 Collective is no longer active and many of its members no longer spin fire on a regular basis. The lack of practice space was only one of several factors that figured into its demise. Jen noted that many members left the city during the mid-2000s. She too had left. After stints in Atlanta and Austin she returned to New York and the Collective, but in 2004 she left the city again, settling in San Francisco. She characterized the Bay Area as being more accommodating of the fire arts and wrote that it was "easy to find practice spaces." But because of these tolerant conditions, she noted, the area was "inundated with fire artists" and thus the practice had lost some of its novelty. No longer burning, she has been a circus arts performer for a decade and is part of the Fou Fou Ha! performance troupe. Similarly, Michael Saab moved on to form the New York–based Modern Gypsies circus company and has performed on television shows and on stage with pop music stars.[18] Like Jen, Erin left New York, moving to Austin in 2003 but returning to New Jersey with her daughter in 2010 to be closer to her family. She still occasionally does fire but mostly for fun or exercise.

March, Burn, and Party: Undesigned Civic Space in Early-Twenty-first-Century New York

As the light faded and a warm afternoon became a very comfortable mid-September evening, the Hungry March Band practice session had already devolved into a social gathering with many friends in attendance. A few members played on while others chatted over beer, soda, and snacks. The barbecue was going and hot dogs and veggie burgers were being distributed. The soccer ball that had been ubiquitous that summer was being kicked around by whoever wanted to join in, including Emily's son, Sam. A few of the band's extended group were spinning batons and flags, and when it got a bit darker someone projected a generator-powered spotlight against the well-graffiti'd back wall of what was once Shantytown Skatepark. Over the spotlight he placed filters that spelled out "peace," "love," and "companionship" in stars across the wall. It was a simple but resonant work of momentary art, and the message was lost on no one gathered on the Slab that evening.

As darkness set in, more people showed up and the crowd was now something close to 150 people. The band's music continued in smaller ensemble, shifting gears toward a more groovy rhythm and blues led by Doug's jammy electric guitar playing, rather than his usual drums. Soon the fire spinners were out, and amid the partiers they found more than enough space to do their thing, while two costumed people walked through the crowd on stilts. The din of talking got louder as members and friends of the band and spinners, guests invited by e-mail listserv just a few days earlier and others who just happened to be there, shared modest libations, got caught up with one another, and made some new friends—a seemingly "ordinary" gathering of New York's creative underground.

Around 9:30 the festivities were called to an abrupt halt. One of the band members had stopped the music and at the top of his lungs asked for everyone to be quiet. To the southwest, large clouds of smoke continued to rise gently and blow across the harbor. Even through the darkness these clouds were visible, and they took on soft and perversely pleasing tones of purple, red, and gray. The smoke, whose awful odor could at times be faintly perceived from the terminal, was from the still-burning wreckage of the World Trade Center. It was just five days after September 11, and anyone who had temporarily forgotten about the lack of normality of those days that followed the attack quickly snapped back into their respective modes of sadness, mourning, anger, and disbelief.

Things quieted quickly, and the band member asked for silence to remember and pay their respects to those who were missing or lost in the attack and honor for those who had valiantly came to their rescue. All were silent for several more moments as the crowd bowed their heads and reflected upon the tragedy that was still playing out before them. At some point heads lifted and those gathered on the Slab awkwardly relaunched the socializing in which they had previously been engaged. The band resumed its playing and poi sticks were relit and spun as the party, still somewhat subdued, moved forward as it had before.

Those who lived through those moments—not just September 11 itself but the weeks and months that followed in New York City—can attest to not merely the grief but also the overwhelming weirdness of trying to get on with life amid this tragedy. For most, it was as close as they had ever been to such a terrible and unexpected large-scale event. But sadness was not the only thing New Yorkers were feeling at that time; there was also a lot of love and a renewed sense of collective purpose in the zeitgeist of the city. The connection between collective spirit and public space was noted by many at the time: Parks were transformed into candlelight vigil sites, and signposts, blank walls, and construction partitions were remade into impromptu memorials for those lost.[19] Some claimed that this was an opportunity to reclaim public space for civic discourse and that the rebuilding of the Trade Center itself could be emblematic of a new sort of urban planning in the city, one that was more transparent, inclusive, humane, and responsive to the needs of a twenty-first-century metropolis.[20] Clearly people discovered that there are other functions to the city's streets, parks, and public spaces than transportation, leisure, and access to commerce.

But what is less obvious now and even then was the connection between civic experience and undesigned space. No one designated sites for these inadvertent shrines to the missing and now dead; they evolved unplanned from where desperate loved ones had placed their signs. Even after it was clear that few if any of the missing had survived, these "Last seen on/at . . ." posters, usually featuring a photograph of the person smiling broadly, proved to be too powerful to take down, and these accidental public galleries were left in place at most locations for many months after.

BEDT had its own set of shrines, along the edge of the water where many people had watched the towers burn on that day. Later they returned with candles, flags, artwork, photographs, postcards, poems, and written tributes—often arranged and assembled against a cardboard or wood backing. Many of the most poignant works were made by schoolchildren who included a handwritten note in combination with other simple media or mementos. These works enhanced the intimate sense that this was a shared experience, a sadness that we all felt together in one space and time. Like the shrines in lower Manhattan, Union Square, and Penn Station, no one designated these spots as being the most optimal or ideal, and placement of a tribute or artwork carried no official approval from the city, its police, or USA Waste, the owners of this part of the terminal at that time.

While public gatherings and expressions of loss were everywhere in New York at that moment and were not at all dependent on finding an out-of-the-way place, the North Brooklyn waterfront had long served as a venue for such discourses. During less trying times, BEDT was one of the few large, outdoor spaces in which people without resources, status, or training could explore creative impulses and practices in a semi-public setting, unconstrained by rules, designations, schedules, and design intent. People explored the boundaries of their own creative limits—in concert with or juxtaposed against others who were engaged in their own forms of discourse or leisure. Providing space to rehearse, perform, socialize, and play, the terminal allowed users to freely mix these conceptions in space and time. It also provided those who just happened to be there with a special or unexpected experience: the sweet sounds of a marching band across the rotting piers and abandoned building foundations of old Brooklyn; or the dazzling display of the fire spinners against the soft glow of Manhattan skyscrapers across the water. Some came to expect and enjoy, but others were surely startled in their "only in New York" moment.

New York needs undesigned spaces like BEDT precisely because they allow for these sorts of creative activities; they provide a laboratory where performers and artists (as will be discussed in the next chapter) can assemble, learn, and experiment, with minimal expense and constraints. The people and practices that exist along the far edge of the cultural production spectrum—whether graffiti and street artists, DJs, rappers and break dancers, or circus performers—are those that define New York as a global center for creative cultures and are synonymous with the longer city's longer traditions of street life. Marching bands and burners can perform in a wide variety of urban spaces, but having rehearsals in a publicly accessible, appropriated setting made them unique and allowed others to experience these art forms in interesting and unexpected ways.

CHAPTER 4

OUTSIDE ART

Exploring Wildness and Reclamation at the Water's Edge

ON THE FIRST DAY OF DECEMBER 2001—a Saturday—dozens of people enjoyed unusually temperate conditions at BEDT. In the fading afternoon light, warm air prevailed and the many who remained—some still in short sleeves—were momentarily distracted from their leisure pursuits when an old beat-up truck with Massachusetts plates rumbled onto the terminal, entering from the usually locked North 7th Street gate. Stopping seventy-five yards in, the truck had already drawn a small crowd of admirers. BEDT's primitive conditions and lack of access made it unusual to see any functioning motor vehicle, let alone a 1948 Ford pickup.

A scruffy man in his early or mid-twenties hopped out of the driver's seat along with a woman of a similar age from the passenger side. Another slightly younger man hopped off the truck bed, grabbing a chain harness and a thick rope. Largely oblivious to the curious onlookers who had gathered around them, the driver attached the chain to the back of the pickup, while the other two ambled down the bank holding the harness. Amid the rocks at the water's edge, they selected a large boulder, perhaps 200 pounds, and wrapped the harness around it, which they attached to the other end of the rope. They stood back while driver, now back behind the wheel, slipped the Ford into gear and stepped on the gas. The engine revved and the wheels spun, but the rock moved only a bit before the harness slipped off. Reattaching the harness, they

Al (*center in left photo*) and his mates harvesting rocks on the Brooklyn waterfront (2001).

tried again—same result. On a third try—the ancient pickup now clearly straining by the drag of the boulder and lack of traction on the loose dirt below—they achieved 10 feet of progress before the rock caught on a lip on the beach. Undaunted by failed attempts and precariously little maneuvering room between the lip and the growth along the eastern edge of the Slab, the driver and his mates gave it another try. Success! The rock was safely pulled over the lip and onto flatter ground.

I continued to watch with several others, still unsure of what to make of the drama unfolding before us. The driver, now out of the truck again, had positioned himself with the other two over the rock. They removed the harness and braced themselves. "Ready, lift!" Heaving upward with all their strength, they deposited the stone into the open bed of the truck. The stone was not only heavy but difficult to grip; a drop could have crushed a foot. From atop the bed, the driver and a teammate awkwardly maneuvered the boulder toward the front of the truck, clearing space for more rocks, and then the crew went back down the bank to begin the process anew. Twenty-five minutes and three rocks later, four large stones were now secured in the bed of the pickup. The team, now out of breath but smiling, gave each other high-fives and called it an afternoon.

BEDT's informal beach was strewn with large boulders, many of which were probably used as fill years ago to incrementally extend the shoreline farther from its preindustrial extent. These stones were now exposed because erosion had taken away the concrete bulkhead whose wood undergirding had been eaten away by marine borers. Al, the driver and owner of the truck, planned to use the boulders for sculptures he was creating. Back at his warehouse studio, he would drill eight holes in each rock, in two parallel rows of four. Each hole would then be plugged with "leg-like" steel tubing, with each pair of tubes forming a truss to carry the mass of the stone. The finished sculpture formed a spider, whose steel legs supported its body (the salvaged boulder) four to five feet off the ground. These rocks when transformed would join the spiders he had previously made on display at the Lunatarium, the art-event space in DUMBO where the fire spinners often performed.

Al had known about the terminal for a few years. He said it was one of the "interesting places" along the Brooklyn and Queens waterfronts and praised the "good granite rocks" it possessed. "There's only a couple of places in New York City where I can get down to the water to actually get rocks," he explained, gesturing to his truck. "Because I can't really drive this thing too far outside the city without it dying. . . . Lately I've been stealing rocks from here because there is no other place to find them."

For Al, BEDT provided the raw materials for sculpture that cannot easily be obtained in an urban environment. For those watching, he and his team provided theater, a display of creative people engaging a landscape that was said to have no productive use. While the removal of the boulders could be considered an act of theft, it was consistent with BEDT's laissez-faire atmosphere, and no one on hand that day seemed to mind. Arguably, it was less of a wanton act than decades of illegal dumping and the multiple hazards produced by a waste transfer station that had operated for years without a permit and in violation of health and safety codes on the south end of the terminal (Chapter 7). Additionally, it was not clear if the state would even bother to reuse these stones in the waterfront park they were planning. Perhaps they would simply be carted off to a landfill somewhere.

BEDT's anarchic conditions allowed Al to repurpose or pilfer (depending on your point of view) objects that had lost their original purpose or value, while at the same time engaging the landscape in a very physical way. (One can only imagine the consequences of similarly removing rocks from Central or Prospect parks.) His art made use of the abundant waste that was inherent in an abandoned site. The boulders he harvested were part of a much larger continuum of found objects that had been repurposed in creative constructions. What was left of the marine-railroad terminal including the piers, crumbling bulkhead, building foundations, and exposed infrastructure plus an untold amount of discarded junk were the remains of a rich material culture exploited by legions of local art makers over the preceding two decades. As Bonnie described,

We used to come here looking for found objects—because I used to do a lot of performances and Vinny is an artist. All the people would dump this "garbage"—you know, this so-called garbage, all over here—you could find the best stuff![]

Bonnie and Vinny had been around this waterfront and neighborhood since the mid-1980s, when the Williamsburg art scene was in its infancy. When I found them sunning themselves at the foot of North 9th Street on a hot July afternoon, they described the rich countercultures that flourished at BEDT. As frequent instigators of varied endeavors including art, theater, music, poetry, and publishing (Bonnie published the well-known 'zine *Misfits Free Press* in the 1990s), they helped establish the neighborhood's creative milieu. Bonnie laughed and Vinny smiled when she said that they were presently artists "in hiding" and had not scavenged at the terminal in years. She did, though, vividly recall not just their own exploits but also the larger creative landscape they encountered at BEDT, including assembled sculptures, graffiti, films and rap videos, and performances in the warehouses that have since been demolished. Like many Brooklyn artists of their generation, they moved to Williamsburg from the gentrifying East Village in the 1980s.[1] And even now as they bemoaned the wave of gentrification that had followed them across the river, complaining about higher rents and replacement of art spaces with bars, boutiques, and condominium units, they still greatly appreciated the local waterfront. About BEDT Bonnie said, "That's what's nice about the neighborhood, it still has places like this."

Unlike Al's spiders, much of the art refashioned from the material culture of BEDT was left on site for others to happen upon, appreciate, rearrange, or dismantle. In a visceral landscape that invited people of all stripes to get their hands dirty, malleability, incompletion, and destruction were indeed essential characteristics of these works. Vinny described the dynamic:

Just roam around and do a little art—a little found object art. Just leave it there and hope someone will come by and say, "Hey! Wow!" And then someone comes by and destroys it. Next time I come by and fix it up again.

By the turn of the millennium, those who still made art or scavenged at BEDT were exploiting the anarchic state of the city's waterfront in what was likely its waning moments. A set of possibilities still existed here, once more common but now scarcely found elsewhere in the city or at least within a large, open setting. Rarely used or abandoned waterfront spaces, including finger piers, wharves, warehouses, and transfer yards common to all five boroughs, formed a network of exploitable spaces for extralegal activity but also creative and recreative pursuits.[2] With the success of the city's waterfront revitalization program, these vacant or lightly used maritime and industrial spaces were rapidly disappearing.[3] Many artists operating at BEDT had a sense of this shrinking geography and the good fortune to create at one of last remaining vernacular waterfront sites in Brooklyn, though it too was changing. Buildings had been cleared, the water had claimed most of the piers and seawall; the terminal was safer and more people were using it more of the time. The landscape had indeed changed since Vinny's heyday, but at the beginning of the millennium, art in multiple and changing forms was still being created at BEDT.

Art in a Waterfront Landscape

Two years before I watched Al and his crew cart off rocks, I had begun my own inventory of art at the terminal. It was still a veritable artists' playground, not unlike what Gordon Matta-Clark and scores of other artists had found along the Hudson River in Manhattan in the 1970s.[4] On a series of blustery March midweek afternoons, when few people were around, I found myself amid a broken-up landscape dotted with provocative installations, small earthworks, and creative gestures. Cloaked by the abundant decay around them, they were modest creations that did not immediately catch the eye, far smaller than and lacking the spectacularity of what I would see that upcoming summer. Yet these anonymously created works, consisting of materials found at the terminal, had a particular power that belied their simplicity and lack of prominence. There

While cloaked by abundant waste and decay, the landscape of the terminal was dotted with simple but elegant, creative gestures in early 2000.

were paving stones piled precariously upon one another, forming slender towers, mocking the vertical landscape of Manhattan across the river; artful arrangements of plastic juice containers hanging from the bare branches of a bush, wobbling gently in the wind; and assorted junk hung from chain-link fencing in careful arrangement. Were these someone's personal effects? I wondered. I also discovered an elegant labyrinth of arranged bricks, covering a five- by seven-foot area, and in a nearby location found a shallow excavation in which rectangular stones had been placed. A small square of inscribed cardboard was held down underneath one of the corners of theses stones. The carefully drawn letters read "Kendra." Was this a tribute to a recently deceased Kendra or an offering to one who was still alive? There was no way to know.

Like many abandoned urban places, BEDT was also a haven for graffiti, which could be found on every vertical surface and on some horizontal ones. I took stock of the hundreds of spray-painted scribbles, elaborate tags, and lurid depictions of power and lust. One tag, a crudely drawn, usually sideways squid, was all over the terminal (and the adjacent neighborhoods). Complexly layered in time, many older tags had been painted over but remained visible while others were now faded or obscured by thick plant growth. The vast sweep of graffiti provided a glimpse into the past, revealing a bit of the rich history of insurgent occupation and use of the terminal. New offerings were a constant, and many of these works were executed in the emerging vernacular, which offered simplified logos, generic imagery, and pictorial reference to pop culture figures like Mr. Spock of the television show "Star Trek."[5] These stenciled and pasted images would soon include an "André the Giant" wheat paste by the not-yet-famous street artist Shepard Fairey. Installed in late spring or early summer of 2001, it sat amid a number of ever-changing works painted on or affixed to a wall of BEDT's only remaining intact building.

By mid-June, the landscape I was observing was both evolving and devolving. Most of the installations of the winter and early spring were gone. At the same time that these were lost, new works could now be found. With the onset of warm weather, participatory or performance art could be experienced every weekend. One such installation consisted of thousands of softball-sized wooden balls that had been dumped onto a corner of the Slab. It provided an unlikely but powerful magnet for many who encountered them and wondered, where did these balls come from and who brought them here? Someone told me that an artist had fabricated them in a basement workshop. Someone else said that they were just discarded production extras from a local factory. Did it matter whether someone created these balls for this art-play experience or merely disposed of them in a convenient place? Perhaps it was just an accidental gesture created by an act of illegal dumping.

The wooden balls were compelling play objects during the summer of 2000.

Whatever their origin, the balls delighted many people who found different ways to play with them. Some arranged the balls into interesting shapes and designs, while others walked on top of them, attempting not to slip or fall. The balls were composed of a stringy wood composite with a hollow core. I watched others derive great pleasure in exploiting the limitations of this design. They hurled them against a wall or the ground, fracturing them into many small pieces. The satisfying smashing sound created from the impact, as I was compelled to discover, added to the visceral joy of destruction. The balls were play objects throughout the summer of 2000 and persisted into the fall, though in ever-diminishing numbers. Like other aspects of this landscape, over time destructive or entropic forces gained the upper hand, and eventually they were entirely gone from the Slab.

Around the same time, I was also beginning to take note of how frequently the terminal was being used as a location by photographers and filmmakers. Already aware of scenes from feature films shot here, including *Laws of Gravity* (1992) and *Hurricane Streets* (1997), I witnessed modest student dramatic productions and full-fledged fashion shoots with on-location crews of ten or more people.[6] The many films, music videos, and student productions that were shot along this stretch of the Brooklyn waterfront (most without the proper permits) prompted a 1997 *New York Times* story entitled "Great Views and Crumbling Piers? Directors Yell Action!" The *Times* understood the location's appeal in terms of contrast and contradiction, noting that directors and film students were "drawn to the jarring combination of man-made beauty and man-made decay."[7]

The openness and deteriorating conditions found at BEDT and their play against the skyline created a *mise-en-scène* that was hard to find elsewhere in the city. In the feature films noted above, filmmakers exploited the terminal's availability and seedy milieu: the abandoned and dangerous waterfront where characters go to escape, hide, engage in rough or destructive play and illicit acts; or simply to reflect in a place that lacked the distractions of structured urban life.[8] Similarly, artists were seeking urban space outside of the expectations and boundaries of conventionally ordered urban experience and used the terminal to exercise similar impulses. The urban waterfront has also long held a power to excite or provoke reflection, and BEDT served this function well. It was not so much "life imitating art" as an intermingling of the real and the unreal, drawing upon the rich trove of fiction, film, and lurid journalistic accounts

A summer 2001 fashion shoot at BEDT. The terminal's unique postindustrial conditions were valued by a range of filmmakers, photographers, and commercial artists.

that has shaped a collective imagination about a waterfront steeped in crime, gangsters, labor strife, urban decay, and human desperation. Brooklyn, of course, lives particularly large in this consciousness: Elia Kazan's *On the Waterfront* (film), Arthur Miller's *A View from the Bridge* (drama), and Hubert Selby Jr.'s *Last Exit to Brooklyn* (fiction and later film) are among the many works that have shaped a dark milieu that artists were seeking to exploit while sometimes making their own contributions to this larger body of works.[9]

BEDT had an additional accidental quality as a strategically located parcel that had withstood the rapid improvement of the city around it. As Williamsburg's desirability and safety increased, more leisure seekers ventured west toward the water. This growing but mostly inadvertent audience added drama and an improvisational element missing from traditional art spaces, even those far off the beaten path. As my own narrative suggests, many found this experience compelling, drawing them into unanticipated encounters that rarely occur in more structured settings. Sometimes works demanded participation from their audience or the events of the moment compelled viewers to make their own contributions. This was surely the case in the immediate aftermath of September 11, 2001. During that day and the weeks that followed, hundreds came to the terminal.

Accessible and offering an expansive view, it was one of the few prominent places in Greenpoint and Williamsburg from which the Twin Towers were visible without obstruction. Compelled by shock, bewilderment, horror, and extreme sorrow, people brought offerings—candles, flowers, photographs, and written and collage tributes to the fallen—and an informal shrine quickly evolved.

As I previously noted, like other inadvertent World Trade Center memorial sites, no one had designated this area as an appropriate public site for remembrance and acts of tribute.[10] It evolved without plan from where people had watched the towers burn and shared a rare collective moment brought upon by tragedy. For several months after, people continued to visit this shrine, adding to the

Around the six-month anniversary of the September 11, 2001, attacks, this sculpture, executed in welded metal, was installed on the Slab. It stood in cardinal orientation as the World Trade Center towers once did (2002).

offerings or engaging in quiet reflection. Around the six-month anniversary of September 11, an anonymous artist installed a white-painted metal-bar, scaled re-creation of the two towers on the Slab. Each tower, ten feet in height, stood in its proper orientation to the other and aligned in space as the original towers. Their lightness and transparency, which allowed views through to the skyline beyond, reinforced a sense of loss. The towers stood intact until the summer.

For more premeditated offerings and actions, practical considerations often guided artists to BEDT. Like the marching band and the fire spinners, the city's great density, competition for space, and rules governing public conduct challenged the logistics of their practices. There were few suitable venues for their works, art not of the gallery and not of traditional public sculpture. Certainly, the traditional and often highly structured parks of New York provide few such opportunities.[11] It cost the internationally renowned artist team of Christo and Jeanne-Claude $20 million of their own money and more than a quarter-century to receive permission to install *The Gates* in Central Park (the 7,500 saffron-festooned gates that lined 23 miles of the park's walkways for 16 days in February 2005).[12] Artists of lesser stature—those without considerable wealth, fame, and the support of New York's art-loving billionaire mayor, Michael Bloomberg (or previous and future mayors)—were surely out of luck, even for significantly less ambitious gestures.

Even Socrates Sculpture Park just a few miles to the north of BEDT on the Queens waterfront, also an abandoned industrial site informally reclaimed for creative purposes, had evolved into a more formal venue for art, as well as a regular community park, with rules and structured programs. The four-and-a-half-acre site, founded in 1986 by sculptor Mark di Suvero as a working studio and display space for his own large-scale steel sculptures and those by other local artists, has been owned by the City Parks Department since 1998 and managed by the park's own not-for-profit organization.[13] Although the park still functions as an outdoor studio and gallery for those selected for its residency program, others are effectively prohibited from installing sculptures, moving earth, or altering the landscape in other ways.[14] Socrates retains a funky and rough-around-the-edges flavor, but it is now part of the network of conventionally structured public spaces in the city, not a place where renegade artists can operate without constraints. As a venue for art, BEDT served this more anarchic niche, providing artists, photographers, and filmmakers with a setting conducive to unconventional, unwieldy, or illicit endeavors. Moreover, participation in these activities was open to anyone regardless of skill, experience, or portfolio. Amateurs and professionals alike were free to create without resources or forethought, though there was no guarantee of permanence for anything created and left at the terminal.

Artists were also drawn to the site to absorb and exploit its wildness. BEDT's edge conditions or "otherness" provoked thoughtful responses from many who took advantage of the lack of constraints to engage in a contemplative dialogue with the city and water. These dialogues were sometimes intensely personal or liberating, blurring social statement with expressions of self. For some artists, their works were meant to be explicit reconstructions of the landscape, building blocks for inciting political or social action, or more simply an opportunity to create something out of the stuff others had thrown out or forgotten. Their works celebrated the joy of creation. But the rawness and lack of rules also made the terminal ideal for bold acts of dissonance, and others created works that were explicit and often visceral rejections of capitalism, consumerism, gentrification, and/or corrupted systems of governance. They understood BEDT as a site of contradiction, difference, and resistance to the dominant forces reshaping the public experience in the city: privatization, security, surveillance, donor-funded improvements, relentless programming, and hollow gestures of grandiosity.[15]

Those who had been around the neighborhood a while also had an implicit sense that the forces which would ultimately transform this waterfront in the name of progress were as corrupt as those who allowed who had allowed it to decay in the first place. The Giuliani plan to greatly expand the transfer station operating at the south end of BEDT and a proposal to build a natural gas burning power plant just to the north reinforced their sense of skepticism and that the deck was stacked against local people (Chapter 7). Less strident artists, those who were not necessarily rebelling against more powerful interests, had a sense that these forces were not so much morally bankrupt as applied with a heavy hand. Those who ran the city knew what was best for all and would never allow for a playful experiment in anarchy even if it was limited in time and space.

In engaging the wildness of BEDT, artists celebrated freedom to create and destroy, and often simultaneously. They expressed ambivalence and contradiction in words or their art, often embracing both constructive and destructive forces. Wildness was clearly liberating and not generally a condition that could be engaged in traditional public settings. Like other informal recreators, artists relished this freedom, but they were also keenly aware that it could vanish at any moment—destroyed or subsumed by forces more powerful and equally opportunistic. And like the skateboarders, artists were motivated by these unpredictable conditions and sense of the nearing end, which encouraged them to make the most of the immediate or short-term aspects of their works.

My encounters with two particular artists—an environmentally minded middle-aged native of Greenpoint and a French-born resident of Williamsburg with a healthy sense of the perverse—explore these contradictions. Their BEDT-sited works were immersions in the creation–destruction continuum and spoke to the moment when the Brooklyn waterfront was shifting from outsider wildness, danger, and decay to mainstream reclamation, revitalization, and lawfully structured use. Characters both, they told stories that encapsulate much of what made art along this part of the waterfront so distinctive, surprising, and pleasurable. Using the balance of this chapter to explore these narratives and the issues they raise, I also attempt to understand the creative dynamic of undesigned spaces—whether on the waterfront or otherwise, in New York or elsewhere—and why they are vital to artists and their city.

Reverse Vandalism: The Vanquished Pirate of the Brooklyn Waterfront

Preparing to leave the terminal on a blistering Saturday afternoon in late June 2000, I heard the deep pulse of a conga drum. From BEDT's beach I caught a glimpse of a procession making its way toward the Slab, about ten people carrying an unidentifiable object of great size. Twenty feet ahead of this group, someone wielded a video camera, walking slowly backward, recording the event. Now reaching the Slab myself, just behind the group, I could see the object they carried: a massive sculpture of a human figure made of fused metal scraps.

Kicking away the wooden balls piled near the corner from where they entered, an unexpected but momentary irritant, they worked their way up the Slab, shouting back and forth in apparent disagreement about where to place this immense work. They stopped 150 feet from the lower edge and slowly tipped it upright. The group and others who had gathered could now fully take in this man of metal, with his menacing face and exposed skeletal frame made up of dozens of identifiable parts: pipes, cables, plates, bed springs, engine and bicycle parts, nuts and bolts, and odd pieces of machinery. It was a remarkable re-creation of human skeletal anatomy in welded scrap, complete with five-fingered hands and five-toed feet. They positioned it facing the river, with its right foot forward and right fist extended raised toward the sky, this animated metal figure now standing in opposition to the Manhattan skyline, mocking its grandeur.

At the base of the sculpture, two flat metal plates supported each of the feet. Holes had been drilled through each of these plates so they could later be bolted or fastened to the ground or a pedestal. The men who had carried the

The artist Ür and some of his co-conspirators attempt to find an ideal place for the Pirate, a sculpture of welded scrap metal salvaged from the North Brooklyn waterfront (2000).

sculpture, many shirtless on this hot afternoon, continued to argue about where and how it could be bolted down so it would not be tipped over or carried away. Several attempts to hammer a railroad spike through each of the feet into the concrete below proved fruitless. They moved the sculpture over a bit to a spot where a seam might provide a better opportunity to drive the stake down. A burly man with a beard and long ponytail positioned himself with a hammer and spike over one of the feet. Hammering the spike repeatedly, he created a rhythm soon joined by conga, accordion, clapping hands, and chanting:

> Pounding the spike.
> He's pounding the spike!
> He's pounding the spike!

Many whacks later the tip of the spike had hardly penetrated the surface. Even at its seams, the Slab was too solid. Eventually they were satisfied with a single spike in each foot driven in only an inch or two, hardly enough to keep the sculpture in place for any length of time.

With its location settled, the creator of this work—a wiry, shirtless Frenchman in his early thirties who went by the name of Ür—was hoisted up by a few of his mates to add the final element to this magnificent work: a broken sword for its raised fist. His sculpture—"the Pirate," as I soon learned—was now complete. This defiant figure of scrap standing ten feet tall, with its body squarely extended toward the river, chin forward, clutching its broken sword in its extended arm, now suggested another New York waterfront icon, the Statue of Liberty, albeit a male version with an angrier disposition.

Even before Ür had a chance to insert the sword, the Pirate had created the impetus for an informal party among co-conspirators, enlisted helpers, and others who happened to be there. The helpers were local men who were hanging

Ür places a broken sword in the hand of the Pirate (2000).

out on Bedford Avenue when the Pirate and its procession came past and gave them the opportunity to provide unsolicited assistance to the cause. Ür humorously referred to these men as "bums and derelicts" who "were happy enough to see some disturbance of the ordered followers" and were expecting beer in exchange for their labor. Another, Chris, a local man in his early thirties, was living at BEDT at that moment—his improvised canopy bed sat on the Slab one hundred feet from the Pirate—was startled by the arrival of the group and its massive sculpture. "Meet your new roommate!" one of the men announced to him.

As the sun began to disappear behind hazy clouds and the canyons of Manhattan, this ragtag group talked, laughed, sang, played their musical instruments, drank beer, and passed around a joint. The "hired" men threw a football around. Some fire spinners who happened to be practicing (unlit) on the Slab also joined the festivities. After a brilliant sunset, they spun fire, complementing the singing and music and adding visual dazzle to this carnival. As the sky darkened, the air still thick but just a bit cooler, I continued to hang out with the Pirate's creator and his crew. Ür lived just a few blocks away, but some of his helpers were Pennsylvania residents. They had collaborated with him in writing and performing "8 Eggs and a Pair of Fur Shoes," an opera that had been staged at the Cave Gallery, an experimental art and performance space on Grand Street, three-quarters of a mile away.[16] In fact, the Pirate had served as part of the opera's set and was on display for several weeks prior in the gallery. After the last of two performances, which was held that afternoon, it was time to return the Pirate to its place of birth.

Nearly three years later, I saw the Pirate's complete journey from the Cave to the Slab on videotape shot by Shige Moriya, the director of the gallery. Shige also put me in touch with Ür, and the three of us met at the Cave on a Saturday in April 2003 to view the tape together. The video well documented this unauthorized parade, which was part performance art provocation and part public mischief-making, while providing a visual chronicle of the millennial, not-fully-gentrified streets of the Northside of Williamsburg.

The journey begins ouside the gallery, where the Pirate is given a goodbye serenade. With the sculpture standing upright on a custom-made two-part dolly—one set of wheels under each leg connected by a long metal rod—Ür and four mates then push it slowly up Grand Street, metal wheels rumbling over the uneven pavement. Making a left on Bedford Avenue, the commercial spine of the neighborhood, the procession slows traffic in both directions, drawing a few honks from motorists and the attention of many surprised pedestrians. The heat of the afternoon had brought everyone out, and the sidewalks were packed. Chanting in deep operatic voices, they wheel the Pirate north past a bodega, a graffiti-covered wall, and open dumpsters. The procession pulls over next to a café. Ür pulls forward his saxophone, which had been slung across his back; two of his mates do similarly with a conga and an accordion, respectively. The group begins to play a song from the opera. From the sidewalk patio of the café, a converted garage, people looking up from their brunch and cocktails are not quite sure what to make of this rolling sculpture and its accompanying procession of musical revelers; some leave their seats and come forward to the sidewalk. Pedestrians along Bedford are now gathering, smiling at the sight of the Pirate and enjoying the soulful music.

Pushing forward again, the men chant as they pass liquor stores, restaurants, a car service, a check-cashing place, and other typical neighborhood businesses. Every other block, they stop to play another song. Farther up the avenue, the Latino flavor of the neighborhood gives way to Polish groceries, bakeries, and a sausage shop, interspersed with bars, cafés, restaurants, boutiques, and the Bedford Avenue Art Mall, all of which reflect the area's emerging bohemian transformation. They continue to sing,

> Steer it with your foot.
> Steer it with your foot!
> You must steer it with your foot!

With unsolicited volunteers joining the procession at North 7th Street, they stop again at North 8th Street and then turn left toward the water. The street is awash in traditional summertime activity. On this typical Williamsburg block—a mix of tenements and townhouses broken up by an occasional garage or detached structure—its multi-generational, largely working-class population is out on the street, sidewalks, and stoops. Many of those inside are perched in their windows. Proceeding forward, the men continue to sing over the ambient din of shouting, laughter, and recorded music, until the Pirate's extended arm brings down a low-hanging utility line. "Oh shit, yo! What are you going to do about that?" someone yells as activity on the block stops and all eyes are intently focused on the group. They disentangle the line from the arm. Some discussion and pointing toward utility boxes and connections ensue, but before long the procession begins again and pushes, undaunted, onto the waterfront.

After viewing the video, Ür and I made our way out to BEDT. It was a warm, cloudless early spring day—perfect for enjoying the waterfront—but we found the gate at the end of North 7th Street locked.[17] Still, we were among two or three dozen people who took no issue with crawling through a hole in the fence to be near the water that afternoon. We went to the spot on the Slab where the sculpture had once briefly stood and Ür quickly found one of the Pirate's base plates, still bearing his signature. We began our conversation; he spoke in French-inflected but clear and often emphatic English, while gesturing and moving around as he talked.

The Pirate was the product of several salvaging expeditions to BEDT, back and forth from the metal shop in which he sometimes worked. Ür was a sort of artistic polymath, a person who could master any creative medium if given a week. Prior to this project he had never used metal in his art and had no experience with welding. Brushing aside any compliments for his skills and sense of composition, he emphasized the good fortune that his "crazy boss" allowed him to use the equipment at night after the shop had closed. After many excursions to the waterfront to collect materials, he began work on the sculpture. For several consecutive days after working a full day at the shop, he would return at 9:30 P.M. and work until 5:00 A.M. and begin the cycle again. After a near-sleepless week, Ür completed the Pirate.

A few people who saw the Pirate at the Cave inquired about purchasing it, including someone who said it would make a great addition to his back yard. But Ür declined, having decided earlier to return the Pirate to the waterfront. (Like sleep, money was not a great concern for Ür and he rarely had any.) Here at BEDT it would be in a publicly accessible setting where people might be able to see and enjoy it, even if only for a little while. He called it a gesture of "reverse vandalism" and hoped it would inspire similar creative acts.

> My idea was really, maybe I can bring a sculpture here and a couple of artists will say, "Hey, that's cool" and go on and put some other sculptures here—and we could have ended up with like twenty sculptures here, [all] totally different, totally weird. But it didn't turn out that way; I guess the destroyers were out before the other pieces would come in.

Ür intended the Pirate to be an explicit symbol of rebellion, a marker reclaiming the BEDT site from the nefarious forces of the city. There was drama in his voice as he continued,

> The sculpture was standing here, waving its fist, angry, with its broken sword, at the dark city. It was kind of a gesture that I wanted to bring—the sort of a angry, defeated warrior stance, "I am still standing—my sword is broken—but I am still here! I still have the stamina to go 'ROAR!'" [He belts out a roar worthy of a tiger.] That was a last, last stance for that poor warrior because the city definitely vanquished him.

With a well-attuned sense of evolution and devolution, Ür harbored no illusions about the permanence of his work. Composed of discarded machine parts and residents' possessions that had been salvaged and reassembled into sculpture, this unified whole would soon be disassembled and destroyed:

Okay, this scrap was taken from this place and I am going to bring it back here and it's going to return to scrap anyway. The idea was really to give it to the people here and say, "Let's see what happens to it." I mean I expected it obviously to go down.

Lasting only weeks before its head was removed, the Pirate was progressively dismantled over a period of two or three months. Ür visited the waterfront every few days to monitor and document its inevitable return to scrap. Intrigued by the various "stages of destruction" in which he found his creation, he complimented his destroyers as "creative" and laughed as he told me of its ruin:

Once the head was torn down—I hear by a bunch of kids who threw it in the river—some people started to come here and installed TVs on the head and started to graffiti it. After that it took a few months and then they just squarely tore it down—and kicked it. I would come here and see these kids throwing rocks at it—kicking it with their feet—it was like an act of rebellion.

For Ür, the Pirate embodied many of the same contradictions that characterized both BEDT and his own tenuous relationship to the city in which it was located. He had come to the United States in 1991 after falling for an American girl who had been studying in France. Following her back to the States (after many months of scraping together the money for a visa and an airline ticket), he settled with her first in Cleveland and then in Maine before moving to Brooklyn in 1993. Soon after, his relationship ended and he found himself living alone in Williamsburg with little money and few resources. However unfamiliar, the neighborhood and its waterfront struck a sympathetic chord within him. The terminal, in particular, became the place where he went to "take some air," relax, and engage in quiet reflection. But he was also drawn to the atmosphere of decay, which fueled his creative psyche and enabled him to reflect upon his own life through the art he created.

On one of his earliest visits to the waterfront, not at BEDT but another abandoned space a few blocks north, he discovered a human corpse. Not anxious to share the grisly details, he said that it was the body of a young man who had frozen to death. After this experience Ür carried a sense of dread whenever he walked along the waterfront, anticipating that he might suddenly come across something gruesome again. At the same time, he found this "warped" feeling strangely exhilarating. It was "like the lichens and mushrooms [were] already creeping up my feet," he said, laughing. These perversities and contradictions would be the implicit themes of the Pirate sculpture:

> From the first time I came here, I immediately associated this space with some sort of weird sense of death—there is this sense of decay—even though at the time, in the early '90s, buildings were still standing and there was still some kind of semblance of cleanliness around here, although freaks were hanging out all over the place. But every time I came here I was overcome by this weird feeling, this feeling of death and of rotten—rot, you know, rottenness—and stuff sprouting from the garbage, and the [Pirate] sculpture is really a perfect symbol of that.

Ür called himself a "reluctant immigrant" to the United States and remarked, "I never really felt quite like I belong here." With only a long-lapsed visa, he found his life further complicated by the heightened level of scrutiny surrounding "illegal" immigrants in the wake of September 11. He valued his trips to the waterfront because, much like him, it was not in total harmony with its rapidly changing surroundings. He called it a "fringe-like utopian grounds" and was able to explore these feelings of otherness at BEDT and through his art. Both Ür and the terminal were rebellious outsiders, out of sync with the world around them but in harmony with one another:

> It was the place that I identify the most with myself—being myself sort of on the fringe, you know. I would come here and just go through my stuff, go through the space, look at the garbage, find some stuff, write some crazy little bits—so basically this became my haven, as it is for a lot of people. After a while, since I also do comics and sort of a graphic novels sort of stuff, I had the idea to lay down on paper and draw and write about the crazy, funny stories that happened to me here and quite a few happened . . . the corpse I found, encounters with cops, the break-ups, the wondrous lovemaking at night, the swimming in the river in the summer when it is too hot and there is no money to go anywhere.

He went on to describe one of these events. One day while collecting bits of metal and discarded objects, he was suddenly overcome with the need to use the bathroom. There were no facilities around and no time to make it to any, so he found a protected corner near an abandoned building. Just as he assumed the required position, he realized he was not alone:

> Suddenly these two big fat cops who probably spotted me a long time before, knowing exactly what I was up to—they stood out right in front of me and said [assuming a caricatured policeman's voice], "Okay, buddy get up now, show us some ID now—you got ID?" Of course, my way to deal with cops is always to fake or pretend that I don't understand English. . . . Well, I got interrogated by these cops for about twenty-five minutes while the work of nature was still going on in my bowels and going out of my bowels while I was being entertained by these fabulous, fabulous cops. And they followed me for a few blocks actually after I was forced to get out of there—walking with very tight buttocks and tightened up anger within me.

The incident, more humorous in retrospect, served as an inspiration for one of his graphic novels. Earlier that day he showed me this work, each moment captured by frame by frame, drawn with striking pencil strokes and captions. It well represented his talent and his own personal ennui while communicating some truth about outsider spaces such as BEDT. Wildness is exhilarating but unpredictable; things do not always end well. Still, he understood that such risks were a part of the fringe experience and part of himself.

Ür was philosophical the future of the place where he had spent so much time and that had inspired much of his art. He arrived in the neighborhood in the early 1990s as an early wave of gentrification was taking off.[18] Even as he watched the neighborhood improve, its waterfront remained a holdout to a previous Brooklyn that was tougher and more dangerous. This provided him with both refuge and inspiration for his art. He laughed as he described the changing scene:

> While this whole neighborhood is changing and becoming cleaner and cleaner, and you have all these galleries and restaurants opening—in the meantime, this scrap of land, this booger of land that stands right in the fringe—and it's being eaten by water, being eaten on the other side by the ever-increasing cleaning up of the neighborhood, but it still stands here. The garbage is still here, the bums still come here and the homeless guys are still here, the crazy band still comes to practice

here, the crazy loners who just got dumped by their girlfriends or whatever come to look at the water or to dream about sirens. . . .

But now even the social dynamic of the waterfront was changing, he admitted, noting that he had lost the sense of dread that had once characterized his experiences. This arc of improvement had already been at work for a few years, making the site slightly less "fringe-like" but still retaining a sense of anarchic possibility:

> After they tore down the buildings [in the late 1990s] it became more and more of a hanging out area, for, you know, more regular people. You would see all people from the neighborhood come down here and just smoke a cigarette and drink a brew and hang out in pretty good spirits. It lost the sort of really dangerous or dirty vibe it had a few years ago, but I mean it became this great neighborhood hangout.

He understood that the social conditions of the terminal were evolving and that it would be impossible to hold on to what he described as its "in limbo" qualities. As an outsider, Ür was reticent about the future of this waterfront. While unwilling to embrace conventional standards of improvement, he acknowledged the value in creating a traditional park at the terminal. "So the future of it—a beautiful park, clean trees and everything—that's great, but it's less interesting," he said. Even as he preferred BEDT's previous state as an "unpoliced place, where you kind of feel free, even though it's dirty and not safe," he knew that this transformation was inevitable.

Ür's art had tapped into this "sense of freedom" and embraced the uncertainty of the waterfront for nearly a decade. "You had this idea that people could take it over and make it into a utopian ground here, which is what I think I was coming here to get in touch with," he noted. "I put the sculpture here to plug into that vibe." His Pirate perhaps represented the climax of this larger moment that by 2003 was about to pass or had already passed.

The vibe at BEDT had indeed changed. If we needed a reminder that greater forces were already at work, we soon received it. As our discussion was reaching its own conclusion, we noticed a squad car 150 yards away at the North 7th Street gate. Two police officers were now out of the car and onto the site. Packing the video equipment away, I noticed a third officer who must have entered the terminal from North 9th Street, approaching from the north. Ür, who was fairly adept at escapes, made his way toward Kent Avenue, where he could find another hole or climb over the fence. I decided to stay, along with Brandon, who had been along to videotape the interview for me. We were called over and detained for roughly ninety minutes while the officers inspected and held on to our identification, perhaps checking it against some remote database. There were about fifteen of us and we simply stood around a police van at North 7th Street waiting for our IDs to be returned. Calling our names one by one, eventually the officers gave each of us our respective IDs *and* a ticket for trespassing. At the court complex in lower Manhattan a few weeks later, I found that all the tickets had been dismissed. The whole event had an air of pointlessness to it. The offenders, many aware that these tickets were routinely issued and almost always dismissed, were more annoyed than upset by all the waiting. For Ür, though, who knew what the consequences might be? Without ID he may have been taken in; and with his questionable immigration status, he might have had a longer detention and eventual deportation.

I saw Ür later that evening and a few times more in 2003, at local Williamsburg art and music events. While maintaining a sense of humor about his situation, he was not at all cavalier about his immigration status. Aside from a few gigs playing the sax, he was without a job and broke. Later that year he returned to France, where today he still practices a number of different forms of art, music, and performance.[19]

Terra Incognita: Dumpster Diving and the Reclamation of the Brooklyn Waterfront

While few installations provided the level of exhilaration of Ür's Pirate, many other artists and their works similarly embraced the informal dynamic of the terminal to explore a range of ideas and feelings, including anxiety, tension, and contradiction. One such artist, an affable man with local roots, used BEDT as a setting for his more minimal, environmentally themed installation, which offered its own form of dazzle and countercultural politic.

On a hazy August 2001 afternoon, I arrived at BEDT to find a series of orange tree-like installations arrayed across the shoreline. Four towers rose from the beach, each approximately fifteen feet high and consisting of plastic tubing gathered and held together at its base by a metal duct anchored by piles of rocks, wood, and chunks of what used to be the terminal's concrete bulkhead. The phosphorescent tubes, radiant even in the eerie haze, brought color to the drab grays and browns along the river's edge. Arcing outward at their tops and gently swaying in the wind, these playful forms were juxtaposed against the vertical geometries and muted colors of the distant Manhattan shore. The effect was fantastic; nearly everyone who visited BEDT that day stopped and marveled at seeing these unexpected sculptures.

The installation had been completed before I arrived, but its creator was still hanging around an hour later, enjoying the waterfront like many others on that hot Sunday. He was a thin man in his fifties, wearing a bright red dress shirt partially unbuttoned, shorts, and sandals. Speaking with a slight Polish accent, he said his name was Zbigniew (on subsequent occasions he introduced himself as Joe) and that he was a "street sculptor" who lived in the East Village. The installation was initially intended for a Village street, but as he set it up along a stretch of sidewalk he was stopped by the police who told him to pack it up or they would arrest him and take it down anyway.

Zbigniew's installation, composed of materials he salvaged from a Manhattan dumpster, calls attention to that which is neither land nor water (2001).

Like Ür, Zbigniew was resilient and used to improvisation. He had grown up in Greenpoint and knew its waterfront well. As a child he fished and swam in the river. "This used to be my playground," he told me. Now he imagined that BEDT would be an ideal alternative location for his work. It was publicly accessible but not so public that he would be asked to remove sculptures at the end of the day. In the work's initial incarnation, the towers were to call attention to the sidewalks as a public space, their connection to the water systems that lie below, and other less-than-apparent environmental concerns. In their new setting, they would call attention to the condition of the waterfront in a somewhat similar way.

When Zbigniew arrived at BEDT that morning, he parked his pickup at the end of North 7th Street and began to unload his materials. Immediately, people became curious and he invited them to join his endeavor. While not everyone was interested—he described with some consternation the "oblivious" Polish men who were drinking vodka and beer nearby—others quickly enlisted and were soon helping him unload the truck. With his guidance, they identified locations along the shore for the towers, gathered the debris that would anchor the materials, and assembled and secured the towers in their appropriate locations. As installation progressed, Zbigniew took occasional breaks to document the work with his old Betacam.

Committed to the shared experience, Zbigniew took particular delight in the instant community he built around his art project. His purpose and method were rooted in the 1960s egalitarianism of his youth and a desire for communally pursued improvement. The project was to

> shed some love and light on this area, which I thought would attract people. And as what happened . . . as people walked by they participated in putting it together. So it was a mutual adventure.

When this "mutual adventure" had concluded, the team, covered in sweat and dirt, took their clothes off and went for a swim.

Like many artists who scavenged the city for discarded bits of culture, Zbigniew had created an installation that reconsidered waste in a very literal way. A veteran dumpster diver, he obtained all the media that went into his sculptures by collecting stuff others had thrown out. "I pull out what I need," he explained. The materials for this installation—unused metal ducts and PVC tubing—he found discarded in a Manhattan dumpster. The find was more serendipitous than usual, as he discovered them underneath some books he was retrieving. (Zbigniew sells books on street corners when he is not making art.) "Wow, hundreds of pipes!" he exclaimed upon seeing this trove of thrown-away materials, presumably left over from a construction project.

The installation was a modest act of reclamation that he felt would initiate processes which would bring more people together to assert their collective rights to the waterfront. While not born of the waterfront like the Pirate, these salvaged materials, Zbigniew felt, had a sympathy with BEDT and the potential to inspire other local reclamations. The Greenpoint–Williamsburg waterfront had long been "a dumping ground where a lot of people had brought things that they didn't want" he said. Even before the marine–rail transfer yard was closed in 1983, BEDT was already being used by the waste-handling industries. He recited a list of the things that had been dumped there over the years, while gesturing to different points along the shore:

Back in the sixties, it was open and there were huge recycling factories here. There were dumping grounds for metal and there were a lot of spaces where people would just drive their trucks and throw stuff out. And there were piles and piles of that here. Actually, you know what [else] they were recycling here? Computer cards, tons and tons, and forests and forests of computer cards, and cartons and things like this. And scrap metal—from old cars—that was the big industry here. Also chemical industries—chemicals, powders, anything that was caustic to people's health—they brought it here, basically because they couldn't put it anywhere else. And they're still doing it today.

In the years after 1983, much of BEDT was open ground that functioned as a veritable auto repair shop for those local residents who wanted to do their own. After repairs had been made, all the old parts were simply left there to rust. The liquid detritus left behind, including motor oil, antifreeze, and corrosive battery acid, was still present in the soil. But the greatest source of pollution, Zbigniew emphasized, came from a legally operating scrap metal yard that had opened at BEDT on the block between North 4th and North 5th streets in the mid-1960s, and then later the garbage recycling and transfer station that replaced it in the late 1980s. For decades, similar facilities operated up and down the North Brooklyn waterfront.

Zbigniew's art was a marker that called attention to this legacy of degradation and neglect. This fouling of the landscape would not be undone by his work; rather, his intention was to *reveal* this condition and incite a local response. The process he initiated by removing the materials from the dumpsters would continue as other people gradually dismantled his art, repurposing these materials for practical uses consistent with the water- or air-related systems for which they had been designed. The next phase in this ecology was already occurring, he claimed, as someone had taken some of the tubing for a repair project. (A nasty storm a week later blew the rest of the tubing away; the well-anchored metal ducts remained in their original locations for many months after.)

The installation was a creative and colorful use of materials that were otherwise headed for the landfill, placed in a prominent location where it could be enjoyed but not so much that the city's laws and governing conventions would ensure its quick demise. The fact that the setting was so striking—where the water, skyline, and decaying postindustrial landscape came into view all at once—not only made the work visually appealing but also attracted much of its audience. Few people probably came to BEDT that day expecting to see Zbigniew's art, but many had come to experience the seductive combination of the contrasting elements (water, skyline, and site) considered in his work. Curious, surprised, or delighted viewers could be (and were) persuaded to take part in some aspect of the experiment, joining his assembly team or carrying away the materials or the ideals it embodied.

The notion that the materials garnered from progressive disassembly of Zbigniew's work would be reincorporated into other things negated some simpler concept of completion and spoke to a longer and more uncertain ecology of the waterfront and its capacity to serve contemporary human needs. Zbigniew argued that the terminal "would always be terra incognita"—a place that was "foul, dirty, and inaccessible" and could be used only as a "dumping ground for industry." His presence along with that of the dozens of others around us enjoying the waterfront in its present degraded state seemed to contradict his own severe assessment, but still he questioned BEDT's viability to be anything other than toxic. The legacies of dirty industries and wanton dumping persisted in the soil and water and would undermine reclamation efforts, he said.

Zbigniew's work and rhetoric—and its relationship to the terminal—reminded me of the installations of the Earthworks artists of the 1960s and 1970s, including Robert Smithson, Michael Heizer, Robert Morris, and Walter De Maria.[20] Its waterfront locale also made it reminiscent of the art experiments on the Hudson River piers on lower Manhattan's west side in the 1970s. While we did not discuss these potential influences at the time, Zbigniew was roughly a contemporary of these artists, and his bookselling table along Bedford Avenue contained many heady offerings about art, philosophy, and cultural endeavor. He was surely familiar with the land art movement and perhaps had first-hand knowledge of the city's downtown scene. What Zbigniew tried to make visible in the "terra incognita" of the Brooklyn waterfront, Smithson revealed in much of his environmental art, including his 1970 construction *Spiral Jetty* on the edge of Utah's Great Salt Lake. While lacking the monumental scale and permanence, Zbigniew's installation on the edge of the East River similarly called attention to a location that was not quite land and not quite water.[21] And like Smithson's mostly unrealized works for abandoned strip mines and other environmentally degraded sites, his installation attempted to reveal hard-to-perceive underlying conditions of the site while inciting longer reclamative discourses or actions.[22] As he described,

I wanted it to be something between water and earth—something that's growing out, something that is really uncertain. What's between the water and in the earth—and we're kind of in the middle of this, right? This guy is saying that you can't really catch any fish here. And I'm sure whatever you grow here will not be edible either. So that's kind of a question mark. Can anything grow? Can anything be placed here? Can we still utilize this space? Any of the shoreline?

Like much of Smithson's art and many of his writings, Zbigniew's work explored the boundary between not just land and water but nature and culture, playing with conventional notions that had arbitrarily separated the two.[23] In writing about Central Park, Smithson revealed its seemingly hidden "constructed" nature and argued that landscapes should be viewed "in a manifold of relations, not as isolated objects."[24] Zbigniew's installation revealed and probed many similar landscape "dialectics" (as Smithson referred to them) at a location where they collided, overlapped, and eluded easy definition.

Historically, urban development practices have often recomposed the water–land relationships. Since antiquity, city builders have gone to extraordinary lengths to facilitate maritime activity, including building docks and piers over water, constructing massive jetties to protect harbors, and dredging shipping channels and wharves. Extending land out into the water, thus creating or enlarging valuable plots of property suitable for urban development, is also among the most common but inherently unstable historic waterfront building practices. Manhattan's landmass is today a third larger than its pre-colonial extent.[25] Similarly, the land that comprised BEDT over the course of its history was extended several times into the East River.[26] But such interventions require regular and expensive maintenance and are often at odds with evolving water standards.

In the New York harbor estuary, the erosion of the bulkhead and the fill behind and underneath it, along with the collapse of piers and wharves, is ironically due to better environmental stewardship of the harbor. Cleaner water has enabled a population explosion of pier-eating marine borers—shipworms and gribbles (tiny crustaceans)—that have undermined wood supports of piers and bulkhead.[27] Just five years before I stood along the broken shoreline with Zbigniew, the seawall at this location was mostly intact, as were the adjacent finger piers. The worms had indeed been doing their work. As the water has now reclaimed some of its preindustrial extent, it has complicated redevelopment efforts. National, state, and local environmental laws prohibit the simple fill practices of the past, even to replace lost fill.[28]

More so than, say, *Spiral Jetty*, whose remote location on the Great Salt Lake removed from settlement and accessible only by a dirt road, art at BEDT—a location at the center of the New York region—was a striking setting for reinterpretation of the relationship between the constructed and natural aspects of our environment. The collision of "nature" and the "city" was indeed what made the terminal so appealing to a range of artists and recreators. Earlier in the summer, Bonnie had noted such a connection—and perhaps summed up how many felt:

> I've lived in the city for a long time, but I love nature and I love getting out of the city. What's really special about this place is that it's got this city and nature combination, like a sort of raw beauty—the very way the bricks are all over the place, the way the docks are falling in, the skyline in the background. It's a landscape that's quite beautiful in a quite rugged way.

Bonnie embraced nature as something malleable, shifting, and inseparable from human endeavor while viewing art in a similar light, as inherent in the changing relationships between everyday objects and their setting. But the complicated or contradictory experience that she and other enjoyed at BEDT was not appreciated by everyone.

At the same time that Zbigniew was making his installation a marker of neglect and potentially a catalyst for local environmentalism, the State Parks–NYU partnership was plotting its own reclamation of the terminal. While not fully aware of the emerging park plan, he had a distrust of political leaders and their connection to land development and stewardship practices that made him suspicious of the endeavor. As I began to describe the plan to him, he quickly launched into his own, more dystopic scenario. Long before the park could be built, a "team of experts" would have to assess the "toxicities" of the site and undertake drastic remediation efforts. As he explained,

> I left this area for a long time. And when you come back you have sensitivity to smells and poisons. Once you have been contaminated and you leave and come back, you are very sensitive to it. And I feel this area is really polluted. I feel it in my bones; I smell it; it's in my system and I know it—it's going to be condemned.

Zbigniew's perspective was colored by Greenpoint and Williamsburg's long history of environmental degradation. Earlier he had referenced the 17-million-gallon underground oil spill along the Newtown Creek, which had slowly accumulated over several decades from petroleum refineries and storage operations before its discovery in 1978. By the

2000s, local advocacy groups, federal and state regulators, and the oil companies, most prominently ExxonMobil, were still arguing over the extent of the contamination, the cost of remediation, and the relative share that each company involved would be forced to pay.[29] BEDT was actually quite far from this disaster area, and its own history was somewhat more benign. The prevailing view of state officials, NYU representatives, and their consultants was, in fact, that the terminal would not require the drastic cleanup that Zbigniew envisioned in order to make it into a park (see Chapter 7). His conviction also seemed to contradict what he had earlier said to me, that the city needed "more spaces like this and Socrates." If the terminal truly was not fit for recreation, why was he here on this day? And what about the others at BEDT that afternoon—were there not risks for them as well? To these questions he laughed and then noted, "Artists can take poisons, you know—but kids and dogs? They'll have a tough time."

Perhaps unwilling to acknowledge the paradox incited by his installations, Zbigniew was struggling to reconcile human activity, including his own, with some larger and more purely imagined construct of nature. The same ecology that allowed people to dump motor oil or antifreeze also allowed for other, less environmentally destructive activities and enjoyment of the waterfront without supervision or constraint of rules. Zbigniew professed a disposition for swimming in the harbor, noting that he had developed "a taste" for the water. Yet activities like swimming—or, in the case of Zbigniew and his helpers on that day, nude swimming—are not permitted in riverfront parks in Brooklyn or Manhattan. Those who try to break the rules in city parks are likely to encounter security to enforce them or obstacles such as railings designed to thwart access to the water.

The Unpark in a Creative City

Zbigniew's dilemma is also our own: How can we create and maintain areas within the city that allow for varied human activity while retaining a more robust, traditional, or salubrious sense of nature—the kind we often imagine being far from the city and untouched by urban development? When I asked Zbigniew why people come to the terminal as opposed to a traditional park, he quickly responded, "Freedom. A sense of freedom—of space." Pausing, he looked out across the well-populated but unstructured landscape around him and added, "People don't like things arranged." If urban art is about uninhibited expression and nature is about malleability, then BEDT was not merely a good place to scavenge or site unwieldy sculptures that have no place in the conventionally ordered spaces of the city. It was also a venue where the wilder creative impulses could be explored and indulged, from the humble earthworks makers who shifted dirt, rocks, bricks, and paving stones to more ambitious artists, such as Ür and Zbigniew, who saw the terminal as an opportune location for renegade sculptures offering explicitly renegade social statements.

The freedom to do things—both creative and destructive—was part of what brought people to the "unpark," as Bonnie had called it. The lack of stability and the presence of risk or perhaps more insidious environmental hazard were explicitly understood; art makers of all stripes had a sense that everything was, as Ür said, "in limbo" and that one day they would arrive to find new fences and bulldozers. Unfazed, they made the most of these conditions. While these artists sought out, engaged, and reveled in this wildness, others held a different conception of what form art might take at the water's edge. As the community planning process began in 2002, participants noted the many artists who lived in the area and asserted that the park plan should respond to and take advantage of this considerable creative community. As the plan unfolded, however, the issue evolved into how local artists might be enlisted to make the plan better, as opposed to providing a ground in which art could be freely created by *anyone* afflicted by a creative bug.

When East River State Park opened in 2007, state officials and their design consultants, like the artists before them, made use of some of the materials that were already on the site (Chapter 8). Large concrete blocks, cleansed of their graffiti, were arranged in a semicircle to mark a playground contained within; old concrete walls were left in place. And while BEDT's beach had been cleared of the once-abundant rocks, wood, and debris that artists desired, the most dynamic of all spaces, the Slab, had been left intact. But for area artists and others, artful arrangement that does not allow for rearrangement and alteration makes this site a pleasant but mostly conventional waterfront park. Enforced regulations prevent any of the sorts of creative activities and events described in this chapter.

The twenty-first-century reappraisal of New York in the 1970s and its abundant and unpredictable art scene remind me of what I saw at BEDT at the turn of the millennium. Better known for dysfunction, deterioration, lawlessness and the financial crisis that brought New York to its knees, the '70s boasted an art scene that is now admired for its audacity, grit, communal spirit, and lack of pretense. Like the manner in which the artists of that era—including Gordon Matta-Clark, Dan Graham, and Richard Serra—made the dilapidated piers along the Hudson River the loci of their art experiments, the lesser-known artists a generation later made BEDT a similar ground for engagement of the waterfront and the city. Matta-Clark, whose work includes *Day's End*—a 1975 transformation of Pier 52 by strategic cuts in its storage shed and substructure to reveal earthly and celestial movements—is often considered the seminal artist of that scene. Of his work Douglas Crimp noted:

> The subject and site of Matta-Clark's art was the city itself, the city experienced simultaneously as neglected and usable, as dilapidated and beautiful, as loss and possibility.[30]

Crimp could just as aptly be describing the Williamsburg waterfront at the turn of the millennium. Unplanned spaces and those publicly available for creative co-option without restraint are vital to all cities but particularly New York, given its status as a global center for creative production. Yet today the city offers no even remotely comparable "official" public art space that is open to all on an informal basis without constraints.

During the Bloomberg era, the city prided itself on global art events like Christo's *Gates* in Central Park and the Danish-Icelandic artist Olafur Eliasson's $15.5 million *New York City Waterfalls* installed in the harbor in 2008 as well as lower-key art programming held on Governors Island.[31] It also promoted more permanent, progressive design in public space, including the pedestrianization of Times Square; the development of the High Line, a park built atop a long-disused elevated freight line along Manhattan's West Side; and Brooklyn Bridge Park. But as wonderful as these spaces are, they provide a relatively limited outlet for the city's own creative agents and in none are individuals free to install art or move the earth. The accidental nature of spaces like BEDT—like the Manhattan piers of the 1970s—cannot be manufactured or planned for, but surely there are opportunities to facilitate unstructured play in the vast network of the city's public spaces.

The creative scene at BEDT would be difficult to replicate, and likewise an urban development policy that simply designates vacant sites as "anything goes" spaces might produce little or no appreciable creative use. The activity documented in this chapter and the previous one—representing just a sample of the creative practices that occurred at BEDT in the years between the yard's closure in 1983 and ERSP's development in the mid-2000s—was as much a product of external factors as its physical conditions and tolerant social vibe. The appropriation of the terminal for art evolved with the increase of creative people living in relative proximity and urban densities that encouraged them to seek out unclaimed or lightly claimed space for their creations, experiments, and events. Spaces like BEDT, publicly accessible but long held by private ownership, are also the product of broad economic and cultural shifts, historic development patterns, local circumstance, and accident, making them unpredictable and difficult to plan. It may be unrealistic for urban parks programs to provide such spaces, and the mere "officialness" of city-sponsored activity—no matter how progressive—de-radicalizes the potential politics of creative endeavor.

Yet it is also clear that this unforeseen arts space offered something different in a city filled with almost every conceivable form and venue for art. Can the planners, designers, and stewards of our parks and public spaces—whether along the waterfront or elsewhere, in New York or other cities—produce informal space and experiences at all like what I have described here? Could they provide a thoroughly open ground that would satisfy the desires of a range of artists, varied in skill, experience, and temperament, from countercultural but accomplished practitioners like Ür and Zbigniew to those who simply moved rocks around or arranged discarded objects? And how should they treat organically evolving but thoroughly accidental spaces, like BEDT? I take up these questions in the last chapter of the book.

Much like the artists, the rearrangement and reconstruction of space is also central to the constituency whose story is told in the next chapter. Far from the mostly young and creatively inclined people described in this and the two previous chapters, the men I spent time with are from an entirely different milieu and mindset. Their stories explore many of the same issues from a different perspective and a few new ones, including the politics of found space, reconciling nature with the city and the value of personal history and tenure in determining spatial claims. They also offer a longer perspective on the vast changes in the social and economic landscape of the waterfront, its adjacent neighborhoods, and the larger city.

CHAPTER 5

LOCAL TALES

Hanging Out and Observing Life on the Waterfront

ASIDE FROM THOSE LIVING THERE, BEDT's most regular constituency was a group of middle-aged working-class men from the immediate neighborhoods who came in good weather and bad, on weekdays and weekends, in the day, evening, and sometimes at night. These men—the "locals," as I will call them—made BEDT their informal social club, spending many hours hanging out, drinking beer, smoking cigarettes and an occasional joint, reading, listening to music, and enjoying the scenery at this waterfront spot. Sometimes they barbecued, and in the cold weather they kept a fire going—burning scrap wood in a rusted fifty-five-gallon oil drum. A few fished and another brought bread to feed the geese and ducks. Although they spent substantial time at the terminal, and frequently while consuming alcohol, their presence was low-key. Rarely the loudest or most boisterous group, they generally kept to themselves and avoided trouble.

The ten or so men who constituted the locals were mostly born and raised in the area; some were near-lifelong residents. A few were also Vietnam veterans, and their experience during and after this war greatly affected their lives and complicated their stories. Their perspectives, when they chose to share them, were intimately intertwined with personal history and often tinged with both humor and sadness. As men who still defined themselves and

Yosh spent many afternoons at BEDT (2001).

others by ethnicity and the neighborhoods where they grew up, they provided a sense of place and time—and time past—that was unique among those who regularly visited the terminal. Their memories provided a connection to a waterfront and social culture that was inseparable from tugboats, barges, freight cars, factories and warehouses, and the rough-and-tumble neighborhoods where their families lived and worked. By the turn of the millennium, that waterfront was mostly a memory, and a decade later that memory is even more faded, as condominium towers rise and parks are built where men once toiled, and working-class families are displaced by better-heeled residents.

With only a few exceptions, they were not that approachable and their stories were rarely complete. Many of these men were suspicious of outsiders. When I talked to them, most were careful not to reveal too much and declined to share basic information about themselves, including their identities or livelihoods. Fortunately, a few were more open and allowed me and sometimes the friends I brought along to enter their social world.

My main contact with this group was Yosh, a quiet, charismatic fifty-year-old Polish-American Jew and a Vietnam veteran. He told me that his given name was John but he preferred to be called Yosh, which was "John" in Polish. Yosh could usually be found in some recessed corner of the terminal, reading or listening to the radio, with a beer in his hand or by his side. Unlike some of the others, Yosh was affable and enjoyed telling stories about the "old days." He always said hello to me (even before we really knew each other) when I saw him at the terminal or on nearby streets. Visiting primarily in the afternoon, Yosh spent many hours at BEDT several days a week, probably more than any other single individual (save for the resident homeless). He spent much of this time alone. Even when in the company of his mates, Yosh would sometimes remain in his own world, reading or quietly listening to the radio while the others around him engaged in loud conversation.

Another frequent visitor was Yosh's friend George, a sixty-five-year-old New York City native of Puerto Rican descent. In spite of this heritage, most people thought he was Jewish or Italian, he said, because of his long nose. He was missing a few of his front teeth, which perhaps accounted for the slight slur in his speech, and his eyes were often obscured by dark prescription sunglasses. George read a lot and was not tremendously talkative; he would usually not speak to me unless I said something to him first. He responded to my questions mostly with simple, no-nonsense answers. But if he thought my question was stupid or had an obvious answer, he would reply with his own rhetorical one. George owned a small building in Greenpoint containing three apartments,

George was a frequent visitor to the terminal (2001).

living alone in one while renting out the others and the two storefronts on the ground floor. But he was neither a Greenpoint nor a Northside native, a distinction he frequently made by saying, "I'm not from this area." (He always declined to say which neighborhood he was actually from.) There was one other important distinction from the others: He did not drink.

Joe, a somewhat slight man of about fifty years of age with a disarming smile, was also a frequent visitor but not nearly as frequent as Yosh or George. Born and raised in Greenpoint, he was like Yosh a Vietnam veteran of Polish descent. Being a veteran was a great part of his identity and one that he felt more comfortable sharing with others in the liberal social environment of the terminal. Charles, a burly man and also a Polish Jew, came to the waterfront with Yosh on occasion to drink beer and relax. An East Williamsburg resident, Charles was not inclined to talk much about himself but enjoyed talking generally and offered his opinions on a range of topics. He also enjoyed "busting my chops" and made fun of me because I was living in Philadelphia. "Did you bring the cheese steaks?" he would repeatedly ask me. Then there was Raul, the gregarious Puerto Rican from the Southside, who liked to play the trumpet and worked at a lithography studio in Manhattan. Other members of this crew included Mikey, a Polish man of around fifty who never said a word to me on the several occasions in which I was in his company. Yosh said Mikey had a keen interest in local history and was involved in an effort to create a maritime history museum in Greenpoint. Another member of this group was a somewhat younger Northside resident named Pete, whose only words to me were, "Are you a cop?" I always told him, "No." But this did little to ease his suspicions.

Less frequent visitors to the terminal sometimes joined the locals. I was familiar with only a few of them, mostly by sight. They included Bob, a twenty-plus-year resident of the area who would visit during the day with his infant son and chat with the others, often about neighborhood affairs. Then there were those who gravitated over for conversation, for company, or in hopes of getting a beer. One of these men, a fast-talking, middle-aged man named Charlie, whom I saw frequently, was often out on the piers fishing. One evening I saw him cooking his catch over an open fire and realized that he had been living in a plywood shack at the terminal.

Creating Social Space amid Waste

As I described at the beginning of this book, one of my first significant experiences with these men came in June 2000, when I discovered their social space amid the dumpsters on the southern part of the terminal (that part south of North 7th Street). Owned by USA Waste and adjacent to their garbage transfer station, this area was a wasteland of equipment and rusting junk. This unlikely setting for the locals' "club house"—one of two they maintained during 2000 and 2001—provided no amenities, other than the views, which could be experienced only when one was standing. In fact, their space, strewn with objects of waste, mildly claustrophobic, and often smelly and noisy, would have been considered unpleasant, even by the modest standards of those who frequented the terminal. But this in fact was what made it ideal for these men: This was space that no one else wanted to claim at that moment. They were left alone and did what they wanted to do out of the gaze of other recreators and the police.

Unpleasant odors notwithstanding, this small, irregularly shaped clearing provided these men with the right degree of intimacy and enclosure on many leisurely afternoons. They each had just enough personal space to be comfortable and were close to arm's distance of their barbecue, radio and music players, bicycles, reading materials, and personal effects. Their beer coolers were always nearby and often doubled as seating for those who had not brought a folding

The locals and others outside of their appropriated trailer in early 2002.

chair. Animated conversations, laughter, barbecue smoke, and the occasional wafting scent of marijuana might draw others to this otherwise hidden spot over the course of an afternoon, including those who were living at the terminal. While the two groups were not friends, the locals knew many of these homeless men and were usually not bothered by their presence.

By spring 2001, the block between North 6th and North 7th streets had been cleared and the dumpsters were gone. The men had moved to a location on the north side of the terminal (farther from the transfer station), where they created a new social space around an abandoned truck trailer. It was a random, rusting ruin covered with scribble and grime. Sitting atop an eroding bank of the beach on one end and a pile of bricks (likely an old building foundation) on the other, the trailer was tenuously married to the terminal. (Two years later I found a postcard in a Manhattan bookstore with a photograph of the skyline taken from its inside, through a hole cut into its side.) Prior to its appropriation, the trailer was a shell with no roof and gaping holes in its sides and base. Using plywood, the locals made some rudimentary repairs, adding a roof, floor, and a lockable front door with a built-in window. But even with these improvements, it was still suspect, being neither flat nor sturdy. Rarely occupying the trailer, they used it instead to store stuff they would use outside, including furniture, a grill, a cooler, utensils, paper plates and cups, clothes, and magazines.

The men spent most of their time just outside the trailer, underneath the shade of one of the largest trees at BEDT, an ailanthus that had taken root in a patch of loose dirt. A path that served as the access point to the piers at the north end of the terminal passed by the trailer and the tree. Arranging their chairs in an informal circle straddling this path, the men acted as informal gatekeepers to the piers, not that they ever stopped anyone from passing. This did, however, give them a chance to check out who was headed in that direction and, more important, gave them a commanding view back to North 7th Street. As one of the men explained to me, this spot allowed them to see when the police were coming well in advance of their arrival, providing them an opportunity to hide or discard beers or other items, or leave the area if necessary. The location also had an excellent view of the skyline and harbor. Much like their previous spot amid the dumpsters, the view was not completely visible from where they usually sat, being obscured by the trailer and the large tree, but it was only steps away.

This is where I often found Yosh, George, Charles, Raul, Joe, Mikey, Pete, and others during the summer and fall of 2001. Yosh also spent time in a few other spots, even when some of his friends were hanging out at the trailer, including a small concrete building foundation about ten yards upland from the trailer, where he would often read, listen to the radio, and sunbathe. This pleasant spot notwithstanding, the men infrequently held more prominent spaces at the terminal. They generally chose spaces that were more recessed, hidden, or marginal than the more desirable areas—the Slab, the piers, and the beach. They spent time in these locations as well but spent most of their time in and limited their constructions to less active spots. So even among the larger group of those who reclaimed space at BEDT, they reclaimed areas that were less likely to appeal to others or create conflicts.

Much like the informality of the spaces they created or occupied, these men visited the terminal on an ad hoc basis, without planning. They came whenever they felt like doing so and usually without specific arrangements to meet one another. If someone went alone and no one else showed up, he would enjoy the site on his own; if others did show up, then he would enjoy it with them. When I interviewed George, he was alone at their spot near the trailer. I asked him where everyone else was and he replied:

I don't know—they come down whenever they want. It could be now and it could be three hours from now or two hours from now. I don't keep tabs. We just come down whenever we feel like it.

Nonetheless, it seemed that when he visited BEDT he had some expectation that others would show, particularly on weekends. When I asked him a different time about Yosh's whereabouts, he seemed annoyed and replied:

We know people are going to be here, so we just come down. Just like you are going to be here and you know we're going to be here. You don't ask us what time we're here—you just happen to find us—and if we are here, we're here and if we're not, we're not.

The others treated their potential social engagements similarly. One afternoon Raul gave me a hard time because I had missed the opportunity to videotape his trumpet playing—he was leaving and I had just arrived. When I suggested that we do it at a future time, he enthusiastically agreed but was unwilling to set a specific date and time. "You'll just have to find me here," he instructed. But I never did, at least not with his trumpet.

A Lifetime Near the Waterfront

Among all the people I met at the terminal, Yosh had the longest and most complicated history with this waterfront. He was also more willing to talk about his past than most. With many stops and starts, he shared much of his story on the day after his fifty-first birthday in early September 2001. He had come to BEDT on that sunny Saturday afternoon with Charles and Charles's wife, Basia, not so much to celebrate as just to enjoy day like any other. There had been no party the day before, and this trip to BEDT was not unlike dozens of others over the past year. Nonetheless, there was a modest sense of festiveness about it and they had brought an appropriate amount of beer, which they shared with me, my friend Brian, and Brandon, who was videotaping interviews. Later that evening, Brian and I joined Yosh and Charles at Teddy's Bar up the street.

After Charles and I argued about the volume of the radio playing in the background, Yosh, who wore his usual neatly trimmed beard and mustache, large glasses, and a brimmed cap, settled into his beach chair and told his story. Other than his term in the Navy when he served in Vietnam, Yosh had always been close to the Williamsburg waterfront. His parents were Polish Jews who met while interned in a German POW camp. His mother had been there longer, making hand grenades and other munitions in a Nazi factory. His father was finishing his tour of duty in the Polish army when he was "caught in the blitzkrieg" near the end of the war. Upon liberation they stayed in Germany (or Poland) and then on December 13, 1950, they moved to the United States with their infant son, Yosh. While they were working-class people, Yosh wanted me to understand that they came by airplane—"a Douglass," he said—not by boat. They settled in an apartment on North 1st Street near the waterfront, not far from where Yosh's uncle lived, joining the large community of Jews of Polish ancestry in Williamsburg.

As a child during the 1950s, Yosh took advantage of living in close proximity to the harbor. Like thousands of men and some women who worked at the terminal, on nearby docks, or in the neighborhood's waterfront factories, warehouses, and refineries, children also found themselves drawn to this edge. It offered them a setting for exploration and play and provided them with the opportunity to get into the water on hot summer days. In spite of safety issues and poor water quality, Yosh, like other neighborhood kids, was a frequent swimmer. He also fished and remembered catching baby eels in coffee cups off the docks at North 1st Street and Metropolitan Avenue.

Like many children, he was fascinated by both trains and boats, the sights, sounds, and rumblings of which were a constant in Williamsburg. The tracks of the Brooklyn Eastern District Terminal Railroad extended from the then-sprawling transfer yard into and across the streets of the neighborhood, terminating inside several warehouses and factories. As Yosh grew older, he frequently played at the terminal with his brother and friends. Sometimes a railroad engineer and friend who worked at the terminal, Kenny, would let Yosh and his brother ride with him as he operated the locomotive. He became excited as he described the thrill of riding in the cab of a locomotive as it moved freight cars about the yard. Another thrill for him was swimming off the piers and idle barges from the terminal. A recently decommissioned tugboat, the *Oleans*—Yosh repeated the word and then spelled it out, "O-L-E-A-N-S," to make sure we understood that it was not "Orleans"—was moored along the bulkhead at BEDT. The boat was easily boarded by neighborhood kids during slack times. "Ahhh—we used to love it down here," he said.

The waterfront would remain an important place for him as an adult. In 1967, a friend of his father's who worked the nightshift helped him land a job at BEDT's Bulk Flour Center. Constructed in 1964, the center helped revive the terminal at a time when its traffic had been declining.[1] Designed to handle as much as 200 million pounds a year, it was the largest distribution center for flour in the New York region and helped sustain BEDT during its last two decades of operation.[2] Yosh's job was to weigh and transfer flour from covered hopper freight cars to storage silos and trucks that served bakeries and macaroni factories across Brooklyn and the region. From the concrete platform on which we were sitting, which Yosh said was once BEDT's tugboat office (historic property maps suggest that this spot was actually the locomotive repair shop), he became animated as he attempted to describe the way the center functioned and how the yard looked thirty-five years earlier.[3] He pointed toward the location of the flour center along Kent Avenue between North 8th and North 9th streets. One of the center's corrugated-metal sheds and connecting gantry had been demolished only a year and a half earlier. He then gestured farther north along Kent to the location of the main office where he picked up his paycheck (the building once located between North 9th and North 10th streets was cleared around 1998) but seemed to lose his sense of orientation as these familiar structures were now gone.

Yosh did not work at BEDT for long. In 1968, he was drafted and soon sent to Vietnam. Returning to the neighborhood upon discharge in 1971, he moved back into his family's apartment on North 1st Street. Aside from stints in hospitals after his service, he lived there until the mid-1990s, when he and his mother and sister were evicted. They found another apartment nearby.

When I'd met Yosh the previous year, he'd regaled me with waterfront stories of the recent past—of crime, drug use, and prostitution, and of dead bodies being dumped at the terminal. He described the ruin of the waterfront and the neighborhood from the perspective of a passionate observer who saw it up close but also with a certain sense of detachment. While his stories were sometimes disjointed or lacking details, he recalled a bygone or rapidly disappearing waterfront of misdeeds, misfortune, and larger-than-life characters, not unlike those in popular fiction and film. Yosh had his own connection to this fictive city of gangsters, violence, and crime. He and his family had been temporarily removed from their apartment so a film crew could shoot interior and exterior scenes of *Billy Bathgate*.[4] The "based on a true story" film depicted the life of the eponymous fledgling gangster who is taken under the wings of the legendary Bronx bootlegger and crime boss Dutch Schultz. Yosh felt that his family was never adequately compensated for their temporary displacement.

Yosh's portrayal of the last years of the BEDT railroad and those that immediately followed had a certain "unreal" resonance and described a milieu that could have been straight out of fiction. Indeed, one of the first stories he told me was about a local man who had been hunted down and murdered. His body was apparently discovered at BEDT a few days after he was killed. I asked Yosh whether it was a mob hit and he quickly replied,

A mob hit? Are you kidding me? It was just one of those things—they just didn't like the guy.

On the day after his birthday, Yosh was full of stories, and few of them had happy endings. I wanted to know more about crimes at BEDT in particular, but just as he began to share important details, Charles would cut him off, directing him to "stick to the hypothetical!" Whatever information was missing, he still painted a lurid picture of the waterfront as a site of everyday crime, desperation, and occasional humor. He called the 1970s and 1980s "the two bad decades." The immediate period after the closing of the terminal's operations in 1983, in particular, was a rough one. I asked Yosh if it was dangerous to come to BEDT in those days and he immediately replied,

Down here? It was very dangerous. You think you'd be down here? You come down with that camera—you think you gonna be walkin' out with that camera? Or maybe all three of youse wouldn't be walkin' outta here. That's how bad it was down here. Now the cops even—didn't even come down here; that's how scared they were too. Yeah, it was bad.

As in other depressed areas of the city during that time, BEDT's vacated freight houses had become, he said, "shooting galleries" for IV drug users and crack dens, and they sheltered a range of other illegal activities. He went on to describe many of the things he had seen or experienced at the terminal and in the neighborhood. It was a somewhat typical story of neighborhood decline in the wake of blue-collar job loss, complete with drugs, prostitution, homelessness, theft, and associated violence:

You want to talk about heavy duty now—right down here. They had these warehouses—they were still standin'. You had a lot of homeless people here during the eighties . . . and people come from everywhere—doin' the drugs, shootin' the drugs—doin' whatever they had to do to survive, this and that. A lot of prostitutes, and a lot of bodies you found—mostly females, prostitutes—ah, this neighborhood was a wreck. It was a total wreck.

Yosh also talked about a "chop shop" operating in one of the warehouses, where "brand spanking new cars" were reduced to parts "one, two, three." Whatever could not be salvaged, he said, was torched on site. (Even in 2001, the terminal was still a place where an occasional car was dumped and stripped—one was only a hundred feet from where we were talking.) Yosh admired the well-rationalized appropriation of another warehouse (or perhaps the same one at a different time). He described a bifurcated interior in which female prostitutes had their "bunks" and more private spaces where they slept and kept their belongings on one side while on the opposite side were the bunks where men slept (the job or role of these men was unclear). Near the entrance to the building were some fifty-five-gallon barrels used for heating and cooking, he said. Food was frequently obtained from the stuff thrown out by local butcher shops, groceries, and bakeries. Yosh described a winter night when he was hanging out with a friend over their own fire when he was overwhelmed by the enticing smell of sausages cooking. He entered the warehouse and a guy named Gregory gave him a sausage sandwich made with "good bread" from the neighborhood. "It smelled good, it was cooked good, so I ate it," he said. Sick to his stomach the next day, he said he was fortunate that his court appearance scheduled for that morning had been postponed and he could return home. (He would not say why he'd had to appear in court.)

Eventually the activities within the warehouses reached the point where, according to Yosh, they were well known and attracting people from other neighborhoods. Of particular concern, he said, was the growing homeless population the buildings sheltered. While Yosh did not mention it, by the end of the 1980s other things also happened in and near these warehouses, including art events, film shoots, and rave parties. By the 1990s, one of these buildings had been appropriated by an artist-inventor who lived and maintained a workshop inside. He had apparently been working on modular living and storage units while acting as an informal caretaker of the terminal and an occasional liaison to the terminal's owners. (The prostitution bunks that Yosh had previously described may have been these modular units.) But Yosh's description of BEDT before and after the warehouses were torn down was consistent with the accounts of others who frequented the terminal during the 1980s and 1990s. When they were demolished, many (but not all) of the illegal activities they housed also disappeared. The demolition also made the waterfront more open, eliminating hidden spots, allowing people to feel that they were less likely to happen upon threatening or criminal activity.

Some of the other locals also noted the connection between changes in the physical and social landscapes and, in particular, the dramatic decline in crime.[5] Joe said that the terminal was safer and more accessible than it had ever been. But at the same time, he lamented the continued deterioration of the piers and the loss of the seawall and the ground behind it. "The erosion went to shit, but the people got friendlier," he explained. Only five or six years earlier the piers were intact enough to allow people to drive their cars onto them; this was an everyday practice in the neighborhood. In the mid-'90s, I too had done this a few times with a friend, who did not mind driving his car over the missing cobblestones, substantial ruts, rocks, garbage, and broken glass on North 9th Street and then out onto the dirt-topped pier. Indeed, it was a special feeling to sit in the car with windows rolled down looking across the harbor and the spread of the skyline.

During the 1990s, the piers along with adjacent areas of the terminal were fine during the day, Joe said, but nighttime was different. The presence of abandoned buildings—and the potential for people to hide out in them—made him feel uneasy after dark:

> You could do more things—cars were parked here—it was cool. But my friend Dave says, at night, you don't stay here—I'm talkin' three or four years ago—you don't stay here at night because there are all kinds of creatures, man you know—there were more buildings. Now, I'm not talkin' about the homeless.

Joe went on to tell me of some horrific crimes at BEDT—about a young couple "getting the shit beat out of them," resulting, he said, in one's death. And another in which a young boy's body was recovered at the terminal. He also said that he frequently encountered weird things, including a noose hanging from a tree and other signs of ill will, that compelled him to leave before nightfall. But now things were much safer:

> I feel safe here, I mean I wouldn't sit in the darkest reaches, but it could be three in the morning— there's always somebody comin' down from the clubs on Bedford Avenue or somethin'—just to see the skyline. . . . I could stay here until three in the morning, walk out here flippin' everybody with a load

on, I got no problem—I got to worry about cuttin' myself when I fall. You know, I feel safe here—and it's only been two or three years.

Joe's conclusion that the terminal had become so safe that the greatest threat to his security was a combination of darkness and his own drunkenness (having "a load on") also suggests that BEDT had evolved into a safer place through the increased use. Making a visual connection with others who happened to be there at the same time was a key factor in making him feel at ease.

While the dramatic improvements in the safety of the waterfront and nearby streets have had many positive impacts, both Yosh and Charles were quick to point out that there was a downside. When Brian asked, "When did things start to get better?" Yosh quickly replied,

Better? When the rents went high—I don't think nothin' got better—it got worse. . . . When the rents went sky-high, the outsiders started comin' in and ruined the neighborhood for us in a way. A lot of old-timers had to go.

In Yosh's mind, the waterfront, the neighborhood, and his family were indelibly linked. On several occasions he referred to being evicted, with his mother and sister, from their apartment on North 1st Street. The eviction stemmed from a dispute with a new landlord who wanted to raise the rent to $1,400 a month:

We lived there all these years—we lived under nine landlords—no problem whatsoever. Now these people are buying up these sections and now we got evicted out of there. Mind you, fifty years [we] lived over there and got tossed out.

He recalled the days of his youth and the modest means his family lived on generated from his father's labor working fifty to sixty hours a week at the slaughterhouse in New Jersey or later at a factory inside the Gretsch Building on Broadway (on Williamsburg's Southside, about one and a half miles from BEDT) where they made porcelain light fixtures. His mother had worked in factories too. But rent was only $17 or $18 a month, which he said was considered high for the time. He associated the current improvement of the neighborhood with "greed" rather than with quality of life and noted that the cost of living was a real challenge for him with his health problems and his mother, who he said was "barely walking" and had only a tiny pension.

Trying to get a sense of the new neighborhood dynamics, Brian asked how longtime residents were getting along with all the newcomers. Yosh replied,

> The majority of the people—the original people that have been here for a lot of years, like in my case fifty years—we're still in shock. The reason why I say in shock is how fast it happened—the invasion.

Charles was also amazed by the rapid social changes. He noted the great increase of people using the Bedford Avenue subway station, complaining that the L train was more crowded than he had ever seen it. He also noted the increased competition for neighborhood parking spaces, adding incredulously, "And all this happened in just the past two years."

Yosh, Charles, and perhaps some of the others (most would not talk with me about such subjects) tended to view the affairs in the neighborhood in the context of broader changes they saw in the country. They felt they were being squeezed on both sides, by gentrification on one end and by runaway immigration on the other. While Yosh himself, a U.S. veteran and near-lifelong resident, was not a citizen, only a legal alien with a green card, he was very concerned about immigration. "We're all immigrants, of course," he said. "But the doors are opening too fast." Later he approximated the sound of a flushing toilet and said, "The U.S. is going down the tubes."

On multiple occasions, Yosh and Charles referenced the 1973 film *Soylent Green*, starring Charlton Heston.[6] This science fiction thriller set in the early twenty-first century portrays life in a teeming and dystopic New York city of 25 million people where the masses have been consigned to live by law. The world had become mostly unfit for agricultural production and the city's poor subsisted on a strange industrial product, Soylent Green, while a small, wealthy elite lived in well-secured Manhattan luxury apartments and ate real food. The movie seemed to explain a lot about the world to them and colored their perspective of local affairs. Perhaps given to hyperbole, Yosh used the movie to explain his own particular vision of New York's future:

It's going to happen. All the poor people are gonna be on this side [Brooklyn], and all the rich people are gonna be on that island [pointing in the direction of Manhattan]. The [Williamsburg] bridge is gonna be sealed off like in the movies.

It was easy to dismiss the conspiratorial banter of Yosh and Charles, but this conversation occurred just three days before September 11. The horrific events of that day seemed to strengthen their established beliefs. Less than a week later Charles told me that it was "a whole new world" and mentioned *Soylent Green* a few more times. (He also chided me for not bringing him cheese steaks.) At a minimum, September 11 brought out their patriotism. George turned out to be particularly moved by the event. When I saw him at the terminal a month later, he was wearing a U.S. flag pin on his jacket and asked why Brandon and I were not also wearing something with the stars and stripes. He showed us the book he was reading, *Beyond the Beachhead* by Joseph Balkoski, an account of the U.S. invasion of Normandy in June 1945.[7] Opening the book to a page with a particularly graphic photo, he asked,

You wanted to see bodies? You got bodies floating in the water—here—that was Normandy—sixth of June.

He showed us a few more pictures accompanied by his own flat narration. "Just imagine that this is New York a week from now," he instructed us. "Did you go to the World Trade Center site or what?" he asked. "Did you get any stories over there?"

With their sense of patriotism and sometimes nativist perspectives, these men also seemed to have a strong libertarian streak. Years, maybe decades, earlier, they had formed an "auxiliary patrol" to protect one another and others who lived, worked, or spent leisure time near the waterfront. They were unwilling to discuss how the patrol operated, if it coordinated with local police, or whether it was still active. In spite of their reticence, the patrol seemed to be consistent with how these men viewed the city and the world around them. These men would trade police protection for the freedom to do what they wanted without being hassled while looking after their own safety. This might involve trespassing, drinking in public, or smoking marijuana. I frequently heard complaints from them concerning tickets for trespassing or drinking in public; these tickets would invariably be dismissed, but not until they made an appearance at a criminal court in Manhattan. As they were mostly in their forties and fifties, they did not usually indulge in behaviors typically associated with these activities, such as disorderly conduct or property damage. They generally kept to themselves and looked after themselves, hoping that others would respect their right to do their own thing, whether it was at BEDT or elsewhere.

Personal Identity, Politics, and Leisure Space on the Waterfront

Other than Yosh, Joe was the only member of this group willing to talk candidly about his life and reflect upon the continuing evolution of the waterfront. Under the high sun of a warm October afternoon I found him talking with a man named Stu, who was representing—or vaguely representing—Louis Silverman, who owned 4Gs Trucking (its truck yard was located on the former BEDT block immediately to the north, between North 9th and North 10th streets) and had a potential interest in a larger development plan featuring an arts center. The three of us talked for a while about this performing arts proposal before Stu received a phone call and walked off, leaving Joe and me alone. Unshaven and with the somewhat golden complexion of a person who had spent much of the past summer in the sun, Joe wore a t-shirt with the logo of the local fire department and a cap emblazoned with a camel, for Camel cigarettes, which he smoked as we talked. As he told me more about himself, he would occasionally pause to consider my questions and take big swigs from a quart of beer that was partially concealed in a brown paper bag.

Joe (*left*) and Stu on a warm October afternoon. Joe noted his appreciation of the diversity and tolerance of the people who spent time at the terminal (2001).

A Polish-American, born and raised in Greenpoint, he still lived just a few blocks northeast of BEDT. Other than his time in military service, he had spent his entire life in North Brooklyn. He well remembered the time when the terminal was filled with freight trains and the harbor with barges and tugs and contrasted it with its deteriorated yet placid conditions we were enjoying that afternoon. He traced the waterfront's demise to completion of the Verrazano-Narrows Bridge in the mid-1960s, which linked Brooklyn to New Jersey via Staten Island, favoring trucks over rail and barge freight. Back then, he explained, the waterfront and the blue-collar neighborhoods adjacent to it were not only more active but also much rougher. While Greenpoint and the Northside, a part of Williamsburg, are relatively seamless today and historically their working-class populations had similar ethnic profiles with many Poles, Irish, and Italians, they functioned more as individual enclaves, and neighborhood "turf" still mattered. "We—Greenpoint—used to fight the Northside: gang wars, guns and all that shit," he said. The social dynamic of the waterfront and neighborhood was different now. "Wow, you know the whole world changed during my lifetime," he noted, still amazed by the apparent speed and vastness of this transformation.

Joe was also a Vietnam veteran. The experience of being at BEDT was important, he thought, because of the variety of people, and their exposure to him and others would perhaps change their perceptions of Vietnam vets and foster more understanding of their circumstances. He believed that the terminal facilitated a sense of respect and an unspoken camaraderie among the people who frequented it. "No matter where you're from or what you do or who you are, everybody's got respect for the head down here," he explained.

As it did for Yosh, the experience of war still weighed heavily upon Joe. At the waterfront, they were joined by other vets and those who had not been to Vietnam but were sympathetic to their circumstances. This shared experience, including the pitfalls they experienced in the years since returning, seemed to color their thoughts and sense of identity. They frequently referred to it in conversation but rarely talked about it, at least not with strangers.

One afternoon George, who had not served in Vietnam, told me, unsolicited, a bit more about Yosh's plight:

> He thinks he came back not the same way—he's seen too many bodies. You know what his job was? To pick up the bodies—dead men that were out there [rotting] from the sun. . . . [He goes on to describe a particularly gruesome incident.] He left here a happy-go-lucky kind of guy; he came back and became an alcoholic. I feel bad for him, too; nobody deserves that.

Without knowing him well, it was clear that Yosh had suffered a lot of pain and misfortune since returning from the war. A few times he had mentioned being "in and out of the hospitals" and made reference to health problems and prescription drugs he was taking. He did not dwell on or really complain about his plight but provided in passing a small sense of the sadness and loss that betrayed his more affable demeanor. As he told stories, on the day after his birthday and at other times, a pattern also emerged: Many of the supporting characters seemed to be deceased. Upon mentioning their names he would quickly invoke, "May he rest in peace." Yosh's younger brother, Raymond—whom he played with at BEDT—and Kenny, the friend who let them ride in the locomotive, were part of this group of deceased people. Another one of his friends, Walter, went down to Florida to "make some easy money" but, Yosh said, doing so shortened his life. He doubted that Gregory, the person who'd handed him a sausage sandwich in a BEDT warehouse years ago, was still alive.

Decades removed from the war, Yosh, Joe, and others were still struggling with physical and mental health issues and economically as well. Yet the area in which they lived had mostly moved on from the Vietnam and immediate post-Vietnam eras. The neighborhoods were no longer the blue-collar bastions they once had been, and these men seemed to feel more comfortable around its edges than in its heart. For Yosh, Joe, and other vets, BEDT was a place where they could gather freely and indulge in camaraderie, sympathy, and other mutual impulses:

> Yosh: [I come] here just about every second day. Because the water relaxes me. I'm a Vietnam veteran . . . this is my medication.

> Joe: It's a place you know—all the guys—the 'Nam vets and stuff like that—and younger guys too—no assholes—we hang down, we do a joint, have a beer and just get away from the world.

The men would often fly a POW-MIA flag (usually along with an American flag) from a pole attached to their clubhouse or to one of the piers. The flag was their way of claiming or reclaiming a bit of the neighborhood's territory, an opportunity they would not have on Bedford Avenue or in McCarren Park.

The Oasis: An Informal Space for Nature in the City

Yosh and Joe had many reasons to come to the terminal: to share and reflect upon their common identity and experiences, to escape the gentrifying neighborhoods in which they lived, and to drink beer and smoke pot and not be bothered.

Yosh (*left*) and Charles walking along BEDT's beach. The locals intensely enjoyed the "natural" aspects of this decaying waterfront (2001).

Closely intertwined with these motivations was their desire to be near the water and nature. BEDT could not be confused with a nature preserve, traditional beach, or large urban park, and it provided little in the way of an Olmstedian sense of landscape. But it did provide enough plant and animal life to convince many that this was a "natural" place removed from urban activity. Yosh sometimes referred to BEDT as "The Oasis" or "Our Oasis," saying it slowly, emphasizing each syllable as he said it. For these men, Yosh in particular, this was their small bit of nature, a garden that provided them with both separation and relief from what seemed to them to be at times an unrelentingly urban city:

> Yosh: It's really been a pleasure to always come down here—and water and trees [make] a person feel like an individual—a human being.

Joe: It's just serenity, solitude—you're in your space.

What the locals appreciated at BEDT was a form of "nearby nature" and "urban wilderness"—undervalued places that are rarely recognized for their beauty, tranquility, and other potentially vital qualities.[8] The terminal's abundance of green, which seemed to grow with each passing year, confirmed their feelings and reassured them about nature's ability to persevere in the city. Other visitors felt similarly. As one artist noted, BEDT was evidence that "nature [was] coming back."

The terminal's largest trees were close to the small building foundations, near the water between North 8th and North 9th streets, also near the abandoned truck trailer around which the locals often congregated. It mattered little to the men that many of these were essentially "weed trees"—they provided ample shade, scenery, and some shelter. Fittingly, some of these trees were the hearty but often scorned ailanthus—"tree of heaven"—the invasive species originally brought to the United States from China in the eighteenth century, which can be found in vacant lots across most American cities.[9] Less than 200 feet to the south was a stand of another invasive, phragmites, a tall wetland grass that is found in most marshes within urban areas in much of the country. Unconcerned about botanical origin, the locals and others were delighted to see this remarkable wetland, created accidentally by an old but still operable fire hydrant under which someone had placed an old clawfoot bathtub for a time. Phragmites have long been admired for their ability to reduce erosion and for their beauty, with their feathery tops and long reeds that sway gracefully in the wind. Ecologists, though, are never pleased to witness their quick spread in wet soil and note their dominance over more fragile native wetland species like Spartina grasses.[10] Yet BEDT was a harsh place for native species (its poorly draining, nutrient-lacking "soil" was essentially landfill). Indeed, in 2006, when State Parks tried to replant the terminal with native trees, grasses, and shrubs, much of this new landscape died quickly and contributed to the nearly one year's delay in opening the park (Chapter 8).

In addition to the greenery, the locals enjoyed the direct and visceral connection to elemental aspects of our earthly existence—the water, air, earth, and sun. Some of the men enjoyed sunbathing, while all enjoyed proximity to the water. Like other recreators, they exploited BEDT's intimate land–water interface. This allowed them to enjoy the water in ways that would not be possible elsewhere: to touch, hear, and smell it; to fish or feed the waterfowl that swam in it; or to be alone with their thoughts under the heat of the sun on one of the crumbling piers.

Much as for BEDT's artists, pliability was another "natural" aspect of leisure that the locals exploited. Being able to move stuff around, use found objects, or add their own insertions into this landscape helped them create their own customized environments. With little fuss or capital investment, their constructions, alterations, and rearrangements of space provided them with varying degrees of enclosure, shelter, and comfort. This pliability also gave them the opportunity to exercise control over their environment in a way that perhaps eluded them elsewhere—in public spaces, at home, or at their workplaces. Staking their claim, they exercised something approximating ownership, even though these spaces were temporary.

Last, there was an implicit sense among some that nature was inseparable from human social nature. Joe frequently mixed his references to the natural systems of the waterfront with its social ecology. He praised both the variety of birds he saw and the people he met at the terminal. Nature, beauty, social diversity, and tolerance were inseparable in his mind:

> It's just a special place. You come off the streets, come down here and it's just a different world—everybody's world. . . [placing his hand on his heart]. It's a soul thing, you know? It's just that way.

But the social ecology that Joe praised and others appreciated was not to last much longer, and soon I would no longer find him at BEDT.

Working-class Colonization and Displacement on the Waterfront

As men who spent most of their lives in close proximity to the waterfront, Yosh and Joe implicitly communicated legitimacy and tenure when they spent time at BEDT. Yet their recent intimacy at this location went back only a few years, to 1998. For years prior, they had congregated at Grand Ferry Park, a waterfront leisure site, which they referred to as "Grand Street." This spit of land, three-quarters of an acre in size, was simply an enlarged landing at the end of the street, featuring little more than a small parking area, some grass and plantings, a few benches, and riprap (a rock-lined embankment intended to prevent erosion). It abutted the Amstar (aka Domino) Sugar refinery to the south, which was still active through the early 2000s (it closed in 2004), and an electric substation and heating oil tank farm to the north, once owned and operated by the famed Brooklyn drug manufacturer Pfizer Pharmaceuticals.[11] Despite its small size, it is a place of significant history where the original Grand Street Ferry connected still-rural Williamsburg with Delancey and Houston streets in Manhattan in 1810.[12] It was from this point that Williamsburg grew; the property immediately upland from the ferry was the first to be subdivided and developed, in the 1820s.[13] And later some of Brooklyn's earliest (and the world's largest) sugar refineries developed to the north and south of this point.[14]

For most of the second half of the twentieth century, though, and perhaps earlier, this landing was considered derelict (ferry service stopped in 1917). Yet even as it served as a "dumping ground for garbage and abandoned cars," for decades local residents regularly gathered amid the trash to enjoy the river.[15] Between 1976 and 1979, local residents worked with the New York City Parks Council and a landscape architect to design, build, and eventually manage this informal recreation space. The design, which included a parking area that allowed residents to drive in and view the river and Manhattan beyond from the interior of their cars, was generated from many observations of how people were already informally using this street end for waterside leisure.[16]

Even though Grand Ferry Park was hailed as a model for innovative community design, after not too many years it fell into disrepair.[17] It was sometime after that, during the 1980s, that Yosh and his group started regularly congregating there. Occupying a space that others had deemed lacking safety and pleasantness, they often spent time drinking beer, barbecuing, and enjoying the waterscape. Joe described the scene:

> We used to hang down at Grand Street park before they fixed it up. It was like this—rats, rocks, the whole deal—but we'd sit there, you know? Who's writin' a book, who's readin' a book, who's readin' the paper, who's talkin' sports, who's just hangin' out listenin' to music and just talking in general?

Until the completion of East River State Park at BEDT in 2007, Grand Ferry Park was for decades Greenpoint's and Williamsburg's only official waterfront park and the only legally accessible spot along the district's entire East River waterfront where it was possible to touch the water.[18] At its edge, it offered perhaps the most majestic view of the Williamsburg Bridge in all of Brooklyn. But the men also enjoyed the intimacy of being next to Brooklyn's last active sugar refinery, and Joe said that they often enjoyed watching the sugar boats come into and out of their dock and unload their cargo of raw cane from the tropics, while the sweet scent generated during the refining process perfumed the air.

After taking formal title to the property in 1997, the city Parks Department redesigned and renovated it in 1998, also adding a sliver of land donated by Con Edison, the owners of the tank farm to the north.[19] This addition included an old smokestack from an early-twentieth-century molasses refinery used by Pfizer in manufacturing pharmaceuticals, notably penicillin. After the renovation, the city increased maintenance, trash collection, and security, which included a crackdown on nonpermitted activities. The locals were forced to find another place to congregate:

Charles: We're here now because Grand Street doesn't suit us.

Joe: They started fixing [Grand Ferry Park] up for the community, which is great—it's nice now, you know, families come down with kids 'n' stuff—but we couldn't sit there and curse and drink beer. . . . Now it's a family thing.

Moving from one waterfront location to another did not seem to faze these men. Before Grand Street, they spent time in a similar space underneath the Brooklyn anchorage of the Williamsburg Bridge. They used it until the reconfiguration of a Department of Transportation facility in the 1980s blocked access. They had occupied other vernacular waterfront sites, and some of the men would occasionally visit the piers and street ends in Greenpoint that also served as working-class leisure spots. Even established spots, such as the India Street Pier, were tenuous. Street ends could be fenced off or appropriated by adjacent warehouses or factories that used them for staging areas or storage for their vehicles, equipment, materials, or products awaiting shipment. Other times, recreators were chased away by police. The piers, most of which were held in private ownership and were in various states of decay, were just as unpredictable. At India Street in 1997, a sudden collapse of a twenty-foot section of concrete dropped seven people into the water, all of whom were rescued. The city then closed off the pier with a razor wire–topped fence, but that did not stop a local Polish man who found a way around this barrier to fish and was later found drowned.[20]

The locals were probably not happy about losing Grand Street at the time, but they understood this larger dynamic and three years later they were not much interested in discussing it, except for Joe, who said he felt no bitterness about it. He felt similarly about the development of a formal park at BEDT. Even if it meant the end of their own informal recreation experience, he appreciated that it would benefit neighborhood children.

While these men spent more time at BEDT and had a longer history along the Brooklyn waterfront than nearly anyone else who frequented the terminal, they were mostly ambivalent about its future. Used to displacement, they had a somewhat fatalistic attitude about what was going to happen. They were not active in local affairs but did have a vague sense of the plans for the terminal from speaking to others who were more informed. George also said he regularly received newsletters from Neighbors Against Garbage (though he did not usually read them), and at least a few of them had seen the large signs temporarily erected for a short period during 2001, depicting the site transformed as an Olympic venue for swimming, diving, and beach volleyball for the 2012 Summer Games. The signs were placed there by New York 2012 Olympic Committee and were intended to impress U.S. Olympic Committee officials who were being given a tour of potential athletic facilities across the city. At that moment, New York's ultimately unsuccessful bid was gaining traction with the USOC and the city was discussing the possibility of a greatly enlarged park that would incorporate the two blocks owned by State Parks plus those to the north to the Bushwick Inlet.[21]

Yosh had been particularly impressed with the renderings on this sign and said on two different occasions that he liked the planned improvements, particularly the depicted marina. On a third occasion he seemed less enthusiastic. Forced to consider the redevelopment of their spot and thus the strong possibility that they would have to go elsewhere to experience the waterfront in the manner to which they had become accustomed, he became more reflective:

> Without this, you know—where the hell are we gonna go? McCarren Park? How many people can fit in McCarren Park? Huh? And then again there's no water over there like over here, the real thing—*capisce*? And whatta view. You can't beat this view. You ain't gonna see this in McCarren Park. [I wish] they could work it out somehow—in a way to keep us in here and enjoy ourselves like always—like we've been doing.

Yosh's sanguine tone at that moment and recognition that their Oasis would not last too much longer did not completely change his mood or his larger outlook. He reflected back on the experience of being forced to move from Grand Ferry Park, from other waterfront spots, and from his longtime home. Having dealt with more trying circumstances over the course of his life, Yosh was not going to worry about finding a new waterfront leisure space. The men had been displaced before; they would find another spot, perhaps not as nice or as large, but they would find it.

While Joe thought a conventional park would be great for the kids, he too wished their needs could also be accommodated. Charles was more skeptical. When Yosh admitted earlier that "We know it ain't gonna last too much longer," Charles added, "We've known that for twenty years." His "wait and see" stance was borne out by all the proposed and rumored waterfront redevelopment proposals that had never come to pass. Charles was not going to worry about having to leave BEDT until it actually happened, which was likely the way Yosh also felt until I induced him to think longer and harder about the subject. Even though he spent a lot of time at the terminal, probably only second to Yosh among the locals, George was less emotionally attached to the space. "I have no idea where I'm gonna go. I guess I'll stay home," he said and then reminded me that as a recovering alcoholic he did not drink and did not require an extralegal outdoor drinking space.

The end of the Oasis came well in advance of any major improvement or transformation of BEDT. In early 2002, State Parks did some preliminary clearing of the future park. They removed all the trucks and construction equipment that were being stored in the terminal's northeast corner and cleared much of the vegetation along its northern edge, including the area around the locals' trailer. The brush around this spot had given it definition, cover, and some degree of privacy. Now that these elements were missing, the men who'd congregated around this spot stopped showing up.

One afternoon in February 2002, I found Yosh alone, reading underneath an old light tower that stood at the end of North 10th Street at the foot of one the piers. The tower's concrete base, which functioned as a bench, was generally a popular spot to take in the views. When I asked him why I rarely saw any of the others, he told me that they were tired of being hassled by the police and receiving summonses. Not long after that, I stopped seeing Yosh too. By the summer, their converted truck trailer was removed as part of another site cleanup. For months, I wondered where they had gone. Walking up North 7th Street toward Bedford after a visit to BEDT in December 2002, I ran into Yosh. He told me they had a new spot at the end of North 3rd Street and encouraged me to stop by.

Behind a bent metal traffic barrier, the very modest landing at the end of North 3rd consisted of only a few feet of hardened dirt and steeply banked riprap. The end of the street was recessed in comparison to the immediately adjacent properties: the previously noted tank farm to the south and the seven-story Austin-Nichols warehouse to the north. These structures towered over this spot so it remained in shadow for much of the day and ensured that its views were less than expansive. But there was enough space between the fence and the rocks to set up a few folding chairs and a barbecue. Additionally, the locals could access, through a hole in a gate that leads to a catwalk, the docks that extended from the heating oil tanks. In early 2003, I saw a few people fishing from those docks but no one I knew. Just as I was leaving, Yosh and Pete showed up. Their new site was not much, but as BEDT and Grand Ferry Park once were, it was a space that few others at that time had an interest in claiming. The men implicitly understood that this space too would be temporary. Yet as with their previous waterfront spots, they were largely unconcerned, living in the moment and without worry about forces beyond their control.

I have often wondered what happened to those men and where they might be congregating now, if at all. I have not seen any of them along the waterfront in spite of many trips in the intervening years, some of which were made on stunning weekend afternoons. Perhaps they have found a spot even more remote or hidden than any previously; perhaps some no longer go to the waterfront. It is also possible that a few of them are somewhere else entirely or no longer living.

Their waterfront has given way to the state park and, to the south, an esplanade, ferry landing, recreation pier, and condominium towers, constructed between 2007 and 2012. Their amid-the-dumpsters spot is presently part of the grounds of the Edge condominiums and the site of a well-attended weekend flea market, though another Edge tower will eventually supplant the market spot. Similar improvements are taking shape farther south and north, and a necklace of green spaces and luxury high-rises will eventually run the entire length of the Greenpoint–Williamsburg riverfront. The industrial waterfront is long gone and the postindustrial waterfront that these men once enjoyed—even as it deteriorated—is also now something of the past.

CHAPTER 6

RESIDENTIAL LIFE

Hardship and Resiliency on the Waterfront

WHILE THE NEIGHBORHOOD LOCALS were probably the longest-tenured recreators of the North Brooklyn waterfront, they were not the constituency that spent the most time at the Brooklyn Eastern District Terminal. As the locals and others socialized, sunbathed, fished, or pursued art or sport, a group of homeless men carried on with the mundane activities of life, often just feet away. Each night somewhere between three and three dozen people slept at BEDT (although usually the number was under twelve) in improvised or store-bought tents or in shanties assembled from construction debris and other found materials.

Many of these men lived communally, and their ubiquitous but mostly nonthreatening presence and occasional participation in leisure activities created not just juxtaposition but also a certain harmony. Most of them—well aware of their own tenuous status and right to space that so many others had also colonized or claimed—treaded lightly, avoiding conflict. Their experience was a more extreme version of the vernacular enjoyed by recreators: living without rules, supervision, or security. Yet it was also was more in keeping with conventional expectations. The appropriation of vacant or marginal spaces for shelter may be discouraged or illegal in many places, but it remains a common practice, particularly in crowded, competitive cities with high housing costs.

Some of the residents of BEDT, including (*clockwise from top left*) Jimmy, Roberto, and Erasto (2001).

While the raw living conditions on the waterfront were far from ideal, these men—and they were mostly men—enjoyed the freedom that it afforded. Living in the open air by the water allowed them a lifestyle and perhaps, at times, a degree of health that would be unlikely in typical homeless milieus, whether on the street or in a shelter. They were also, in a sense, liberated from the degrading stereotypes of being homeless bums or "street people" who panhandle on corners and in the subway and sleep on city sidewalks and in parks. Additionally, they were freed from the expectation that those who want to do the right thing will seek out not just work but also social services while living an abstemious life. As such I got to know them on more personal terms and not just within the context of their own misfortune. Yet it was still difficult to fully understand who they were and what had brought them to the waterfront. My encounters were rarely straightforward, complicated by language barriers and other issues. Thus their stories are incomplete, missing important details, and, at times, ambiguous.

The men I came to know did not represent everyone who was living at BEDT at that time. Individuals and an occasional family, like the young Polish couple who lived in a sturdy store-bought tent with their young son, came and went. For a while a wooden Guinness Beer sign leaned against their tent and toys were often strewn around the perimeter, but they were almost never around when I was. Some people living at BEDT simply kept to themselves or avoided me, and others were not around much during the day, even on weekends. And few wanted to advertise that they were homeless. Over the course of three years, I rarely found more than four or five tents or shanties arrayed across the terminal. This was not a major homeless encampment or "skid row," and conflict between those living here and police or property and business owners never approached the level of conflict of notable 1980s–1990s homeless spaces, such as Tompkins Square Park and "the Hill" on the Manhattan Bridge ramp embankment in Manhattan, or those in other American cities.[1]

The Residents of BEDT and Their Dwellings

The residents of BEDT were a group of men nearly all of Latin American descent ranging in age from about twenty to forty-five. They lived communally, pooling part of their limited resources, and mostly slept in a single shelter that was rebuilt a few times at different locations. The majority were natives of Mexico, but among them were also native El Salvadorans, a Puerto Rican native, and occasional mainland American natives. They were a diverse group, and most had found the site independently of one another. Most of these ten or so men were also undocumented immigrants, a status that greatly complicated their quest for work, housing, and a more stable way of life. Their existence was generally day-to-day, focused on pursuing life's basic necessities—food, shelter, and income. During good times, many worked as day laborers on nearby construction sites. In leaner times they simply stayed at BEDT, venturing out into the neighborhood only to find or buy food, scavenge for materials that they could sell in second-hand shops, ask passing strangers for change (although this was not their general habit), or to look for work. These men were not the chronic homeless who lived on the streets for years on end; they were itinerant laborers without a place to live, all of whom greatly desired to return to a regular life of steady work, permanent housing, and, for some, reunification with their families.

My first substantial encounter with them came on a hot afternoon in July 2001. The men were hanging around the edge of the seawall on the southern portion of the terminal. By late afternoon, the waterfront was filled with people, perhaps more than a hundred. Many people were fishing or hanging out on the piers in front of us, while inland, less than fifty feet from where we stood, a fashion shoot was occurring amid the weeds and abundant summer wildflowers of this otherwise featureless portion of BEDT. Makeup artists and assistants attended to three models who were attired in retro, peasant-inspired clothing while the director, photographer, and others, numbering ten people in all, played supporting roles. Entertained by the scene around them and the sonorous Spanish-language music that played from their portable stereo, the residents were in relatively good spirits, in spite of the many significant problems they would soon describe. Our long conversation that evening enabled me to establish some credibility, as did the photos I took, which I delivered to them on repeat visits. Later, these same photos would generate laughter and commentary (in Spanish) among them.

On that day I met George, a copper-skinned El Salvadoran in his mid-thirties who usually wore dark pants and a tank top that showed off his muscular physique. George would turn out to be my most frequent contact among the residents. There was something unsettling about George, some underlying anger that occasionally came to the surface, but usually he was friendly and his English was stronger than the others'. Another El Salvadoran, Jaime, a thin young man barely older than twenty, also spoke reasonably fluent English. He said to just call him Jimmy, the English equivalent of his name. Wearing his hair slicked back, clean pants, and collared short-sleeved shirts—when he wore one at all—Jimmy was fastidious and pretty fashion-conscious for a man living on a vacant lot.

These men from El Salvador were joined by four from Mexico: Erasto, Roberto, and two others whose names I never learned. Erasto, a short, slightly heavy, dark-skinned man who was missing two upper front teeth, was eager to talk about his life and misfortune, but his English skills limited his ability to do so. He was older than the rest—in his forties probably—and frequently talked of his estranged family, which was still in Mexico, and relatives who were scattered across metropolitan New York. Roberto and two other men were in their mid-twenties; none of them spoke much English and consequently did not participate in our conversation. They came and went and goofed around as I talked and got to know the others. These men bore the darker skin complexion and facial features of native Mexicans as opposed to Hispanics of European or mixed descent.

As I talked with the residents, a local man, Doug, also hung around and occasionally said something to advance the conversation. Probably in his mid-forties, he was an anomaly—a white native-born man from the neighborhood who apparently had a contracting business and occasionally hired the others. Doug was careful not to say much about himself and did not want his picture taken or to appear on video. Spending days and evenings with these men or occasionally alone on the piers, after a while I suspected that he too sometimes slept here. Soon I would meet Alfredo, a friendly Puerto Rican native whose poor English often inhibited his ability to communicate with me. A relatively thin man in his early thirties, he always wore a neatly trimmed beard and mustache and a variety of caps, including a Red Sox cap he had brought back from Boston after working there for several weeks. Manuel, a native of Mexico who also spoke little English, was likely the youngest member of this group, at perhaps nineteen or twenty. Finally there was Chris, a sweet-talking thirty-two-year-old of Puerto Rican descent, born and raised in the neighborhood, who ostensibly lived in an apartment nearby. I had met Chris the summer before when he was sleeping at BEDT and had serendipitously joined the festivities when Ür's Pirate sculpture was being installed on the Slab (Chapter 4). Charismatic and confident bordering on cocky, Chris was not at all like the others, but somehow he fell into this group and stayed at the terminal when he may have been unwelcome in his own nearby apartment. Other men of this group, mostly Mexicans

I believe, drifted off to the periphery when I was in their presence. Aside from Alfredo, Jimmy, and the neighborhood natives, most of the residents were undocumented immigrants, and as their stories unfolded, this became a defining characteristic of their existence.

On that Saturday in July, they described the relatively peaceful vibe of living on the waterfront. The men had lived itinerantly in locations across the city, but they said that this one was superior, praising the breezes that kept them cool during the heat of summer. BEDT was not easily found by those unfamiliar with the neighborhood as George, Jimmy, and Erasto had once been.

The shelter occupied by the residents during the late summer and fall of 2001.

They had learned about it by word of mouth. A mostly plywood shanty located just off the north edge of the Slab served as their sleeping quarters. As they talked about this shelter, another large, squarely built shanty of mostly plywood stood behind us. I thought this was what they were referring to, but George said it belonged to "a Puerto Rican guy" who slept there alone each night. I had already met this feisty, middle-aged man named Charlie; he was often fishing out on the piers and successfully so. The river provided much of his food, and his oversized bucket was often filled with fish or crabs. At times Charlie could be ornery or antisocial, valuing his privacy and security, and thus kept the single entrance to his structure padlocked when he was not there. While the residents' shelter was not as large or sturdy as his and had to serve more people, they seemed satisfied and did not complain about apparent discomfort, crowding, or lack of privacy.

Later that summer their shanty burned down, along with a second shanty nearby. They would not say much other than that it was a purposeful fire lit by two men who doused the structures in gasoline. The residents quickly built a new tent-like structure at a different location, on top of the second and less-used concrete foundation that sat parallel to the Slab on its south side. A three-foot-deep groove separated the two slabs. This cut, less than twenty feet across, was a two-track railroad bed that once serviced the warehouses that sat atop these foundations. The tracks were long gone, and except for a small cleared area adjacent to the residents' tent, the groove was thick with weeds, garbage, and debris. The men used this railroad bed as a general waste space where they would usually dump their garbage, as it was created, one item at a time. Most of their daily activities, including cooking and recreation, took place on the Slab "proper" just on the other side of this divide.

The men had constructed their shelter from scrap plywood and beams, disassembled freight pallets, a large plastic tarp, and rope, all materials that they found or salvaged. The tent's wood frame gave the dwelling a definite rectangular geometry. The ropes, fastened to trees and anchored to the ground under various objects, held the tarp in place. Plastic chairs and other possessions were usually strewn around the outside of the tent. Inside were rudimentary bunks for four people and floor space to accommodate more when needed. During the summer the tent was ideal. Keeping the covering tarp partially open facilitated air flow through the tent, which made for comfortable sleeping, George explained. Their previous shanty was hotter and stuffier, he said. On really hot nights, some simply slept outside on the concrete. Its strategic location underneath a few ailanthus and poplar trees that were growing from the groove also provided some shade from the sun, although rarely could they be found inside the tent during the afternoon. There were usually between three and six people who slept in the tent each night, though George said at times it slept as many as twelve, even though there did not seem to be nearly enough space.

When I asked the residents to compare their experiences on the waterfront with those of sleeping in homeless shelters, they responded quickly and dismissively. They did not like shelters and did not want to talk about them. On a subsequent occasion when I asked again, they became quite agitated, cursing and carrying on in Spanish about their bad experiences at these places. Shaking his head, George could say only that the shelters were not good and it was better to sleep elsewhere. Alfredo mentioned that the shelters were better in Boston but could not say why. In the summer and early fall, these men were not willing to consider going to a shelter. For the moment, life was good here and they all thought they would have permanent housing in the near future. So why worry about the weather turning cold?

In the fall, George told me, he sometimes slept in an encampment at the Manhattan anchorage of the Manhattan Bridge (probably the Hill). He complained about the crowded conditions, noting he had to share quarters (in a tent or shanty) with anywhere between three and fifteen others. He stayed there for a stretch of time in November and upon returning to BEDT he was upset about the way he had been treated by the police who visited that well-known encampment. He cursed frequently about tickets they had given him, although he would not say what these tickets were for.

Plight of the Residents: A Lack of Steady Work

These men were homeless for a variety of reasons. Some were uncomfortable talking about their personal circumstances and others found it hard to talk about their own complicated histories in English. But a few wanted me to understand clearly that their lack of permanent shelter was tied directly to their inability to find steady, fairly paid employment:

Jimmy: We are here because we need work. We need [to be] working. We need to be working every time.

George: I go to look for job, I don't find nothing; I have to come back here; because I live over here—what can I do?

The residents found occasional work as day laborers doing various construction jobs and other tasks. Some also worked for Doug on occasion, when he had work for them and for himself. They claimed to be experienced in a number of different construction jobs, and they were willing to work hard and under difficult conditions. When I asked them how they made a living, I received many replies:

George: Landscaping, painting, construction, demolition—whatever comes, whatever comes. But I don't work for less than eight dollar an hour.

Jimmy: We work anyplace, anywhere—we stay there any day. You need work? We go to work. We know sheetrock; we know framing; we know painting—anything about the construction work. You need cement, we do it. You need brick, [we do] brick.

Some of the men also had worked in restaurants, though none did at that time. They were nomads of a sort, following the work wherever it required them to go, doing whatever it required them to do. On many mornings they would head to a day laborer pickup spot at Division Street and Bedford Avenue, on the Southside, about a mile away. The conditions were unpredictable and they were usually forced to compete against others, some of whom might be willing to work for less. Wages were low and when they were lucky enough to get picked for a job, it could last for several days or merely hours; the really fortunate would be hired for projects lasting several weeks. Other times the men would find work through their own network of friends and family members, and occasionally their work took them well beyond the city. Alfredo had relatives in Boston who also worked in construction and contacted him when there was work there. Buying a one-way ticket on the Chinatown bus (which for a while offered one-way fares for as little as $5), he stayed in Boston until the job ran out. From there he might go to other places; his home was wherever he happened to find work.

The men emphasized the hazards of being day laborers without any workplace protections and complained about people who tried to take advantage of them. I had a sense of the dangerous work they did and the low wages and poor conditions they were forced to endure. Their pickup site on Division Street was a well-known spot for construction jobs, mostly on housing projects in the booming ultra-orthodox Satmar Jewish community that spanned South Williamsburg and was expanding into parts of the Southside as well as Clinton Hill and Bedford-Stuyvesant. While working for the Department of City Planning in the late 1990s, I had indirectly facilitated a few of these construction projects through a rezoning initiative that I managed, which covered some of the blocks near the pickup spot. This project was among several intended to stimulate residential development in areas formerly zoned for manufacturing and serve this growing community that was aligned politically with Mayor Giuliani. As planners we did not get involved in the construction or approval of building projects (that was responsibility of the Buildings Department), so we were insulated from some of the egregious and often illegal construction practices that occurred in this area.

These practices made headlines when in November 1999 a twenty-two-year-old Mexican laborer was killed and eleven others were injured in a structural collapse involving the pouring of concrete and the laying of concrete blocks at a construction site in South Williamsburg. The laborer was one of many undocumented immigrants from Mexico or Central America working on this project, which paid only $6 to $10 an hour, even though the prevailing union wage for such work was $20 to $25 an hour plus benefits.[2] The builder was notorious for dangerous working conditions, shoddy construction, and low wages and had previously accumulated many violations and warnings from the city's Buildings Department.[3] This was not an isolated incident, and these practices were fairly commonplace; the residents attested to similar experiences at other construction sites in this area. As the *Times* reported, the Mexican and Central

American men were well aware that conditions were unsafe but were used to "low pay and bad conditions," and, as undocumented workers, they were "not going to complain about dangerous practices."[4]

The residents were particularly incensed by potential employers who tried to pay them less than the prevailing wage or cheated them out of promised money. At the end of a job sometimes employers would pay only half of the agreed-upon compensation; other times they would insist that the men work longer hours than was originally agreed upon for the same pay or renege on promises like providing them with lunch. The men had no recourse and often could do little more than argue. "What are we going to do?" George said with resignation. Erasto, who formerly did restaurant work, said that his earnings from day labor were neither large enough nor steady enough to enable him to rent an apartment. "Some people want to pay $5 an hour, no lunch, no nothing, it's not very much," he complained.

Even though they worked in environments effectively beyond the protection of labor laws and had no union to protect them, the residents thought of themselves as skilled workers and thus entitled to fair wages and fair terms of employment. George became particularly agitated when discussing those employers who wanted to take advantage of their low status as day laborers, as immigrants, as Hispanics:

> Listen, you are a white guy. I am a Spanish guy, but I don't let nobody get me like a sucker. You know what I mean all right.

As he talked, Erasto, who was sitting next to him, nodded in agreement. George said he could do just about any construction job and had been in the United States for eighteen years, to which Erasto quickly added, "Twenty! I've got twenty years in this country!" Jimmy said employers typically wanted to pay only $7 an hour for skilled construction work when $10 an hour plus lunch was the prevailing rate for such tasks among day laborers. Yet at the same time, he said, these employers expected unreasonable levels of productivity under difficult conditions. "I'm no Superman. I'm no Spider-Man," he said mockingly. George went on to describe one particularly positive but brief job he'd recently had for which he'd received $36 for two hours of labor. The person who hired him also bought him two pizzas—one plain, one pepperoni—and a six-pack of beer. He expressed dismay that there were not more employers like that. "Listen, I don't drink no coffee," he explained. "I'm sorry, I need a beer!"

Their lack of housing was connected to both limited employment prospects and individual problems. It was difficult to disentangle or establish causality, but many of the residents suffered from a punishing combination of factors that fed upon one another: no regular employment, no green card, poor English skills, familial strife and failed personal relationships, and, in some cases, substance abuse. Some had a fatalistic sense of how they wound up living on the waterfront and attributed their problems to forces largely beyond their control. George described the cause of his homelessness:

> Let me tell you something! I pass some kind of spirits when my wife left me and she go with somebody else—and what the hell? What can I do? I just lose my apartment, my bank account and everything.

As George interpreted his own misfortune and its consequences, Erasto smiled and added, "Me too." Erasto's story was particularly complicated, and his poor English made it even more difficult for him to tell it. In his twenty years in the United States, mostly working low-wage restaurant jobs, he managed to send money on a regular basis back to Mexico, where his four children lived. In a brief period of time a year earlier, he lost his job, was thrown out of his apartment by his wife, and went on a drinking binge that lasted forty-five days. The exact sequence of these events was unclear, but now he had been living at BEDT for six months. In an effort to reconstruct his life, he no longer drank and he worked as much as he could, usually three or four days a week as a day laborer. He hoped he could find a regular job and get a room or an apartment soon after that and eventually be reunited with his wife. A family man, Erasto had relatives scattered across the city, in New Jersey, and in White Plains and spoke of them dearly and with what seemed like a bit of regret. "I love my family. I love my wife, my sisters, my nephews," he said, describing the locations, occupations, and accomplishments of various loved ones. He told me about his children in Mexico: His oldest son was in college studying engineering; a second son was in high school, studying to be an accountant; his daughter and youngest son were also doing well in school. He had not seen any of his children in at least a decade (given that his wife lived in Brooklyn, it was unclear who was raising these children or if they were from a previous relationship). Erasto was once a permanent resident, but his status had since lapsed or had been rescinded, complicating his search for work. "I lost my papers," he said. "I have no papers; they no give me job, no social security card—I don't have nothing—very difficult for me to find a job." The others spoke only vaguely about green cards or issues related to immigration. Jimmy was a permanent resident, but he said that George, Manuel, and Roberto were not. Many of the men's poor English skills also contributed to their difficulties in finding work and shelter.

As with Erasto, social, familial, or substance abuse problems also played a role in the homelessness of some of the others. Manuel and Roberto spent much of their time drinking. Manuel, the youngest of the group, was demonstrably intoxicated many of the times I encountered him, often staggering or slurring his speech. On a few occasions, I found him passed out at random spots on the Slab. Chris, who usually lived with his wife and son in a nearby apartment, seemed to be sleeping at BEDT on an occasional basis. "I come here to hang out, sometimes I spend the weekend here," he explained. But given the frequency with which I saw him, I sensed that his situation was more complicated, and later he told me he was having some problems with his wife.

Finding itinerant employment in different locations and not knowing in advance where they might finish a day's work had implications for where these men might sleep. They often expected to sleep on or nearby their work site. This was what made BEDT a viable place to live: It was close to many of the area's construction projects. In jobs that took them far away or required them to work late into the night, they often expected that their employer would provide a place to sleep. Jimmy spoke about their struggle to find consistent work and the variety of places he had worked in New York and beyond. When I asked him about where else he had slept, he repeatedly substituted work sites for places to sleep. I thought it might be a mistake before I realized he was referring to the same place. As we talked, Jimmy stood up on the bulkhead with the water and, farther back, the FDR and Stuyvesant Town behind him. He turned and looked out over the water toward the city and began to recite dramatically the place names of the various locations he had worked (and often slept), while swinging his body around and pointing in the corresponding directions, almost as if he were conducting a symphony:

Downtown Brooklyn. Queens! Midtown! Brooklyn! Southside sometimes. Northside sometimes. Manhattan sometimes. Chambers Street and Church [Street]. . . . Midtown! Chinatown! In Chinatown, I was mixing cement on some roof there.

He was proud that he had worked in all these different places and knew the geography of the city.

By mid-August, I could find neither Jimmy nor Erasto at the terminal. When I asked their whereabouts, the others just shrugged and acted as if they did not know who I was talking about. In October, I showed Alfredo a picture of

Jimmy I had taken in July, he laughed and said, "I know this guy!" Still he had no idea where Jimmy might be. I saw Jimmy two years later, but I never saw Erasto again. None of the remaining residents knew Erasto's whereabouts; a few could hardly remember his name.

These appearances and disappearances were part of a consistent pattern. Nearly every time I visited the waterfront a different combination of men was residing there. Some individuals stayed for a matter of weeks, then disappeared, before returning a few weeks later. Others, like Erasto, disappeared altogether. The residents' habit of sleeping at or near work locations was evident by the varying number and combination of group members I encountered on each visit. As people who lived outdoors and had to be at their day laborer spot early in the morning, the residents were early risers and usually early to bed as well. My visits usually lasted until after sunset and often into the darkness of night, so I was fairly certain that when I left, it was unlikely that any other members of the group would appear. On the first Saturday in October, I found George, Arturo, Manuel, and Alfredo at the tent. On the following Saturday I found only George, Alfredo, and Roberto. Alfredo said that he thought the others had found work in Manhattan and were probably sleeping there as well. On a Thursday evening nineteen days later, I found only Alfredo and Roberto. This time, Alfredo said that the others were all working in Manhattan and George was living in a hotel in Chinatown. He and Roberto also had work for the week. "Everyone was happy" to have work, he said. In mid-December, I found George, Roberto, Manuel, and Alfredo. In the full darkness of night (it was just after eight), Alfredo tried to sell me some old Polaroid cameras that he had found as Manuel stood by his side, silent, wasted, with his cap and sweatshirt hood pulled down over his eyes. Alfredo had also salvaged a valve to a large boiler and a few related parts. In the morning, he would bring them to a shop where he hoped to get a few dollars for them as there was little work for day laborers at that time.

Communal Life at BEDT

The residents enjoyed several advantages living at BEDT as opposed to their other, very limited options. As a place to sleep and live, they felt that it was superior to the streets. In particular, they could sleep in relative comfort and peace, undisturbed by the police, other people, or the constant activity of the city. The waterfront was quiet at night.

They made good use of a still-operational fire hydrant, under which someone had placed an old clawfoot bathtub, located at the northwest corner of the Slab. They used it as a source of drinking and cooking water and for washing

While living conditions were less than ideal, the residents enjoyed their autonomy and the camaraderie of the waterfront (2001).

clothes and household items. They also bathed regularly in the tub or used a bucket for personal cleaning but complained about not having hot water. George in particular repeatedly expressed the desire to take a hot shower. (They used the weed- and garbage-strewn crevices to urinate and used toilets up in the neighborhood during the day or, if need be, remote corners of the site to defecate.) Most of the men placed a premium on cleanliness and rarely did any of them have noticeable body odor or wear dirty clothes. There was also plenty of space for them to go about their daily activities, such as cooking and eating meals and engaging in recreational endeavors. Scrap wood was also available for building fires. Up in the neighborhood were warehouses and businesses where other materials could be salvaged. And perhaps most important, BEDT was close enough to the day laborer site while remote enough (as opposed to the streets or a park) to lessen the chance that they would be hassled by police or others. Its expansiveness and remoteness also gave them the opportunity to store personal possessions safely.

The residents usually seemed to be in good health. Most of the men were thin but not overly so. With his muscular arms and broad shoulders, George looked particularly fit. Judging by the way they usually dressed and carried themselves, it was hard to know that they were homeless. Most of them had at least a few changes of clothes, which they wore with brand-name sneakers or shoes. Most of their clothing looked to be recently purchased and of contemporary fashion. Some of the men also wore jewelry: George wore a watch and Manuel wore a gold stud in his nose. They bathed regularly, brushed their teeth, shaved, and kept their beards and mustaches neatly trimmed. They also possessed a variety of personal or portable entertainment items including radios, tape and CD players, and a battery-operated television that they watched inside their tent at night.

The residents may have been homeless, but their lives on the waterfront were far from joyless. When not at work or sleeping, they engaged in a leisurely lifestyle and enjoyed the camaraderie of their encampment as well as the larger scene. Sometimes they were boisterous—talking loudly, laughing, and singing and dancing to Spanish-language music they played on one of their radios or CD players. When they had money, communal activities sometimes involved the consumption of alcohol. While it did seem to be a problem for some—Manuel and Roberto, and maybe George on occasion—the others were generally able to imbibe without engaging in destructive or self-destructive behavior. They were a sociable group generally not prone to violence, predatory activity, or antisocial behavior.

No one else I spoke to at BEDT in the early 2000s reported a serious problem or incident involving these men. A few of the residents spent time on occasion with the neighborhood locals sharing conversation, beer, or the warmth of a fire. Sometimes these men would be out on the piers fishing or trapping crabs side by side with those who came to the waterfront solely to do so. On Sundays, the Hungry March Band and members of their social group would kick a soccer ball around with the residents. Like the band, the fire spinners and the skateboarders—those with whom they often shared the Slab—all expressed some measure of respect for the residents. Members of these groups regularly shared food or drinks and were rarely bothered by their presence. Though there were minor conflicts, most of the people who used the terminal respected the residents' right to dwell in this marginal space.

The residents too appreciated the vibe and tried to keep their social relations with others positive. At times, though, George could be bitter about the scene around him and what he considered a lack of generosity and understanding of others who were there for leisure. When I asked him how he felt about all these other people with whom he shared what was in effect his living space, he replied,

　　　　　　　　　　　　　　　　　　　　　　　　RESIDENTIAL LIFE

What do we got to do? Nothing about it. You ask somebody for some food, they don't give it to you. They say you gotta work to feed yourself. . . . We go to Division [Street, for work], we don't find nothin'.

Later, when I asked Jimmy, Erasto, and George about their relationship with local police, they all began to talk at once, mostly in animated Spanish. George's voice carried over the others. He was upset about having received a $50 trespassing fine the day before. It had been given to him on the same day that he had saved, or at least helped, someone who had fallen into the water:

> I got a ticket for trespassing. I asked the cop to give me a chance. A lot of people fall down in here [pointing to the edge of the water] and we pick them up. Even yesterday, we saved that lady's life. And what the hell does that mean? [Rapidly shaking his head back and forth in dismay.] It's no fair to give me a ticket for that. Why do I got to pay $50? They give me fine, what the fuck can I do?

This averted drowning occurred just feet from where we were talking, and thinking about it now, George became even more incensed. He recited the entire sequence of events for me. No one had recognized his possibly lifesaving action, he claimed:

> I don't know why the cops don't say something—say they appreciate [it]. The lady just goes away; she don't give me one penny or nothing. Now I tell you the truth; now you know how things are going—when you help somebody and they put you worse than the way you [were].

Unlike the others in physical appearance and temperament, George seemed to have a darker side to his personality. The more I got to know him, the more wary I became in his presence. I often brought food to give to these men—some doughnuts, bakery bread, or sometimes beer—or I gave them a few dollars toward their evening meal. It was a gesture of good will and sometimes functioned as a way to buy their access (though the others mostly did not hesitate to talk to me and did not ask specifically for compensation). When we rolled video, George would say that we had to give him ten or twenty dollars. I generally brushed those "shakedowns" aside as humor but understood the dynamic. As George got to know me better, he became more aggressive in asking me for money. The amount he wanted escalated over time and was always more than I could or was willing to give. I took note of the pattern and that his demeanor changed when he was alone with me as opposed to when the others were around, when he was more amiable. I remained aware in his presence and minimized the time I talked with him alone.

But George was not always this way, and often he was not only jovial but also quite gracious. He was the cook of the group and often took it upon himself to organize the evening's meal. He genuinely enjoyed cooking and was very proud of the meals he could put together with no real equipment and very limited resources. "We eat really good," he said to me. On a Sunday in mid-August, he was in good spirits, and I had an opportunity to watch him in action and taste the product of his labors. It was only he, Alfredo, and Chris that evening. I was joined by my friends Brian and Brandon, who recorded the evening's events on video.

Like other aspects of their life, their approach to eating was pragmatic. Nearby there were a number of places where they could buy a meal for just a few dollars, including pizza, deli, and Chinese or Mexican takeout. In the evening when enough of them were around, they cooked and ate communally. While those on the street or in shelters eat mostly pre-pared items (whether purchased or given to them) from stores, restaurants, or soup kitchens, the residents had the satisfaction of preparing some of their own meals. Their communal meals often had a leisurely quality to them; it was as if for a little while they were no longer homeless and were just cooking out. The men also took occasional advantage of soup kitchens or places where food was distributed and praised the food served at a Manhattan church. They would sometimes make a subway trip there just to eat and occasionally stayed overnight nearby (whether in a shelter or on the streets was not clear). While none of the men explicitly made the comparison, my sense was that the meals they ate in soup kitchens like this one or from takeout restaurants—even those that were particularly tasty, satiating, or nutritious—lacked the enjoyment and camaraderie of those at BEDT.

On this particular evening, George was preparing a pot of Sopa de Mora, a dish adapted from his native El Salvador, made from branches and leaves that he had foraged from somewhere nearby, a "special place," he said. Later I learned that the English translation for this dish was mulberry or blackberry soup. Mulberry trees are somewhat common street trees in New York City; the berries themselves make a sticky mess of the sidewalks underneath. There were probably a few mulberry trees in the adjacent Northside neighborhood. The branches, leaves, and flowers that I watched George

George cooks Sopa de Mora on the Slab (2001).

put into the pot may well have been from a mulberry tree, though there were none of the berries that should have been available in August. Perhaps the branches were from a different tree or this recipe did not make use of the berries; I did not know enough to ask at the time.

George cooked the soup in a big metal pail with a looped handle, over an open fire that made use of the two-foot wall that, where it was still intact, ran along the edge of the Slab, creating a partial oven effect. It was also a convenient place that few would stumble over. The pot sat on a beat-up metal grill that was supported by rocks and pieces of concrete and wood. It took a while to get the fire going, but no one seemed to be in a rush. As George cooked and talked with me, the Hungry March Band was rehearsing just one hundred feet down the Slab. When he heard a song that he particularly liked, he said so and moved his body to the music while tending to the pot or the fire. He also commented on the way they were able to eat at BEDT when times were tough:

> When there is no money coming—what we gotta do? We don't die if we are hungry. . . . Sometimes we cook all vegetables. When somebody go to work, we cook chicken—and we cook fish—we catch the crabs over there [pointing to the river]—sometimes like this and sometimes like this [gesturing to show different small and large-sized crabs]—it's the best thing you can do with this kind of soup.

Soon after the greens were in the pot, Chris returned on his bicycle with a modest bag of vegetables: onions, potatoes, garlic, and lemons. Earlier he had taken up a small collection for this purchase to which we contributed (we also gave a six-pack of beer). Nonetheless, he joked with us afterward about having possibly stolen them. To the others, it did not matter how he obtained the vegetables; they were content with this contribution. George peeled, cleaned, and cut the vegetables with a plastic knife and then added them to the pot. He then cut the lemons, squeezed out their juice over the pot, and then threw the rinds in too. Once all the ingredients were in the pot, the soup needed to cook for forty-five minutes, George said. He then asked Chris for salt. Chris said he had thought about it but did not want to steal it. While George replied he would make do, Chris sensed his disappointment and said he knew where to get some—in some shack somewhere—and off he went again on his bike. Later he came back with a pile of salt wrapped in a newspaper. It was coarse salt and George threw some in the soup, preserving the integrity of the dish. Later he told us it was also important to sprinkle it liberally onto the greens when they were in your bowl.

Chris sped off on his bicycle again and returned a short while later with a bag full of breads from a local bakery. He pulled each loaf or roll out of the bag one by one, slowly announcing every item of his inventory. They were of all different varieties, including Polish bread and sweet bread with powdered sugar. He was particularly proud of the chocolate bread; the others too thought that this was something special. After going through the contents of the bag, he asked, "Did I do good or what?" Chris had taken the breads from the back of a commercial bakery in plain sight of several bakery workers. He refused to say whether it was an act of theft or charitable acceptance. "I told you, I'm a wanted criminal," he declared for at least the second time that evening, but then said later that he was only joking. Unlike the others who were non-natives, Chris carried himself with confidence, demonstrable street smarts, and a well-developed sense of humor. Having grown up in the area, he knew where and how things could be procured without paying. He liked to draw attention to this special skill but was careful not to share too many details. The others were unconcerned and accepted whatever he brought without asking any questions.

When the soup was finished, large amounts of vegetables were doled out into various receptacles with a little of the broth. George used a large, battered metal pan for himself while Alfredo was given a tall can that may have once been used for chemicals and Chris, a plastic bowl. Brian and I were also given a plastic bowl. Plastic forks or spoons were distributed and Chris went around and gave each person their choice of bread. George encouraged everyone to eat up and noted all the people he had served the soup to, many of whom were strangers. About the soup's value as sustenance and nutrition, he said, "That's why I am still alive." Chris was less enthusiastic. Before we could eat, he wanted to make sure we shot some close-up video of the fully cooked product. As he held the handle of the pot underneath the video camera, he gave us his assessment:

> That's what you eat when you're on the street. As long as it fills your belly and gives you some nourishment. It's not about tasting good and it's not about being a good meal. It's just to fill your stomach—that's all it is.

Everyone seemed to be content eating the soup out of their given receptacles with plastic utensils, munching on the large tangles of this foraged plant whose grayish-green color after cooking and bitter taste were somewhat like those of dandelion leaves or broccoli rabe. Alfredo made a sandwich, placing the greens, a chunk of potato, and a slice of onion inside one of the rolls. Chris ate his soup using large pieces of bread to soak up the liquid. I had only a little but Brian ate an entire bowl.

After they were finished eating, we hung out with the residents a bit longer as they cleaned up and prepared to retire inside the tent for television and sleep. It was nearly 10:00 P.M. when we left and headed directly up North 7th Street to a local Bedford Avenue bar to deconstruct our experience. Chris decided that he would come along with us. We knew he had no money, but I was willing to treat him to a few beers. The bar was dark and hardly crowded; we settled into a booth and drank tap beer from the large and inexpensive styrene containers that this establishment was known to serve. Chris was one of those New York City neighborhood characters who talked fast, humorously, authoritatively, and often about others. As he entertained us with his stories and jokes and asked a few questions of us as well, I tried to learn something more about his life and why he spent so much time at BEDT.

I was surprised when Chris said he was only thirty-two; he carried himself as someone who was a bit older. He did not have a job at the moment but frequently mentioned that he had been in the armed services. His relationship with his wife was complicated and they had an eighteen-year-old son who lived with them. He said he would like us to meet her sometime and that she would like us. By the time we had left, almost two hours later, Chris had not provided many details, but some of his bravado was gone and I could sense that there was some sadness in his life and circumstance that he could not control. Back on the street, Chris headed toward BEDT. He said he was just going to get his bicycle but it was likely that he too would be sleeping in the communal tent.

Winter and the End of Comfortable Living

Life at BEDT offered the residents many advantages that they were unlikely to experience elsewhere, including a communal lifestyle and proximity to potential work sites. The "amenities" available to them were difficult to beat, and living at the river's edge in the summer and early fall provided them with cool breezes, a place to cool off when it was hot, and an occasional source of food. But the waterfront was far from an ideal place during the winter. I frequently asked them what they would do when the weather turned cold or when construction began on the park. They usually responded with shrugs or said something about finding an apartment. It was generally a mild fall and they were able to live in relative comfort through the end of the year.

Winter 2001–2 also turned out to be one of the mildest on record with high temperatures in January and February often reaching well into the 60s. But there were still a few extended cold spells and the nights were still relatively cold. I visited them during one of these cold spells toward the end of January. Sometime earlier, they'd moved into a shanty they had constructed just below the Slab. It was actually a shelter that had been constructed by someone else who had left the waterfront earlier that fall. The builder was a young man from upstate New York who lived in it with a large, aggressive dog. No one knew where he went or was sorry to see him go, including members of the spinners and the Hungry March Band, one of whom noted the man's antisocial behavior and speculated that he had a serious drug habit that left him strung out much of the time. Once I had a conversation with this person who told me his name was "Hub-Cap Man" and that he was involved with the music industry. He talked very fast, starting or ending every utterance with the word "man."

Nonetheless, he'd built a fairly solid and neat shelter using the side of the Slab as one of the walls, which provided some protection from the wind off the river. The group expanded and insulated this structure. Scarcely four feet high, the shanty had a few compartments including one in which they created a stove using an old oil barrel. Plywood sheets made up its walls and roof. To increase the warmth of its interior, they hung blankets, discarded rugs, and a plastic tarp on the exterior of every wall and on the roof. Copious amounts of electrical tape and car tires, which sat atop the roof, held these layers of insulation in place. They also used blankets to insulate the interior walls of the shanty and separate the compartments.

Roberto (*left*) and George outside their winter shanty (2002).

While the residents may have thought that their shanty was their best option given limited choices, it was not a very healthy place to live during the winter. When I visited them in late January, George, Manuel, and Roberto were sleeping there at night as was another man of Mexican origin. Their general appearance and health were in stark contrast to what I had seen during the previous summer and fall. All wore hats, gloves, and winter-weight jackets or several layers of lighter clothing. While they had some protection from the cold, their clothes and faces were filthy. The inside of their shanty and the immediate surrounding area reeked of burned wood and body odor. Garbage was strewn in every direction around the shelter. Both George's and Roberto's faces were swollen. When I saw him in the fall, Roberto seemed to have a broken nose (I tried to inquire as to what had happened, but he did not understand). Now his nose was even more bent. All of the men coughed frequently. Also gone were their frequent smiles and the playful demeanor I had observed throughout the summer and fall. Their lives were clearly more difficult in January than in July.

The swollen faces probably had something to do with the emissions from the oil-barrel stove in their shanty. The carbon monoxide poisoning they were likely suffering from may have also been responsible for their sullen and slow demeanors. While the stove was ventilated through an opening in the roof, some of the smoke stayed trapped inside the shanty. The walls of the compartment in which the stove was located were covered in thick soot and the ceiling boards were black. When I stepped down into this space, the fumes were overwhelming. I could not imagine staying there for more than a minute, let alone sleeping there an entire night. The stove was also undoubtedly a fire hazard, but the men seemed unconcerned. While the men slept in two other rooms that were connected to the stove area, only a blanket hanging from the ceiling separated these compartments and the stove room. The men were spending a good deal of their time exposed to the stove's noxious emissions, whose impacts to their appearance, behavior, and health were significant.

In my own estimation, the cost of maintaining their autonomy was likely outweighed by the benefits of being in a heated, emissions-free environment that a shelter would provide. But for these men, having control over the terms of daily life, even at the cost of their own self-destruction, was difficult to give up. Later that afternoon, sitting in the comfort and warmth of my brother's apartment, I began to feel regret: Why had I not been more emphatic about the health hazards to which they were being exposed and pushed them to go to a shelter? I doubt they would have listened to me. I again considered their circumstance and options: What did I really know about the shelter system in the city other than what I read in the papers? Maybe there was no space; maybe they were putting themselves at risk of deportation; maybe the conditions were deplorable and unsafe; maybe there were other things I did not know about these men that made them fear authority or those who kept records and asked for identification. Perhaps their choice was more rational than I had initially thought and possibly still the best of their very limited options, even in cold weather.

Resiliency and Return after Expulsion

I was not able to visit BEDT much during the late winter and spring of 2002. In May and June, I spent two nights there with the fire spinners, but did not arrive until dark and presumably after the residents were asleep in their shanties. On the second of these occasions, a homeless man made himself heard when he yelled about the drumming and other noise the spinners were making (Chapter 3). He had been sleeping in the same shanty off the edge of the Slab that the residents used during the winter. I never saw the man, but his voice did not sound like that of anyone I had come to know from my previous visits. Perhaps some of the residents were also in the shanty; I could not tell. In mid-July I saw George only briefly and for what would be the last time. Later that month, a site cleanup prompted by State Parks but carried out by a city sanitation crew included the eviction of those living at the terminal and the leveling of their shelters (Chapter 7). On subsequent visits, I could find no more shanties, though on occasion I did see Manuel or Roberto. Perhaps they were still sleeping in a more cloaked structure or in a tent that could be disassembled in the day. The last time I saw Manuel, he was sleeping, passed out, face down on the Slab in the middle of the afternoon.

By the summer of 2003, BEDT was still in a transitional phase. State Parks had yet to construct anything and their plans were stalled by budgetary problems. They kept the gates locked and occasionally sent personnel to monitor conditions and ensure that their property was indeed secure. In addition, the city police department visited more frequently and was more aggressive in keeping people out and handing out tickets. But enterprising people still found a way onto this waterfront, particularly on weekends, though not anywhere near the number as two years prior. By then homeless men had also returned. They were young Latino men, much like those I had gotten to know two years earlier, but I did not know them and could recognize only one by sight.

At the beginning of September, I saw Roberto and Jimmy, but neither was living on the waterfront. Roberto was sharing a Southside apartment that he rented with three others for $600 a month. He was working in a restaurant in Manhattan but as this was Labor Day, the restaurant was closed and he had no place to go, no money or food, so he went to the waterfront to visit his friends who were living in an improvised tent that took advantage of one of the long concrete walls north of the Slab. Using the wall as one of its sides provided protection from the wind and, more important, made the tent hard to see from the street or from other spots at the terminal. Roberto said that four people regularly slept inside, all of whom were Mexican. None were around at that moment. Roberto's English had improved slightly and he tried to update me about his life and answer my questions about the other one-time residents. While talking with him, I noticed that his broken nose had never healed correctly and his face was well weathered and more gaunt. The preceding years must have been difficult him. In two years' time he appeared to have aged ten.

Roberto left but soon Jimmy appeared. He was on his way to use a fire hydrant to wash up. Different from the one they used previously, this hydrant was located near Kent Avenue along the edge of North 9th Street, hidden behind one of the large mounds of debris created by the previous year's "cleanup." The mound was now green with weeds and small trees: Insurgent, "non-native" nature had returned as well and robustly so. Many bicycle parts were strewn about the area around the hydrant, some chained to the trees. Unlike Roberto, Jimmy looked healthy and was as outgoing as he had been two years earlier. We talked as I watched him methodically go through his hygiene routine. He was no longer doing construction and worked for his father as a mechanic and car service driver in East Williamsburg. He had been living in his father's house but had to move out because he did not get along with his stepmother. He was now sleeping in the back seat of a car that was parked in the rear of the parking lot of the garage.

We continued to talk as Jimmy changed into a new set of clothes, brushed his teeth, and thoroughly scrubbed the black shoes he was wearing. When I asked him about all the bicycle parts, he made some reference to the men who were living in the tent. Apparently, they were from stolen bikes and the men were running a small bicycle "chop shop" here at the terminal. Jimmy was fastidious and did not let the light rain that

No longer a resident, Jimmy stopped at the terminal to use its facilities (2003).

RESIDENTIAL LIFE

began to fall upset his routine. When he was finished, he carefully closed off the hydrant with a pair of pliers and left them and the bar of soap he had used for the next person who might need them.

We exited BEDT together through a hole in the fence onto Kent Avenue and walked a few feet up North 9th Street where he showed me the car he was driving. It was a large, black four-door sedan car his father owned, one that is ubiquitous throughout the city but particularly in the outer boroughs where car service often takes the place of metered taxis. He proudly showed me some his mechanic's tools neatly stored in plastic cases in the trunk of the car. Within a few minutes Roberto and one of the tent dwellers joined him at the car. They were all going to buy food that they planned to cook and eat at Roberto's apartment. Jimmy gave me a card for his father's car service and said to call the number and ask for car 36, and they took off. Six weeks later, I ran into Roberto again, this time on Wythe Avenue, two blocks from BEDT. He told me he was out of work but planning to move to Chicago in two weeks. He had a brother who lived there and could get him a job working in a restaurant.

Freedom, Companionship, and a Lack of Options in Outsider Space

The residents of BEDT were resilient; in spite of great personal hardship and almost untenable circumstances, they were able to carve out a temporary niche for living in a landscape in flux. The terminal was not an ideal place to live, but the men made the best of it and probably had a better quality of life than those out on the streets or bedding down in shelters, at least for eight months of the year. It enabled them to live in relative comfort and privacy and carry out a communal existence that would not be possible elsewhere in the city. Companionship and shared living made their lives a bit easier and more joyful and provided additional stability for these men who had little of it. And for those whose lives were severely constrained by multiple factors and had little opportunity to influence their own predicament, the terminal was a space of last resort.

Not unlike the local men from the neighborhood, the residents had found a freer place to conduct their lives, a place where they would largely be left alone, unburdened by rules, expectations, and authorities. When not working they could do what they wanted without anyone looking over their shoulders, making sure they followed a prescribed routine for achieving some far-off, unknown, or unavailable outcome. On the waterfront, these men enjoyed autonomy over the few things that they could control, including the terms of their eating, sleeping, personal hygiene, leisure, and social life.

In the way they shaped the landscape for their own personal needs, they were not unlike other constituents of BEDT who made their own environments: the skateboarders, artists, and even the marching band and fire spinners. They all shared and reveled in the companionship of outsider space, and thus the residents were often afforded a high degree of respect from these people with whom they had little so in common. Additionally, the residents' largely copacetic presence at the terminal suggests that those places frequently used for leisure can simultaneously serve other needs, including providing shelter for those with nowhere else to go.

CHAPTER 7

NEIGHBORS AGAINST GARBAGE

Activism and Uneasy Alliances on the Waterfront

MANY OF THE INSURGENT AGENTS that appropriated BEDT for recreative and other purposes were largely unaware of or unconcerned about the broader conflict over the future redevelopment of the Williamsburg waterfront. As the 1990s progressed, more people began to discover and use the Northside waterfront for more activities, more of the time. And by the turn of the millennium, the sheer volume of users and the regularity of their activities surely suggested, as a few told me, that this was "the people's waterfront." Only part of this circumstance was accidental. Behind the scenes a group of local residents had been fighting for a decade to permanently secure this waterfront "for the people" while fighting off less desirable counterproposals made by more politically connected parties and City Hall.

By 2003, the conflict over the waterfront's future and which parties would determine and control its use seemingly reached its nadir when Mayor Michael Bloomberg and his planning department introduced a sweeping proposal that would rezone 170 blocks of Community District #1, including most of its East River frontage, from manufacturing to residential and mixed-use districts. By the time the City Council approved the controversial measure in 2005, several large waterfront properties, including those that were a part of BEDT, had already changed hands in speculation of the transformation the rezoning would enable. But the "underutilized and vacant land" that became the rationale for the city's plan was not inevitable, nor were 30-plus-story residential towers arrayed in a necklace of green spaces the only potential vision for redevelopment contemplated by city agents.[1] In fact, the conflict over the rezoning and the transformation it soon facilitated obscure an earlier conflict between local residents and government-allied interests.

The glass and steel condominium towers constructed between North 4th and North 7th streets after the 2005 rezoning and the breezy esplanade that now links them betray the radically different vision of the waterfront held by Bloomberg's predecessor, Rudolph Giuliani. A decade earlier, when residents (both those new to the neighborhood and longtimers) began to envision a waterfront reclaimed for public recreation, light industry, and revived maritime uses, Mayor Giuliani and his administration saw this same edge as the key to the city's seemingly intractable solid waste problems.[2] I retell the story of this conflict here, largely from the perspective of the Northside residents who formed Neighbors Against Garbage to fight the expansion of a waste transfer station at the south end of BEDT and a later proposal to build the city's largest waste-handling facility across all seven blocks of the terminal. By the end of the 1990s, these activists had emerged victorious, keeping the water's edge from becoming a walled-off dump. NAG's actions allowed the unplanned occupations to flourish at BEDT for a few years more while it fought and sometimes collaborated with city and state agents. But the defeat of the waste carters also allowed the Bloomberg administration to later pursue its own vision for this edge. In effect, NAG members and other local activists were enablers of the rezoning and its results, even though many of these same residents bitterly opposed this action.

NAG's story as told in this chapter begins in the early 1990s and continues through the immediate aftermath of the garbage controversy in the early 2000s, when these activists working within the context of an unusual alliance of a state agency, a national not-for-profit land trust, and a prominent university formed a novel partnership to develop the waterfront park they had long envisioned. Even though the partnership fell apart in 2003, the larger vision of a public park at BEDT anchoring a larger ring of recreation spaces to the north and south is becoming reality. But it comes at a cost: the condominium towers that were never a part of the vision of these activist residents.

Their story differs from those previously told in this book: It is not about on-the-ground insurgency of opportunistic recreation seekers. While most of the constituencies of the undesigned did little if anything to advance their cause through protest or participatory politics, NAG members by contrast vociferously asserted their rights to the waterfront through these modes of contestation. For nearly two decades, these residents were the terminal's most vocal stakeholder and a forceful advocate for local interests across the entire Greenpoint–Williamsburg waterfront. Even today, as

NAG (which now stands for Neighbors Allied for Good Growth) has evolved and the stakeholders of the waterfront have greatly expanded, many veterans of this earlier conflict retain a role in the ongoing redevelopment of the water's edge, even though the larger terms of what it will be and who will use it have been largely settled.

I learned much of the story of the long conflict over the Williamsburg waterfront by spending time with NAG principals and attending their meetings and events. This included interviews I conducted with NAG leaders in 2001 and 2002. This chapter also draws upon my own observations and notes taken during several public forums during the early 2000s, including a BEDT

A 1994 Neighbors Against Garbage protest at the Nekboh transfer station on the Williamsburg waterfront. (Photo courtesy of NAG.)

site walkthrough led by State Parks officials in 2001, and many communications and conversations in the decade that followed, along with a review of related planning documents and print and electronic media.

Brooklyn Waterfront Legacies: Fighting Waste Transfer

Residents of Brooklyn Community District #1, comprising Greenpoint and Williamsburg, long complained that their neighborhoods were dumping grounds for waste, sewage treatment, and noxious, toxic, or nuisance uses.[3] As industry and maritime uses receded from the water's edge beginning in the 1950s, they left vacant land and M-zoning (manufacturing), which permitted waste-related uses. Looking to stimulate the redevelopment of underutilized land, multiple administrations during the 1980s and 1990s examined the city's M-zones, which had been in place since the passage of the city's 1961 zoning resolution.[4] They argued that the preponderance of these zones did not adequately foresee the decline in manufacturing and the rise of containerized shipping cargo and truck-based freight hauling, trends that were already underway by the early 1960s.[5] The Department of City Planning had determined that vast swaths of the city's M-zoned waterfront could be remade into desirable middle-class residential districts, office and retail areas, and parks.[6] But as the amount of M-zoned land in the city shrank (both at the water's edge and inland), the number of places where garbage could be processed, sorted, compacted, or transferred shrank as well.

For decades the city had brought most of its residential garbage by truck to waterfront transfer stations in all five boroughs where it was loaded onto barges destined for Fresh Kills Landfill on Staten Island. The incremental redevelopment of the city's waterfront over the 1980s and 1990s and gentrification of nearby neighborhoods challenged the continued operation of barge transfer stations at the same time that the unpopularity of Fresh Kills fueled a secession movement on Staten Island. These developments threatened the city's larger waste-collection system, which had been in place for half a century.[7] Bowing to political pressure in 1996, Mayor Giuliani announced that he would close Fresh Kills and develop a new system of disposal built around a few large, privately operated transfer stations. These facilities would compact trash and send it to out-of-state landfills via barges and trucks that would connect with rail systems on the west side of the Hudson River.[8]

Years before the administration announced the closure of Fresh Kills and a new municipal solid waste plan, Brooklyn Community District #1 was already playing an outsized role in the city's trash-collection systems.[9] With M-zoning still in place along the edges of nearly the entire Greenpoint–Williamsburg peninsula, much of it in the form of privately held property, the district's waterfront was already a repository for what was not wanted elsewhere: solid waste transfer stations, recycling and scrap yards, warehouses for storage of hazardous materials, sewage treatment facilities, and trucking terminals. Discontent among residents was already coalescing around the local concentration of these uses when, in 1987, the Barretti Carting Corporation of Hoboken, New Jersey, opened a transfer station on the southernmost block of the sprawling BEDT property, replacing a scrap yard that had been in place since the mid-1960s. The operation, given the name Nekboh, which approximates "Hoboken" spelled backward, sat just blocks from the Bedford Avenue spine of Williamsburg's Northside. Just as the area was beginning to experience a modest revival in the early 1990s, Nekboh expanded its operation across a second BEDT block. As its size and capacity grew, so too did its environmental impacts. In response, five aggrieved Northside residents formed Neighbors Against Garbage in the summer of 1994. (Later NAG would expand its focus to provide advocacy for environmental and open space issues in all of CD #1.)

"There were all kinds of problems coming from the garbage transfer station—we were having smells coming to the neighborhood, dust, trucks lining up in our streets, rats in our basements," said Peter Gillespie, one of NAG's founding members. He was an artist and construction worker by trade, and his position with the group would eventually evolve into his being its only paid employee. Peter spoke with an assured sense of conviction that suggested he would use whatever means were available to him to defend his constituency and fight for what he believed was right:

> When the garbage transfer station started operating, it was only on one block; it was relatively small.... [Nekboh] rented out [an additional] block north of their site, and then they rented out still another block; so they went from a three-acre site to taking over about nine acres.... It was at that point, in that second expansion phase, that the community realized that either they were going to stop this transfer station from expanding and operating or the entire waterfront would be taken over by this industry.

Peter frequently called the facility "illegal," noting that its operating permits had been acquired improperly—without undergoing the environmental reviews and vetting required by New York City and state. Fellow NAG member Bob Bratko, a retired New York City police officer and lifelong area resident, agreed, noting that frequent complaints lodged with the city's Department of Environmental Protection received "very little satisfaction."

NAG fought Barretti on multiple fronts, with on-the-ground protests, aggressive lobbying, and legal challenges. At the same time, they sought to build local awareness of Nekboh's environmental impacts. They wrote letters appealing to elected officials, circulated petitions, rang doorbells, hung posters, staged public events, and enlisted local businesses and organizations into the cause. "We really went after these guys," said Cathleen Breen, an environmental lobbyist who moved to the Northside during the 1980s. "Every day was a fight, every day was picketing, every day was leafleting; the community came out in force."

In November 1994, NAG organized its first of many large protests. On a Sunday afternoon, members marched through the neighborhood, gathering supporters en route to "Mt. Nekboh," the pile of dirt, construction debris, and garbage rising by the river. By the time they reached the waterfront, the group had grown to 200 "delightfully rowdy" protesters: young and old, longtime residents and new arrivals, artists, business owners, and members of all of Williamsburg's prominent ethnic groups.[10] In early 1995 they rallied at City Hall, after sending hundreds of provocative postcards (designed by Peter) to Mayor Giuliani and his Commissioner of Sanitation, John Doherty. One depicted the two men handing a permit to Nekboh owner Phil Barretti allowing him to "pile more garbage on the East River and further pollute North Brooklyn." Deputy Mayor Fran Reiter told the *Daily News* that it was "the most eye-catching campaign [she] had ever seen."[11]

The postcard campaigns became a frequently employed tactic used by NAG to confront elected officials who, these activists felt, had for too long ignored their concerns. At the same time, NAG took directly to the waterfront, appropriating parts of the terminal not just for protest but also for festivals and cleanup events. NAG's fall 1995 waterfront festival on the north portion of BEDT was attended by several hundred residents and brought needed publicity and press coverage, while raising a bit of money. More important, Bob said, it encouraged local residents, many of whom avoided the neighborhood's edge altogether, to "realize what the waterfront contained and what it could possibly be."

While its operation was legally dubious, Nekboh's expansion plans were backed by Giuliani and Doherty. Hoping to show how much opposition there was to Barretti's existing operation and proposed enlargements, and to provide evidence of the operation's impact on Northside residents, NAG invited Doherty to the neighborhood to meet with residents. Much to their surprise, the commissioner accepted the invitation and in February 1995 met with them in the basement of a local church. As Peter described,

> We were thinking of telling people we're gonna cancel it because it was just too bitter cold and we were afraid that nobody was gonna show up, and we realized that it was too late to do that. And it turned out that hundreds of people throughout the neighborhood showed up to this meeting and we really let the Commissioner of Sanitation know that this community was united and that they were going to fight this transfer station.

A few days prior to the meeting, NAG's campaign received an unexpected and somewhat painful boost. To provide Commissioner Doherty with visual evidence of the transfer station's lack of legally required hazard controls, Peter had intended to videotape Barretti's operation. From an adjacent street, Peter began shooting, but his session was quickly interrupted when a group of facility workers that included Phil Barretti Jr. confronted him. They demanded he leave the Nekboh property even though he was actually on a public street. When he refused to comply, they assaulted him, took his camera, and destroyed the videotape it contained. The event led to Barretti Jr.'s arrest, reports of which soon appeared in local newspapers.[12] As Peter, who did not sustain any major injuries, described:

NEIGHBORS AGAINST GARBAGE

Postcard campaigns were a frequent tactic employed by NAG in their fight to reclaim the Northside waterfront. These cards were designed by Peter Gillespie and ultimately sent to Mayor Giuliani in 1995 (*left*) and 1999 (*right*).

It got sort of ugly, but in a certain way they played into our hands, because it sort of demonstrated very clearly to the community and to the city, particularly the Sanitation Commissioner that night, that the people that we were dealing with were not people that the city should be doing business with.

But the fallout from the assault was only one of several problems now facing the Nekboh operators. Phil Barretti Sr. was also facing an indictment related to his participation in larger organized crime rackets within the carting

Peter Gillespie (*foreground*), one of NAG's founders, loads a truck with the garbage and debris collected during a waterfront spring cleanup. (Photo courtesy of NAG, 1999.)

industry. In June 1995, Manhattan District Attorney Robert Morgenthau brought an indictment against Barretti on thirty-three different counts, including arson, grand larceny, and coercion, all allegedly facilitating the growth of his waste empire, which was valued at more than $40 million.[13] A day later, with a state Department of Environmental Conservation determination that Nekboh had been operating without an official permit for more than six years, city and state regulators shut it down.[14] After it was allowed to partially resume its paper and cardboard operation a month later, regulators shut down Nekboh again in October, after they discovered that it was handling more than double its legal limit of paper.[15] Also in October, Barretti Sr. was arrested and accused of assault by his Morris County, New Jersey, mistress (the charge was dropped when the woman declined to press charges).[16] "Between community pressure and the way he ran the facility and his other problems, we were able to close down the original operation and stop the original owner from running the transfer station," Peter reasoned.

It was a significant victory for residents of the Northside, but their joy would not last long. In January 1996, the USA Waste Corporation bought Barretti's company and all of its assets.[17] The Houston-based company was the second-largest garbage carter in North America and seemed to have the ear of the Giuliani administration. The mayor, once an organized crime–busting U.S. deputy attorney general, had been elected in part for his commitment to clean up the seemingly intractable corruption connected with industries that did business with or within the city, such as trash hauling, construction, and the operation of the Fulton Fish Market. In waste carting, he was eager to rid the city of locally based companies operating as a cartel and replace them with national operators. Assuming Barretti's lease at BEDT, by May USA Waste had received a permit from the state to resume its Williamsburg waterfront operation.[18]

NEIGHBORS AGAINST GARBAGE

Backed by the mayor, in 1998 the company applied for a permit to expand the size and scope of its BEDT transfer station, proposing to handle more than 5,300 tons of residential garbage per day.[19] The waterfront facility was among the most important components of the Giuliani administration's solid waste plan, which proposed turning over much of the municipal sanitation system to private operators and would help the mayor fulfill his commitment to close Fresh Kills Landfill (the main repository for the city's residential trash until it was closed in 2002).[20] USA Waste's mega-station proposed for BEDT and a second similarly sized facility proposed for Linden, New Jersey, were to receive and compact most of the city's residential garbage en route to out-of-state landfills.[21] As Cathleen described:

> USA Waste had come into the New York market and they not only wanted to have the Barretti site, the North 4th to North 5th [Street] site, but they also wanted . . . to expand their facility from North 4th to North 12th Street, to encompass the entire Brooklyn Eastern District Terminal. So we would have had eight blocks of a huge garbage-hauling facility. And it would have been countless trucks that would have been coming through the neighborhood. And as trucks so often do, and we knew this from Phil Barretti's operation, [they] idle along the streets. It was touted as the largest facility in the Northeast.

With the administration firmly behind the USA Waste proposal, NAG directed its efforts toward state government rather than to City Hall. They hired an attorney to serve as their lobbyist in Albany and traveled to the capital to meet with the staff of Governor George Pataki. Gaining in knowledge and influence, they began to flex their newly developed political muscle. As Peter described:

> The previous owner didn't have a permit to operate a transfer station; they just had an agreement with the city and state to do it. So we said, "You have to get a permit and you have to dot all the 'i's and cross all the 't's on that permit." And once the city and state agreed to that, we were able to stall it, slow it down, and we required them to do an environmental review and suddenly their permit application began to unravel. And even though they claimed—USA Waste—they were going to open up their [expanded] operation a few months after taking ownership of the site, they were never able to do that.

Cathleen took on much of the responsibility for soliciting donations, organizing events, and getting local businesses involved: Neighborhood restaurants provided food for two NAG block parties, a local company produced and donated NAG shirts, elected officials were lobbied and made contributions from their discretionary budgets. She also tapped into Williamsurg's growing art scene, working with a few of the area's galleries to enlist local artists to donate works. In all, artists donated "a couple of hundred works" that were randomly given to people making a $100 donation at a fundraiser held at the Brooklyn Museum.

At the same time, NAG's political efforts in Albany were beginning to pay off. In February 1998, Pataki signed a memorandum of understanding, naming BEDT a "priority site" for the state's open space plan, eligible for acquisition using money generated from the 1996 Clean Water/Clean Air Environmental Bond Act.[22] But much like NAG's earlier victory over Barretti, celebrating would be premature. Even with the terminal on the state's purchase list, USA Waste and city officials continued to push ahead with the permitting and environmental review for the waste transfer facility.[23] Though the mayor and the governor were both popularly elected Republicans, they infrequently saw eye to eye and often undertook major initiatives without the backing, coordination or involvement with the other. This rivalry now threatened to scuttle the hard work and park dreams of NAG members and their growing resident constituency.

As NAG encouraged local residents to attend a local hearing required as part of the permitting of the proposed facility, city officials were apparently unaware of just how large and vociferous the opposition had grown. The April 1998 meeting held at a local high school turned out to be a watershed event with an estimated 1,200 people in attendance, nearly all to protest or speak out against the mayor's expansion plan.[24] As Peter recalled:

> That put the nail in the coffin . . . it was the [state] Department of Environmental Conservation hearing on the permit application. And it turns out that the number of people . . . was the largest showing in the history of DEC; it was the largest number of people to attend a hearing in New York state's history. And that message . . . was heard up in Albany and that was really the beginning of the end of [their] opening up their transfer station.

While these events were happening locally, larger events were reshaping the waste disposal industry. A proposed merger between USA Waste and another carting giant, Waste Management, Inc., of Oak Brook, Illinois, was making its way through the U.S. Securities and Exchange Commission's approvals process. Regulators were concerned that this new entity, combining the industry's largest and third-largest waste disposal companies, could control entire regional markets. Under a July 1998 settlement reached by the U.S. Department of Justice and thirteen state attorneys general (including New York's), the merged corporation would divest itself of a number of its properties to be in compliance with federal and state antitrust regulations. The divestiture of the Williamsburg site was part of this agreement. At a foreclosure auction just days earlier, Waste Management had purchased two-thirds of the southern portion of the BEDT property (from North 5th to North 7th streets) for $6.75 million to pursue its expansion plans.[25] As the divestiture list could have potentially included any combination of USA Waste– or Waste Management–controlled properties in the city, the impetus behind including BEDT was largely political. In its reporting of the divestiture agreement, the *Times* noted the "tenacious battle local residents waged to keep the transfer station from being permitted" and reasoned that "even without the merger, the site's future as a transfer station remained questionable."[26] NAG members, of course, felt similarly. "There was just so much community opposition they just decided to go elsewhere," Cathleen explained. "It just wasn't worth the fight."

Even with this battle won, area residents would still need to push the governor to purchase the terminal and begin planning its redevelopment as a park. Cathleen noted that because BEDT was zoned for industrial use, and not in public ownership, it was still a viable site for other undesirable uses, such as warehouses and big-box stores. There were also other possibilities. During the five years that residents had been fighting waste transfer on the Northside waterfront, their neighborhood had been evolving into a bohemian extension of Manhattan's East Village, just one stop away on the L train.[27] Pleasure seekers streamed into the neighborhood each weekend, supporting ever larger numbers of new stores, restaurants, nightlife establishments, and art venues. At the same time, those priced out of Manhattan and Brooklyn's brownstone belt to the south were placing upward pressure on the area's real estate market. The tree-lined streets filled with nineteenth-century townhouses, tenements, and loft buildings suitable for live-work or just live provided a variety of housing options for those who wanted to purchase, rent, or share living space.

By the late 1990s, a coalition of local community groups led by the CD #1 Waterfront Committee had been working for more than half a decade on a community-based "197-a plan" for the Williamsburg waterfront. Such plans, the names of which refer to the corresponding section of the city charter, were intended to empower local residents, businesses, and civic groups to become active agents in planning their respective neighborhoods. The Department of City

Planning was to provide technical support for these efforts. Once approved by the City Planning Commission, these plans, though not binding, were to serve as a blueprint to "guide future actions by city agencies in the areas addressed by the plans."[28] Although the *Williamsburg Waterfront 197-a Plan* was not approved by the Commission until December 2001, the Department of City Planning was aware well in advance of the recommendations it would contain and ostensibly supported them.

The plan called for park uses on the entire BEDT site (from North 4th to North 11th streets) *or* a rezoning to a mix of park space and "contextual, medium density residential, high performance light industrial, and neighborhood-scale retail" similar to the mix and scale of development found in the Northside.[29] These recommendations were consistent with the Department's own 1994 *Plan for the Brooklyn Waterfront*, which called for rezoning BEDT to permit "residential and light industrial uses."[30] Given the mayor's insistence that this waterfront be developed for waste transfer and his later refusal to take any contrary action even after his plan was defeated, the Department of City Planning was not at that time contemplating a waterfront rezoning on Williamsburg's Northside (or in neighboring Greenpoint). As we planners in the Department's Brooklyn office worked on rezoning initiatives to facilitate the development of housing, community facilities, and parks just a few blocks away on the Southside and in South Williamsburg, the Northside was off limits. Rezoning measures to facilitate neighborhood interests were pursued in support of only those groups in active alliance with the mayor.

Even without a zoning change, by decade's end speculation was already occurring on the individual parcels that made up the larger BEDT property as gentrification was sweeping through the Northside. High-rise luxury condominiums might ultimately be considered "highest and best" use by a future administration. NAG was adamantly opposed not just to garbage transfer but also to high-rises, and its leaders understood that the longer the waterfront sat in a state of underutilization, the more likely these towers would become. Not far to the north, in Hunters Point on the Queens waterfront, a state development agency was overseeing the implementation of the 1994 Queens West Plan, which included property that was once the Brooklyn Eastern District Terminal Railroad's Pigeon Street Yard.[31] By the late 1990s, two residential towers had already been constructed, with several more in the planning stages. Cathleen said Northside residents did not want to see their waterfront become another Queens West. We want "to make sure we don't have 400-foot Trump-like towers" she explained, acknowledging that efforts to secure as much waterfront park space as possible would also stoke development interest in adjacent parcels. NAG and other local advocacy organizations, she said, were committed to obtaining "more open space *and* making sure that those in the community who fought so hard to get this park don't get priced out." In the short term, the M-zoning still in place along Williamsburg's waterfront ensured that residential development could be pursued only through a "variance" in which the owners claimed a financial "hardship" that prevented a fair return on their investment. But in the longer term, absent state money and forceful support, high-rises were a distinct possibility.

There were still remaining impediments to the state's purchase and development of BEDT. The state bond fund would provide an allocation for purchase, but there was not enough money for the entire site, let alone enough to cover the cost of building and maintaining a park. A legislative act authorizing a budget allocation for purchase and the dedication of state parkland was also needed. As state representatives have difficulty representing public interests in an auction environment or in live negotiation, the state prefers not to purchase land directly; it would need a land trust to act as a conduit for the sale of the property. Any or all of these impediments could jeopardize the park project or stall the process indefinitely.

FGH Realty, the owner of the terminal, was also eager to sell. As the principal mortgage holder since 1987, FGH had received the entire BEDT site from a consortium of owners who had purchased it during the 1980s real estate boom with the intent of building a 2,500-unit residential community with additional light industrial development.[32] But this development proposal failed to attract investors in the slumping economy of the late 1980s and early 1990s and encountered substantial local opposition. Through a series of bankruptcy proceedings, FGH came to control the terminal and in 1998 assumed full title to the northern four blocks of the property (North 7th to North 11th streets) with a winning bid of $5 million at auction.[33] In a related auction the same day, USA Waste purchased most of the southern portion of the terminal for $6.75 million.[34] (The initial value of the mortgage was $10.5 million for the entire terminal, and it is unclear how much of this money was paid back to FGH over the decade before foreclosure.)

While the Giuliani administration's proposed waste transfer facility was near-dead, the administration was still unwilling to consider a broad rezoning initiative for the Northside waterfront. At the same time, the mayor's push to ease zoning restrictions for big-box retail made selling BEDT to a commercial developer perhaps the most expedient way to realize the fullest value of the property.[35] In March 1999, FGH signed a contract giving commercial developer Blumenfeld Realty an "option" to purchase the property for the purposes of developing big-box stores, a multiplex cinema, and a parking facility.[36] As in the past, NAG countered with postcard campaigns aimed at the mayor and the governor. The 5,000 signed postcards from area residents and concerned citizens sent to Albany in June urged Governor Pataki to keep the promise he had made during his 1998 reelection campaign to create a park at the terminal, a pledge he reaffirmed when he added BEDT to the state's open space acquisition list.[37]

A Novel Public–Private Partnership

The state was willing to acquire BEDT only if it had a partner who would share the development costs and stewardship responsibilities. Officials were already working with the Trust for Public Land (TPL) to identify a potential partner. "The state was willing to do some, but they can't purchase the land; they can't do it alone," Cathleen explained. "And at the time it was the full BEDT site."

By early 1999, the Trust had matched State Parks with New York University, which was looking for a place to build sports fields for some of its athletic teams. A meeting was quickly arranged during which NYU representatives made a presentation to neighborhood residents. According to Cathleen, the meeting was a surprising success. Residents were pleased to learn that NYU was willing to work with them to establish a shared vision for the park. In agreeing to move forward with this partnership, NAG members also felt that NYU could use its own considerable sway with city and state governments to help bring the project to fruition and would serve as a forceful advocate and fundraiser for the park's eventual expansion.

In October 1999, NAG and NYU received some good news. Issues concerning the state Department of Environmental Conservation–mandated remediation persuaded Blumenfeld to stop pursuit of its multiplex cinema plan and allow its option to expire.[38] But even with the Trust for Public Land working behind the scenes on behalf of the state and NYU, other interests were also eyeing the property. FGH Realty placed the northern four blocks up for auction again in December, but the Trust had neither the cash nor the full commitment from the state to bid on the property. At auction the property was sold to Jallco, Inc., whose winning bid was $5 million.[39] Jallco was controlled by a local businessman, Norman Brodksy, who desired the property for expansion of CitiStorage, his document-storage business, located just to the north of the terminal, between North 11th and North 12th streets. BEDT's new owner immediately leased and later sold one of the blocks to Louis Silverman, who had helped Brodsky finance the purchase and was the owner of 4Gs Trucking (a truck-leasing company).[40] Brodsky constructed a large one-story warehouse on one block while Silverman cleared, paved, and fenced the other for use as a storage yard. With Brodsky now in possession of the four northernmost blocks and probably speculating that his property would eventually be rezoned for residential development, the park coalition was forced to try to negotiate an agreement with him to sell the remaining two blocks to the state. Brodsky eventually agreed, but the offering price was significantly higher than what it once could have been.

A complicated purchase agreement between the state, NYU, and the TPL with Jallco was completed in June 2000. The state would pay $8.3 million for the central portion of the BEDT site, from North 7th to North 9th streets, approximately seven acres.[41] With money borrowed from NYU, it was actually the TPL that took title to the property that October.[42] It then transferred it to the state in January 2001, after the state paid NYU back the entire purchase price. As part of the deal, NYU agreed to pay for most of the park planning and development costs, with the rest coming from the state and city governments. (Later in 2001, the city backed out of its entire funding commitment.) Under the agreement, NYU would hold a forty-nine-year lease but be co-stewards of the property. The agreement between the state and the university also stipulated that NYU athletic teams and the "community" equally share the use of these facilities.

Some local residents grumbled both at the diminished size of the prospective park and the involvement of NYU. Others wondered how the state had been outmaneuvered by Brodsky, who essentially bought a four-block site for $5 million and then a year later sold half of it to the state for $8.3 million. But Cathleen offered a more pragmatic view of the partnership:

> For the exact same price that we would have gotten the entire BEDT land [seven blocks, over twenty acres], we are now only going to get two blocks and seven acres. Still, it was starting to look like not such a good deal for NYU, and part of the concern was that NYU would pull out and we wouldn't have any open space. And we would have a developer . . . who would build luxury housing across the entire [site]. So there were a lot of compromises along the way. We'll have to make do with two blocks for now and strive for more. . . . [L]et's not lose this opportunity because it's not going to come along again so readily.

Her perspective was shared by others who had been involved in the negotiations, including Erik Kulleseid, who had constructed the deal for the TPL. Erik had been involved with the Williamsburg waterfront since starting as a TPL intern in 1993 and included the terminal in a 1995 report he wrote, *New Parkland for New Yorkers*.[43] When I talked with Erik in 2012, he explained that the Trust had for several years wanted to acquire BEDT for public park development and had approached the owners on several occasions about such a purchase. "They wanted us to put millions on the table and of course we didn't have it," he explained. Cash up front (rather than a state commitment to pay for property pending authorizing legislation) was not the only issue that stood in the way. TPL's leadership was "very nervous" about the extent of the terminal's contamination and need for remediation, he said. Thus, the prevailing view in the organization at the time was that the purchase might expose the Trust to untold liability. In purchasing the northern portion of BEDT, Brodsky had "taken a calculated risk," Erik explained. By the time NYU was brought in and the state legislature took up the necessary legislation to allocate funding and dedicate the site as parkland, Brodsky was able to dictate the terms of the TPL-brokered sale.[44] Brodsky left the two northernmost two blocks for his own profitable business as well as that of Silverman's 4Gs, which he knew would appreciate in value by being adjacent to a public park (and spectacularly so; see Chapter 8), while justifying his price for the remaining portion of the property based on an appraisal he had commissioned.

The BEDT purchase and partnership were lauded by all the parties involved, the local press, and the *Times*.[45] NYU President L. Jay Oliva called it a "historic partnership" that would provide "the kind of athletic program that our students deserve, and for the community to have important new recreational opportunities.[46] New York State Assemblyman Joseph Lentol, who played a key role in bringing the parties together for the deal, called it a "triumph for all the residents of Williamsburg."[47] In a story entitled "Taking Back the Waterfront" appearing in their publication *Land and People*, TPL downplayed the dealmaking aspect of the partnership, focusing instead on the long struggle of area residents to reclaim their edge of the river.[48] Peter said that having NYU involved was probably the "best scenario" for the neighborhood. Fellow NAG member Michelle Rodecker, a lifelong North Brooklyn resident who met her husband, Jim, during the 1970s at BEDT when they were both employees of the railroad, said the deal was "unique" and could "serve as a blueprint for the creation of more parkland along the Greenpoint and Williamsburg waterfronts."[49]

By fall 2001, with the various parties in general agreement about a vision of shared use for the waterfront park, the planning process could begin in earnest. Over the next eighteen months, NAG members and local residents working with NYU representatives, state officials, and their hired consultants engaged in a sometimes contentious public planning process that would test their novel public–private partnership. By mid-2003, NYU had pulled out of the agreement.

What caused this historic partnership to un-ravel and what were the implications for the residents of Williamsburg who had for so long fought for this modest swath of waterfront? The rise and demise of this unlikely but much-heralded marriage would ultimately result in radical changes in the design and program of what would become East River State Park.

During a November 2001 BEDT walkthrough with NAG members and local residents, Jim Moogan (regional director of State Parks) points in the direction of the planned sports fields.

But at the onset of the park planning pro-cess at the end of 2001, the mood among NAG members was quite optimistic. In anticipation of the work ahead, it was becoming clear to NAG leaders that they were not well equipped as an organization to fully represent local interests. Their mission, ex-perience, and expertise were focused on environmental concerns, and their tactics were more confrontational than collaborative. Their advocacy was also still very much needed in Williamsburg and across Community District #1. In addition to ongoing issues involving waste transfer, hazardous materials, air and water pollution, truck traffic, and petroleum storage and distribution, NAG now needed to spearhead the campaign against a power plant proposed for a waterfront site a few blocks north of the future park.[50] At BEDT, waste haulers and the city had been defeated, but a new community-based mission—built around park design, development, and administration—required new skills, a broader set of participants, and a more collaborative approach. With some largely undefined but permanent role in the planning and stewardship of this new waterfront park yet to be determined, NAG members decided to spin off a dedicated group to advocate for neighborhood interests in this venture, and thus the Friends of BEDT Park was formed. The mission of the Friends was to ensure that the "future use of the shared recreation fields and park areas occurs in a fair and just way that serves the public's interest" while serving as an advocate for the development of more park space along the waterfront.[51]

Building on their meetings over the previous eighteen months and the November 2001 BEDT walkthrough, State Parks, NYU, and the Friends agreed to stage a series of community design meetings for the spring of 2002. The purpose of these forums was to collectively develop a design for the park and deal with environmental and operational issues, while involving a broader swath of the public in the project. Among the Friends there was a feeling that few people beyond a familiar cast of residents and business owners knew about the project at all. These meetings were also intended to build a larger working relationship between the partners. While public–private partnerships could be found throughout the city—NYU was involved in several such development initiatives in Manhattan—none had principally involved the building and shared use of a public park between a private university and local residents. Could groups with such divergent interests successfully build and share the park in a mutually satisfying way—and one that would require little funding from the state? The meetings would provide some indication.

The forums were largely orchestrated by State Parks and their hired "design team" consultants, comprising Sasaki Associates, an internationally renowned urban design firm based in Watertown, Massachusetts; URS, a New York engineering firm; and AKRF, a New York engineering and planning firm. State representatives and their consultants, NYU, and the Friends agreed on three meetings held over a period of three months. An agenda distributed at the first meeting, held in a church basement that April, laid out this progression: The first meeting would determine the programmatic elements of the park; the second was to evaluate and select from the alternative schematic designs generated by the team based on the programmatic elements and constraints of site and budget; and the last was to "confirm" park design and determine treatments for building materials, plantings, furniture installations, and other details.

Many of the approximately sixty people in attendance at the first meeting were learning about the project for the first time. Accordingly, much of the evening's proceedings—led by Cathleen Breen and Jim Moogan, the project manager for State Parks—was dedicated to introducing the project and its partners. Later, Kathryn Madden, the project manager for Sasaki, discussed some possibilities for the park's design; and Bob Marman, an engineer from URS, described the environmental issues.

The presentations elicited several questions from audience members, who were balancing a sense of excitement with guarded caution. Even before NAG's waterfront transfer station battle, the politics of Community District #1 had long been contentious, with the use and redevelopment of the waterfront a particular source of friction and distrust. While many audience members seemed happy with the project and expressed genuine gratitude to those who had facilitated it, the tone of others suggested that there was something that they were not hearing, a catch or "fine print" that might make the plan a poor deal. Attendees wanted to know about the use of the park for community events, the size and form of the park building and bleachers, and the fate of the small "in-holding" building along Kent Avenue (a property not part of the state purchase that projected into the park footprint). They also asked if the piers at North 9th Street, which were rapidly sinking into the river, could be conserved and incorporated into the park. Additionally, was there a way to maximize the general-use space as opposed to the space occupied by the ball fields? Where would entrances, fencing, and lighting be? Would the final design call for the use of green technologies, and would local laborers be employed in the park's construction? Moogan responded to all questions and comments positively and offered to "look into" every suggestion.

Probably a veteran of many such community meetings, Moogan had a particular way of quickly defusing more difficult questions. This included an inquiry from one of the eight skateboarders present concerning the rationale and parties responsible for the destruction of their self-built skatepark. Evasive and vague, he could acknowledge only that State Parks was aware of the popularity of skateboarding in the area. The intention of the meeting was not merely to introduce and answer questions but also to begin the process stated in the agenda of "generating ideas for the programmatic elements of the park." But the main elements of the plan—a soccer field, softball field, and facilities building—had already been agreed to in principle by NYU, State Parks, and NAG.

Prior to the second public forum, one month later at the Brooklyn Brewery (two blocks from BEDT), many of the nearly 100 people in attendance mingled, snacked, and drank while studying several large boards and a model prepared by Sasaki. The three schematic design options were each represented by a board. Each featured a softball field, a soccer field, and bleacher seating for 1,500 spectators with the same location, dimensions, and orientation. A building to house equipment, locker rooms, and public facilities also figured strongly in all three schemes, while each contained only a limited amount of general-use space, mostly in a modest-sized spot along the river, respectively developed as a playground, picnic area, and amphitheater. The schemes elicited tepid reviews from some audience members who were beginning to realize that the plan was dominated by the non-negotiable programs required by NYU. Some attendees were also disturbed by the lack of meaningful decisions concerning park design that were left to be made collectively.

The twenty skateboarders, most of whom showed up with their skateboards, seemed to have the biggest issue, as none of the three options contained a skatepark. As the formal presentation began and expressions of gratitude were dispensed with, Moogan became aware of this palpable sense of dissatisfaction. He hastily acknowledged that the plan would not feature a skatepark but said that he had "good news." The state, he said, would be working with the city to build a skatepark at a city-owned property in the neighborhood, but it was too early to discuss or share important details, such as its location. Seemingly pacified, the skateboarders remained quiet throughout the rest of the meeting.

The forum proceeded and Madden guided the audience through the details of the three schematic designs and treatment options for the water's edge and park installations, such as fences and lighting. Moogan and Marman described the status of the ongoing environmental review. Well aware that many in this audience were particularly wary of anything concerning environmental hazards, Moogan cautioned that the forthcoming report was not yet complete, but said it would likely conclude that a few buried oil tanks would need to be removed and the "relatively benign" levels of contaminants in the soil could be remediated without jeopardizing or delaying the project.

After the presentations, Madden reminded audience members that they needed to select their *preferred* scheme by the end of the meeting. Up to this point there had been no discussion about just how attendees would decide, and few, if any, were at that moment prepared to select among the options laid before them. While mostly polite, audience members instead used the opportunity to take issue with the program and design of the park. Several asked questions or made suggestions concerning how general-use space could be maximized within the design, including reducing the size of the ball fields and bleacher seating. Another asked why the facilities building had to be 15,000 to 18,000 square feet, which prompted a suggestion that equipment storage could occur under the bleachers, lessening the need for a large building. Madden said that they would consider reducing the impact of the building and bleachers, but the size and placement of the two sports fields were not debatable. An audience member again asked about the fate of the two piers at North 9th Street. Someone else recalled that those piers were (mostly) intact a few years earlier and were long used informally for fishing, sunbathing, and taking in the views. Moogan said the piers were not part of the project and there was no money in the budget to rebuild them. They were *city*, not *state*, property, he added, noting that the state would support a city-funded effort to rebuild them.

A related issue, brought up frequently by the Friends throughout these forums, concerned the possibility of rebuilding the bulkhead and reclaiming some of the land lost to erosion over the past decade. Moogan answered that it was not possible to reclaim this lost land; multiple federal and state environmental laws made it difficult to re-extend the shore once a body of water has reclaimed a previously filled area. As for how the water would meet the land, Madden expressed surprise that some audience members were not happy with the proposed design of this edge, which sought to build upon the informal and intimate nature of the shore as it then existed. The treatment options included ripraps and graded banks that allowed for some interaction with the water. Apparently uncharmed by BEDT's inadvertent beach, one questioner noted that "the community deserved" an esplanade similar to what could be found in Battery Park City in Manhattan. Moogan again noted that funding was limited and an esplanade required lengthy permitting from the Army Corps of Engineers and the state Department of Environmental Conservation.

Audience members also expressed dissatisfaction with the state's decision not to include in the plan the privately owned "in-holding" parcel. The property was a small three-story building (containing illegal residential apartments) located in the middle of the Kent Avenue frontage of the park, potentially preventing the most efficient layout of the two sports fields.[52] As he had done previously, Moogan explained that the state was interested in purchasing the parcel if funding was available and the price was right, but for now they had to assume it would not be part of the park.

While the size of the sports fields was the primary concern among attendees, there was little discussion and few answers about *how* the fields would be managed. When someone asked about the "spontaneous use" of the fields for pickup games, non-athletic activities, or by the Hungry March Band (though none of its members were present), Moogan replied that there would be time allotted for "community groups" but declined to say how such groups would place themselves on the schedule. About the potential for nighttime use, Moogan answered that for special events, like July 4th fireworks, the park could be open beyond dusk, but the general hours of operation would be consistent with those of other state parks, which are open from dawn to dusk. Moogan and Madden also stuck to the mantra that was repeated throughout all three meetings: that the use of the fields was to be divided between "the community" and NYU, with community using the fields 51 percent of the time and NYU 49 percent, and that NYU would have "priority" during the academic year and the community would have priority during the non-academic year. What exactly did having "priority" mean in terms of the use of these facilities? Who would determine and monitor the scheduling, making sure that all parties would receive their contractual share? Who would decide which members of "the community" would be able to use the fields and when? Many resident participants were so focused on the designs that they seemed to lose sight of these governance issues.

With many issues unsettled, the Friends realized that little negotiation, decision making, or resolution of responsibilities could be accomplished within the more purely public structure of the meetings. They decided to develop their own proposal outside of this process while continuing to object publicly to what they saw as the more egregious aspects of the State Parks–NYU plan. Drawing upon local talent that included artists, designers, and a landscape architect, they organized their own design committee to analyze, critique, and develop alternatives to the plan that could satisfy the needs of all stakeholders, including NYU.

The eighty people gathered in the Brooklyn Brewery for the last meeting quickly found out that Jim Moogan had taken another job and was no longer representing the state. His interim replacement, Warren Holliday, had driven down from State Parks headquarters in Albany that afternoon and was still learning the particulars of the project. He said that eventually someone from the regional office would assume the responsibilities that Moogan once held. As the meeting began, one of the Friends whispered in my ear that they were disappointed that the consultants had failed to act upon or modify the plan according to any of the changes suggested by the Friends' design committee. Indeed, the graphical material on display, including the three schematic design options, seemed to be identical to those of the preceding session. To help press the point, one of the Friends distributed slips of paper to its members each with a different question written on it, to be asked at an appropriate moment.

The Friends again pushed for increasing the space dedicated to general public use. At opportune moments, they asked the consultants to reconsider previously made suggestions: Rebuild the piers at North 9th Street, rebuild the bulkhead to its farthest extent (the Friends calculated that this would add more than 45,000 square feet to the size of the park), reduce the size of the sports fields or include the "in-holding" parcel on Kent Avenue. Holliday replied that none of these suggestions was likely to be feasible but said the state would explore the possibility of building a mini-pier platform at the end of North 7th Street.

Concerning access and security, one attendee wanted to know why it was necessary to have two sets of fences, one around the perimeter of the property and then others around the individual fields. Madden said the interior fences were necessary to keep balls from escaping the playing area. Another person pointed out that the new Gantry Plaza State Park, a mile to the north on the Queens West waterfront, had no gates or fencing, so why should this park be treated any differently? Holliday said that State Parks needed to "protect the property." To a similar question, Holliday responded that the gates to individual fields would likely remain open when these fields were not being used by NYU or community leagues.

The size of the sports fields continued to dominate the discourse. After someone asked if the fields could be reduced and still be in compliance with the NCAA, Madden replied that the fields would *not* be the "maximum," only

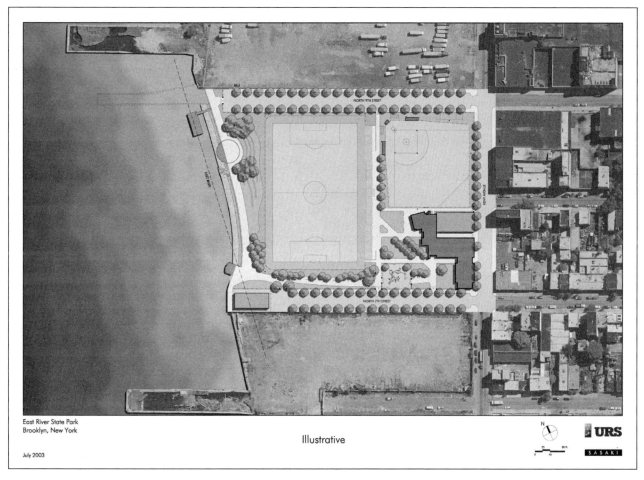

An unrealized plan by Sasaki Associates for the part of the terminal that would ultimately become East River State Park. (Graphic by Sasaki Associates, 2003.)

the "optimum," size for competition. Someone raised the issue again, noting that the Friends' design committee had calculated that approximately 56 percent of the park was dedicated to the sports fields and the facilities building, leaving only 44 percent for more purely public areas and circulation. However, this individual noted, much of this public area was in the form of residual or leftover spaces that were too small or oddly configured for significant recreational use. Could NYU live with sports fields that were the "minimum" allowable size for NCAA competition as opposed to the "optimum" standard that was currently planned? The committee had calculated that reducing these dimensions to their minimum allowable size would yield an additional 22,000 to 25,000 square feet of general-use space.

The discussion that ensued concerning the difference between these NCAA-defined dimensional requirements was abruptly halted when an audience member stood and declared that the state bought the property to increase public waterfront park space available to local residents rather than to build athletic facilities for a Manhattan-based university. This was met with loud applause, to which Madden responded that NYU had its requirements and without the university there would be no park at all. With both confusion and tension in the room rising, NYU representative Chris Metzger quickly stepped to the podium to clarify the university's position. He repeated what others had already said: that the dimensions were not the "maximum" recommended, just "optimum," and the university was not willing to go any lower.

While many of the Friends left the meeting dissatisfied, they were still committed to working with their partners to resolve these issues. Later in 2002, the Friends' design committee also produced *Form and Matter*, a document that offered alternative concepts for the design of the park.[53] With its many original analyses, illustrations, and photographs, the plan, Cathleen said, was well received by State Parks and their consultants.

Leaving the agreed-upon park program intact, *Form and Matter* argued that the terminal could still be a "model riverfront development through the integration of innovative science, landscape design, community history and citizen participation" and "serve as a teaching tool" for sustainable practices. While its goals were lofty, in essence the document presented a catalogue of mostly modest ideas that could be incorporated into the design of the park. Consistent with previously voiced concerns, it contemplated reductions in size and more efficient arrangements of the sports fields, ecologically sensitive treatments of the water's edge, the incorporation of green infrastructure, and potential programming that would emphasize environmental education, local history, and art. Its programmatic suggestions also included a tidal pool, oyster farm, "green" water storm water filtration, solar and wind power generation, earthworks and interactive sculpture, engaging play equipment, and a community garden. While *Form and Matter* did not substantially address the vernacular use of the waterfront in recent years, it did suggest programming and design that would "allow for a maximum of open space leaving the how and what up to the visitors."

The Friends also continued to lobby for the purchase of the "in-holding" parcel, and by September, State Parks had agreed to pursue the property.[54] But negotiations with the parcel's owner never proceeded, and by mid-2003, state budget cuts and a spending freeze stopped all planning work on the park. A few months after the public meetings, a member of the Friends' design committee told me there was still dissatisfaction with the plan, but the group had decided not to oppose it. Many of the Friends had decided to focus their energy on a more pressing waterfront issue: fighting the proposed power plant just three blocks to the north. The Friends also believed that the State Parks–NYU sports facility could be leveraged into obtaining a much larger waterfront recreation space, if New York were selected as host of the 2012 Olympic Games.

Backed by a powerful coalition of civic and business interests, the New York Olympic bid was gaining momentum.[55] In July 2002, as the partnership was struggling to realize a plan that would satisfy both the university's concerns and neighborhood interests, New York was selected over San Francisco to represent the United States in the final bidding to be host city of the 2012 games. The 600-page plan submitted by NYC2012 envisioned building the aquatics center and beach volleyball venue on the Northside waterfront, using the two-block state park property and additional property purchases to the north. The 24-acre venue would stretch from North 7th to North 14th streets, incorporating the two-block State Park site *and* the rest of the northern portion of the original BEDT property (owned by Brodsky and Silverman), plus all the properties west of Kent Avenue, north to the Bushwick Inlet. The entire site would be turned back over to the city at the conclusion of the games and rededicated as a multipurpose public park. If the city were selected, the locals would achieve two of their goals simultaneously: The amount of waterfront park space would be greatly enlarged, and the power plant (proposed for the Inlet property) would be defeated. It was not clear how the State Parks–NYU partnership and its resulting design might play into the dynamic of the proposed larger Olympic facility, but new NYU President John Sexton was an enthusiastic supporter of bringing the Olympics to the city and sat on the NYC2012 ethics committee. By April 2003, there had been only "preliminary conversations" between the university and NYC2012, and the final selection by the International Olympic committee was still more than two years away.[56]

Even as the Olympic bid represented momentum toward creating a much greater expanse of waterfront parkland, the Friends continued to advocate for their interests within the more limited footprint of the State Parks–NYU plan. During the spring and summer of 2003, the Friends continued to generate new ideas for the park and communicate regularly with their development partners even as work was officially suspended because of state budget cuts. By the fall, the Friends learned that NYU had pulled out of the partnership.

The partnership's dissolution was announced with none of the fanfare of its formation. There were no press releases or major newspaper coverage. Apparently the university pulled out because it could not reach consensus on the design and use of the park working with State Parks and area residents.[57] The heralded partnership had failed. While few wanted to discuss the failure, many of the Friends viewed it in a positive light. They were thankful that the university had lent the money to the Trust for Public Land that had enabled the sale, but without NYU the project was far from doomed. With State Parks still in ownership of the site, the Friends felt that they could build upon their efforts over the past two years and now get the park they really wanted.

The Friends were not the only ones feeling a sense of relief. Cathleen said that State Parks had also been disappointed by the designs generated by the consultants and their inability to identify the measures and cost estimates needed to open the park for safe interim use.[58] Absent formal pronouncements, State Parks was now apparently committed to both a more locally generated long-term design and some form of interim use even if the park itself was less than the grand waterfront space they once had promised. State Parks and the Friends would soon convene another meeting with elected officials and representatives from neighborhood groups to identify potential sources of money for interim and permanent improvements. By December, the Friends received additional good news: The J. M. Kaplan Fund had decided to the fund their grant request. The $30,000 award would help underwrite their continued planning efforts and pay for a design competition for the park.

Partnership, Public Safety, and the End of Informal Recreation at BEDT

While the Friends spent much of 2003 and 2004 building their organization and generating ideas for the park's design and use, less informal activity was occurring at the terminal itself. Incremental interim development had claimed the blocks immediately to the south and north of the State Parks property. In 2000, the bifurcated BEDT site was seven blocks large. USA waste was using one of the three blocks south of North 7th Street (two of which it owned) for its waste transfer operation, the other two for equipment storage, staging, and parking. This also allowed for some unauthorized appropriation of the space adjacent to the waterfront for recreation and other uses on these blocks. The four-block expanse to the north was more open territory, the "make your own experience" space colonized by the people whose stories are documented in much of this book. By 2004, the accessible part of the terminal was much smaller. At the south side of BEDT, the transfer station was gone. In its place, though, was a large parking lot leased to the New York City Sheriff's Department, which it used for impounded vehicles. On the northernmost blocks of the terminal (between North 9th and North 11th streets) was another impound lot, 4Gs's truck parking, and the CitiStorage warehouse.

By 2004, it was also becoming more difficult to access and use the remaining two blocks owned by State Parks. The main gate of the site on North 7th Street was locked most of the time, and those who ventured through one of the holes in the fences risked a ticket or arrest from local police, who periodically patrolled the site on foot. Thus, most of the groups or individuals I'd interviewed over the previous four years had gone elsewhere. State Parks officials had little sympathy for informal recreators or those living on this waterfront. They kept the gates shut and the police on notice that the future park was off-limits.

Since the beginning of the decade, I had wanted to better understand State Parks' vision for the terminal and the policies that would guide its development and governance. Multiple state officials denied requests for an interview or to answer questions by e-mail or over the phone. They also refused to provide me with plan documents, agreements, contracts, or communications that might have explained their vision, development strategies, or policies. (In 2011, State Parks finally consented to an interview session, but I was still forced to file a Freedom of Information Law request for project documents; see Chapter 8.) Even without an interview, however, their perspective—communicated through press releases, presentations, and discussions during public meetings and quotation in the press—was reasonably clear. They viewed their own actions in near-heroic terms, promising to provide long-aggrieved residents with access to the waterfront and recreational space where there had previously been none. Pataki's 2000 press release about the partnership heralded state actions:

> A new waterfront park for Brooklyn will breathe new life into the community and surrounding neighborhoods, providing open space for residents to enjoy and much needed playing fields for university students' outdoor athletic activities. By converting this underused site into a recreational opportunity for the community, we are taking one more step toward re-connecting residents and visitors with one of New York State's most important waterfront resources.[59]

During the public forums, state officials discussed the plan and partnership in a tone and tenor consistent with the governor's announcement. Jim Moogan, the Regional Director of State Parks in 2001 and early 2002, rarely displayed any sense of modesty or intimate knowledge of the local context. He repeatedly described the park plan in superlatives; it was a "win-win situation," and the sports fields would be "state of the art," he boasted. In response to nearly every resident suggestion made during public forums, he said that he or his colleagues would "look into" it. Yet few of these suggestions were incorporated into the NYU partnership plan or the "in-place" park that was ultimately developed and opened at the terminal in 2007.

In all of the meetings and communications, state representatives refused to acknowledge that the vernacular users of BEDT had created environments that were special and in some cases extraordinary, and that they valued the terminal for more than its views and the scarcity of traditional recreation spaces in the area. Warren Holliday expressed the state's perspective in an e-mail message sent to the Friends group in July 2002:

> Note that an all agency meeting was held on the site yesterday to seek cooperation for cleaning up the site, clearing up the brush and opening up site lines for police patrols. It appears that the site has become a haven for the homeless and for crack parties.

To the state, BEDT was derelict, in need of cleaning and full of undesirable users, the presence of whom threatened more generally lawful people who desired a safe waterfront park experience. Later I e-mailed Warren to ask specifically about the state's view of some of the interesting uses of the terminal over the past years, including fairly unobjectionable activities such as marching band practices and art installations. I later asked these same questions of three other state officials, but they all declined to respond. Eventually I was able to reach Wendy Gibson, State Parks' Director of Public Affairs, by phone, but she was evasive and our conversation lasted less than two minutes. She did say that the state was "not in the business of providing skateparks" and noted that they needed "to protect the park and provide for public safety."

During the 2001 community walkthrough, Moogan referred to the recreation space planned for BEDT as an "economically insulated park operation," meaning that NYU was going to pay for yearly maintenance and management costs. Budgetary constraints and political expediency were the driving forces behind the NYU partnership. On several occasions, Moogan boasted that the $8.3 million that New York state paid for the BEDT property was the most expensive land acquisition in state history (on a per-acre basis). While the acquisition costs may have been a record, total state investment in BEDT totaling $11.3 million was dwarfed by its investments in other New York City park projects that began during the late 1990s and early 2000s, including $85 million in Brooklyn Bridge Park and $100 million in Hudson River Park.[60]

When the site cleanup that Holliday had referred to was carried out (actually by a city agency), it cleared most of the vegetation that so many people had appreciated, including a few trees that had been planted by NAG members during one of their own cleanup events in 1999. What Holliday had referred to as "brush," others called "nature." The cleanup did not ultimately remove the brush as much as push it around, with vegetation, debris, and the dwellings built by the homeless (their residents now evicted) indiscriminately bulldozed into fifteen-foot mounds. This left BEDT bereft of green except along some of the edges and crevices that could not be reached with earth-moving equipment. A year later, those mounds were still standing, though they were now covered with thick layers of weeds. Nature had returned and so too had some of the informal recreators. The homeless returned too, as I found a few men living in a small tent in an inconspicuous spot.

Whose Waterfront? Informal Communities and the Limits of Advocacy

Tempered by their experience and history, the Friends were also cautious about pushing the informal "make your own experience" aspect of BEDT. A few used the waterfront in such a way and others appreciated it, but in establishing a formal vision for the terminal and in negotiations with their development partners, politics was for now separate from on-the-ground experience, and the Friends pursued their vision through traditional channels of community action, mostly removed from the locus of BEDT in the immediate present. Perspectives among the Friends were far from uniform, and some shared the view of State Parks that the terminal was derelict and its users were mostly engaged in unwholesome or illegal acts. Others were just hoping that the formal recreation space they were promised would be better, grander, safer, and worth waiting for. They would have to wait for several years, as the site itself did not officially open for recreation until summer 2007—and even then it was far from the park space they had envisioned.

The Friends continued to work patiently toward achieving their community-based vision for the park while awaiting the fate of New York's Olympic bid, the news of which would be announced in August 2005. Meanwhile, larger actions away from the terminal were reshaping the political landscape and potentially offered a far larger transformation in the form and use of the waterfront. The plan to build a power plant on the Bushwick Inlet and the Bloomberg administration's waterfront rezoning proposal were now the priorities of the resident activists of North Brooklyn.

The Northside residents who formed NAG and later the Friends of BEDT State Park adopted a pragmatic approach toward the terminal's redevelopment. After enduring and emerging victorious from the long campaign to end waste transfer, they immediately refocused their concerns on other perceived threats to their larger vision, mainly the power plant and the rezoning, the details of which were just beginning to emerge at the time of the breakup of the NYU partnership. Thus, their vision for the waterfront was tempered with the knowledge that there were many redevelopment possibilities and those that were most feasible and expedient involved undesirable or potentially noxious uses allowed under the site's M-zoning. They were also concerned that a large rezoning would open up the entire Williamsburg waterfront to residential development without any reasonably-sized waterfront parks and only the minimum permissible open space at the edge of the river as required by zoning. The Bloomberg administration's rezoning proposal, introduced in 2003, served to confirm the validity of their larger set of strategies, which focused on a comprehensive vision for the entire CD #1 waterfront and argued for maximum public access and park space, with less concern about design and program details. So when the earlier partnership with NYU seemed less than ideal, these resident advocates still embraced it. They believed that the waterfront's larger potential for locally oriented public recreation was under far greater threat from those who viewed the same stretch of the river as a good place for potentially noxious and other unwanted uses.

During the public meetings and my interviews and conversations, Williamsburg's resident activists frequently used the word "community" as a way to claim possession of the waterfront. As Bob Bratko said to me, "This has always been the community's waterfront." But my experience with other BEDT constituencies, including those that did not regularly participate in CD #1 proceedings, suggested that "the community" for the waterfront was far broader, more eclectic, and less unified than that invoked by the Friends. These activists could speak for only so many, and their sense of community was largely formed around local residents who shared geography and a traditional sense of advocacy and betterment. The waterfront had no one rightful community, and assertions otherwise, implicit or explicit, were often at the expense of other constituencies that might have a similar claim. But those who did not assert themselves within the established forums of community politics would simply lose their claims. With the exception of the skateboarders, the eclectic users of the accidental park, when informed, gave State Parks' public planning process only a shrug. On the ground and in the moment, these informal recreators had asserted their right to occupy and use the BEDT property. Now removed from the immediacy of their occupations, they had acquiesced.

Without their presence, the community of the park and waterfront was defined by those residents and others who partook in these exercises.

The Friends did not forcefully advocate for these absent, informal constituencies, but this was less a conscious exclusion than a consequence of making the most of already limited circumstances. And some remained hopeful that the new park would still have the capacity to accommodate spontaneous use, including those that had made it a destination for both eclectic and everyday leisure practices. But with many interests to balance, advocacy for informal uses fell toward the bottom of their priorities. In their minds, the NYU partnership was, at least for a while, the best that could be achieved given the larger realm of possibilities. If the waterfront lost some of its eclectic character and characters, that was a reasonable price to pay in return for the guarantee that some of the BEDT site would be forever open to conventional passive uses or sports.

CHAPTER 8

UNPLANNED POSTSCRIPT

Dogs, Sunsets, Rock Bands, and the Governance of a Waterfront Park

IN EARLY 2005, I received an unexpected e-mail from Chip Place, the recently hired director of Capital Facilities and Planning for the New York City Regional Office of State Parks. He had inherited the BEDT park project and was interested in my research. Now that the NYU partnership was dead, he wanted to discuss ideas for the design and program of the terminal, particularly those involving interim use. I had been pursuing State Parks for more than three years at that point; my numerous requests for interviews and planning documents were all declined, unanswered, or passed along to another party in the bureaucracy without ultimate satisfaction. Now they were calling me for something— an interesting development. I called Chip back and we chatted. I suggested they could inexpensively craft a park with minimal improvements, leaving the landscape more or less as is. The conversation was pleasant and I forwarded him my 2002 article "Brooklyn's Vernacular Waterfront." Knowing that Chip represented an agency that would likely find my ideas unworkable, I did not push hard. Given the state's relative inaction as owner of the site over the preceding years, I thought it would wait for another partnership to emerge—even if it took several more years—and then launch a new plan that might transform the waterfront into something very different from the sports fields envisioned by NYU.

When I did not hear again from Chip or anyone else at State Parks during the balance of 2005, I just assumed that my ideas had indeed been dismissed. But on a visit to the terminal in May 2006 I found a landscape of freshly contoured soil imprinted with bulldozer tracks. The cobblestone streetbed of what was once North 8th Street had been partially repaired and was now flanked by a row of freshly planted seedlings. Other surfaces had been smoothed, repaired, and/ or cleaned. Attending a meeting of the Friends of BEDT State Park the next month, I formally learned that State Parks had been quietly moving forward with their own plan to open the terminal for interim or possibly longer-term use, without a partner or a grand plan. The Northside's long wait for a waterfront park was almost over.

Upon my arrival at this meeting, held at the NAG office across the street from BEDT, Cathleen Breen greeted me warmly and, as she had done in the past, invoked her own variation on an adage generated from a children's book about a little train. "I told you," she said with a smile, "it's The Little Park That Could." The five Friends in attendance excitedly discussed who should be invited to the ribbon cutting and how to set up a naming contest for the park. They also talked about commissioning one of the many graphic designers of Greenpoint and Williamsburg to create a logo for the park that would recall the BEDT Railroad diamond logo. Cathleen said they might also be able to bring back a retired BEDT engine that was apparently sitting in a Sunset Park rail yard. While excited, the Friends were also a bit apprehensive, as Chip Place would be by soon to show them the damage to the park's fledgling plantings caused by the previous week's storm.

The Friends had hoped to have the official opening on Independence Day weekend. Over the years, neighborhood residents had gathered at the water's edge, in whatever condition it was in and wherever they could find or create access, the night of July 4th to watch the fireworks display over the East River. Instead of attending, Chip phoned in. Cathleen took his call and relayed the message to us: The opening would have to be pushed to late July, to give State Parks a chance to repair the ground cover. The Friends were disappointed but understanding; some of them had been fighting for a waterfront park, in one form or another, for a dozen years, so they could wait another month or so. Ultimately it would be another year before the park would open.

Around that time I had all but given up on interviewing a State Parks official. But in 2011, I began again and reached New York City Regional Director Rachel Gordon, who eventually agreed to let me talk to Chip at their office in Manhattan. The day I met Chip for the interview at the State Office Building on 125th Street in Harlem, October 31, 2011, was nearly ten years to the day since I first asked state official Jim Moogan for such an opportunity (at the BEDT November

2001 walkthrough). The State Parks regional office was on the seventeenth floor, towering above and insulated from the hubbub of the street below. Through the wall-to-ceiling plate glass windows, I could see Central Park to the south and Marcus Garvey Park just below us to the southeast. In the distance were the East River and the elevated expressways that feed into the core of the Robert Moses–built Triborough Bridge complex atop Randall's Island. The office seemed well suited for an agency that grew out of Moses's Council of State Parks and corresponded well to his top-down style of planning.[1] But before I could get a good look, I was shunted off to Chip's desk, which was in a less prominent position closer to the core of the building and lacking a commanding view. Perhaps this location suited Chip's focused working style and attention to detail—no spectacular views to distract him from the tasks at hand. I sat down across from him and he told me the story of East River State Park, from the beginning of his involvement in the project in 2004, not long after the dissolution of the NYU partnership.

As we talked, the state's dilemma quickly became clear: How could this agency, well accustomed to command and control management and firmly ensconced within government bureaucracy, design, build, and administer a formal recreation space where an informal one formerly flourished, while *also* satisfying a range of well-invested stakeholders with divergent perspectives and expectations? This is the central question that I too struggle with in this chapter, in which I chronicle the waterfront's history from 2004 forward. Given that State Parks possesses only two of the seven blocks that once constituted the BEDT rail yard, this chapter also examines the larger transformation of the Northside waterfront, from both garbage transfer and the informal uses that I have documented to condominium towers and formally developed waterfront parks and public spaces, facilitated by the city's 2005 rezoning. As part of this action, New York City committed to the development of an additional thirty acres of waterfront parks, esplanades, and recreation spaces in Community District #1, in a combination of public and private ownership. While the largest of these spaces, Bushwick Inlet Park, is still years from completion, the first part of the park—a soccer field just north of ERSP, as well as the developer-funded three-block-long esplanade and the city's new recreation pier and ferry landing—was completed by 2012.

Informal by Necessity: Planning a Unique State Park

Chip Place had come to State Parks in 2004 from his own land-use law consulting firm located in Garrison, New York (ninety minutes north of the city). With the demise of the NYU partnership, the development of the Williamsburg waterfront park had slipped into a bit of a vacuum. It was "not high on anyone's priorities," Chip said. Reduced by budget cuts, regional staff were focused mostly on the development of Clay Pit Ponds State Park on Staten Island and the upkeep of the major parks of the region—Riverbank State Park atop a sewage treatment plant on the Hudson in West Harlem and Roberto Clemente State Park on the Harlem River in the Bronx. Anticipation of the selection of the host city for the 2012 Olympic Games (granted to London in August 2005) was also cause for delay. Had the city been awarded the Games, the terminal would have become the aquatics center and beach volleyball venue and, after, would have been transformed into a public park. Neighborhood residents viewed the millions of dollars that would be invested as a silver bullet that would result in the development of a much better and larger park, even if it was still many years off. The state viewed it similarly, and as a way to build it without spending much more money.

Both an architect and an attorney, Chip was an ideal person to champion what would become East River State Park. Earlier in the decade he had worked under Jim Moogan for the Brooklyn Bridge Park Development Corporation (Moogan had taken this position after leaving State Parks in 2002) and guided this project through its crucial stages of design, funding, and permitting. As a land-use law consultant he was also instrumental in facilitating the state's purchase of a 5,000-acre estate straddling the border of Westchester and Putnam counties that is now part of a larger nature preserve. Yet he was also sympathetic to the undesigned conditions he inherited at BEDT and knew of the site's history, before and after the demise of the transfer yard.

When Chip visited the terminal in 2004 he found it in a "totally derelict state" and noted the homeless encampments, crumbling surfaces, and piles of garbage and debris. He complained that every time workers repaired the chain link fencing that surrounds it, they would soon find freshly cut openings. Yet he also found himself drawn to this deteriorating edge of Brooklyn, captivated by not just the views but also its primal, postindustrial conditions. "It was developing an interesting quality," he said. "Nature was taking over." BEDT's exposed infrastructure also intrigued him. The loss of the bulkhead and continued erosion of the landfill behind it exposed the "cribbing"—the boxlike, wood-framed structures built incrementally over perhaps 150 years to extend the land into the water. It was like "building log cabins underneath the water," he said of this nineteenth-century construction method. Standing atop one of the warehouse foundations, which had been demolished in 1990s, he marveled at the gently sloping concrete under his feet. He had never seen a sloping building foundation before. "You could do a lot of things with these slabs," he said, noting its potential for concerts, festivals, and flea markets.

Around this time he was in regular contact with Cathleen Breen, who was still the leader of the local advocacy group that was now calling itself The Friends of the Williamsburg Waterfront Park. Similarly, the Friends were now calling the site the Williamsburg Waterfront Park as opposed to BEDT State Park (neither name really resonated with State Parks). In early 2005, Cathleen invited Chip to a waterfront community design forum hosted by the Friends and the Brooklyn Architects Collective, paid for by NAG's grant from the J. M. Kaplan Fund. Walking into the main space at the Collective's office three blocks from the terminal, he was immediately taken by the looped slide show being projected onto a wall. The presentation chronicled the history of the waterfront, including its more recent vernacular use as the "Brooklyn Riviera," and considered its future, noting both locally generated development concepts and constraints. The slide show and his dialogue with attendees, many of whom were designers or artists, served to stimulate his own imagination and resolve for a more minimally developed park. He also sensed that participating residents were eager to move forward and were not interested in another drawn-out planning process, like the one involving NYU.

Chip's approach to developing the park site would leverage the public's desire for immediate action while making the most of the state's limited resources. It also reflected and somewhat reconciled his own conflicting impulses, being both an architect and an attorney. BEDT provided an opportunity to playfully engage an interesting urban landscape but one in which he could apply his insight gained from shepherding land development and conservation projects through legal vetting and public review processes. With most of the permitting already in place by 2005, he believed he could build a park without additional administrative delays, new state appropriations, or major partnerships. His plan, as outlined in an internal document he shared with me, would be "a celebration of the site's industrial past combined with an appreciation for nature's effect on the urban landscape."[2] At the same time it recognized the need for efficiency and minimal review:

> Rather than spend a great deal of money and time on a master plan for a park it could not afford to build, the region instead focused in the interim on reclaiming what was already there. . . . [T]he approach offered . . . a cost effective means of providing safe public access to a treasured waterfront site. It also precluded complex programming decisions that inevitably become politically contentious and extremely time consuming to resolve.

With a concept and some local support, he drew upon the modest but not insignificant resources he had at his disposal. From the environmental bond fund the state had allocated $10 million for the park, but the purchase price was only $8.3 million, leaving $1.7 million for planning and development (NYU had paid for most of the planning costs associated with the previous partnership plan). The regional office had succeeded in obtaining an additional $850,000, earmarked for the park, from various city and state budget allocations, including $300,000 from the discretionary budgets of state Assemblyman Joseph Lentol, the park's greatest champion in Albany over the preceding decade (who had been instrumental in arranging for the purchase of the site), and Brooklyn Borough President Marty Markowitz. Chip thought these funds could pay for basic contracting to make the site usable in its "as is" but cleaned-up condition. The environmental review completed for the NYU plan showed that the terminal needed little remediation other than the removal of buried gas tanks and replacement of some of its fill.

He also had access to RGR Landscape, State Parks' "term consultants," who were on hire to produce drawings, studies, and plans for parks throughout the region. He asked them to create a plan that made the most of the site's informal conditions. The plan they eventually developed in November 2005 accentuated the prominence of the two intact slabs and strategically used fill to bring the level of the ground to their edges where necessary and filling in the gaps between them. It also included a number of small repairs and clearings, adding only minimal plantings. The beach, for now, would be cleaned but mostly left as-is, even if it was still eroding. While still pursuing their own larger vision for the Williamsburg waterfront through a design competition and other community outreach events, the Friends embraced RGR's plan based on Chip's "in place" concept.[3] With the plan, local support, and the remaining money in the budget, he pushed forward. By December 2005, Chip had obtained the internal approvals to put out for bid the contract for the remediation and landscaping of the park. The winning bid of $1.7 million was awarded to the WWC Construction Corporation in early 2006, and work was underway by March.

By June, State Parks was preparing for the park's imminent opening. The contractors had just laid the "hydro-seed"—the native grass mixture that was to provide ground with its green cover. The mixture has a neon green, powdery quality when it is first applied, and Chip said it looked weird against the buildings and features of the site. But the grass produced from the mixture never had a fair opportunity to take root—a torrential June storm destroyed the would-be lawn. BEDT, even in its "improved" state, did not have functioning sewers, and its capacity to absorb surface water was poor. During storms, runoff that did not make it into the river simply collected in puddles (and sometimes gave rise to wetland grasses). While the site's new landscaping had been graded to facilitate storm flow in a predictable fashion, it was overwhelmed by volume. The runoff from the slabs was particularly heavy—as was the unexpected runoff from Kent Avenue, which was then under reconstruction and had been milled down in a way that did not direct the flow of water into its catch basins. The absence of mature grass to help absorb and hold the water also contributed. Assessing the damage the day after the storm, Chip decided the park could not be opened for the July 4th weekend as planned. Cathleen Breen and other neighborhood residents also took in the mess and agreed with his assessment. "Everyone was pretty understanding," he said.

I asked Chip why it took another year to open the park. He explained that the contractor, WWC, was unwilling to do much more than reseed the grounds even though the site needed additional remediation, re-grading, and landscaping. State Parks went "back and forth" with WWC, and by the fall he had concluded that the state would not get much more from the firm. Devising a new work strategy, he sent an "in house" maintenance crew out to do some planting of meadow grasses that would help absorb runoff and enhance aesthetics. The grasses took quickly and he decided that the crew could handle other landscape repairs and plantings similarly. With the onset of winter, work was suspended until the spring with a new target of opening in advance of July 4th weekend, 2007.

The actual opening in late May was a low-key event, with local elected officials, community board members, and advocacy groups receiving letters only a few days in advance.[4] The park did not have an official name yet, even though once the word spread a steady stream residents came to the waterfront to check it out. State officials and their communications going back to at least 2000 referred to the project as "East River State Park," as do citations of it encoded into state law.

Local activists Peter Gillespie and Cathleen Breen (*far left*) join their elected leaders and representatives from State Parks and the Trust for Public Land at the ribbon cutting for East River State Park in July 2007. (Photo by Nana Taimour.)

It had been an interim name, Chip explained, adding that "B-E-D-T State Park [did] not exactly roll off the tongue." While they were committed to a public naming competition they had been planning with the Friends, once the park was open, state officials just kept calling it by its interim name. Consumed with more pressing details about its continued development and operation, they decided to stick with this name, even though there was already an East River Park on the Manhattan side of the river.

Whose Park? Conflict and Contradiction at ERSP

The official ribbon cutting was held on July 3, one year after it had initially been planned. Residents were invited on July 4th to bring their barbecues and to watch the fireworks over the river. After years of dreaming, fighting, and planning, the neighborhood had its waterfront park. But not everyone was happy. Later in July, local complaints prompted press coverage, including a *Daily News* article subtitled "Too many rules, too few hours!" "You miss the most beautiful part of the day," a resident who wanted to watch the sunset told the *News*.[5] Residents also complained about the 7:45 P.M. closing and "odd regulations" such as the ban on dogs.[6] Community Board #1 District Manager Gerald Esposito told the *Brooklyn City Paper* that residents also felt "burned by the state's lack of communication" and were dissatisfied with the park's lack of greenery and amenities. "We're not happy with the outcome," Esposito said. "They cleaned the property and planted a couple of trees—a park, that does not make." The irony that no dogs were allowed even though dog walking had been one of the pioneering and most frequent activities at the terminal before the park was opened was not lost on some of the residents. Rachel Gordon, who had been named the director of the State Parks' Regional Office only two months earlier and was a dog owner herself, defended the prohibition. "This isn't a place I would even want to take my dog," she told the *City Paper*, suggesting that canine owners use the dog run at McCarren Park.[7]

Thinking both about the park *and* the city's waterfront rezoning that had had been approved two years earlier, the *Times* took a longer view, calling it "the early fruit of an ambitious plan to refashion the North Brooklyn waterfront from a postindustrial wilderness to a bustle of high-rises, green space, and public trails."[8] Indeed, the state's plan was incremental, and over the next few years it would add improvements to the park as budget and donations allowed. By winter, State Parks had deemed the first season a success and plotted future improvements, including enhanced plantings, a series of interpretive plaques that honored the history of the BEDT site (installed in 2010), a small playground

The collapse of the NYU partnership enabled State Parks to craft a more minimally designed park that made use of existing building foundations and retaining walls. The concrete area in the foreground was once BEDT's locomotive repair shop (2008).

set in a new grove of trees (constructed in 2010), and solar-powered lights (installed in 2011). The playground, funded by Nestlé Juicy Juice, featured equipment evocative of BEDT's past, including a wooden train placed in alignment with the railroad tracks there previously, and made use of salvaged concrete blocks and other found materials.[9] The state, Chip said, was also committed to stabilizing the shoreline while preserving visitors' ability to touch the water. He described the eventual shoreline as a something akin to riprap but with smaller, smoother rocks—a "friendlier edge" that parkgoers could safely navigate. The state also wanted to bring a waterline down North 9th Street and into the park for watering the trees, shrubs, and grasses. (Maintenance crews had been watering plantings by connecting a hose to a fire hydrant.) This would enable State Parks to build a permanent comfort station to replace the trailer in use through the park's first years.

Chip was proud of this novel park and its engagement with the bygone transfer yard. While it was not the realization of a grand plan nor was it the sports facilities promised by the NYU partnership, he felt the park had its own postindustrial charm that well suited Williamsburg and simply honored the waterfront's history. From a planning perspective it was also less likely to break down into conflict over use, he believed. "Just by reclaiming the site at first, you don't get into a programmatic discussion," he explained. "You don't have the people who want the soccer fields versus the people who want something else—it takes all that discussion away."

The constructed park landscape had some of the same qualities as the vernacular one it had replaced. The design was incremental, still evolving; and the ultimate final design was unknown. Chip noted that the poplars now growing in various places throughout the site were unplanted, self-seeding trees—an unanticipated but intriguing development. (Some similar poplars had been taken down by state parks as part of its 2002 cleanup.) What else would blow across and ultimately take root? How would the adjacent park being developed by the city ultimately affect this one? What programming would local residents desire? And would there eventually be money to rebuild the water's edge and connect it to the East River Esplanade taking shape to the south? Chip was unable (or unwilling) to answer these questions. Instead he emphasized the state's desire for more immediately realizable, targeted improvements and programming for one year at a time only. The terminal was developing its own uncertain ecology, one that was far different from the sports-programmed park envisioned by NYU or the aquatics center and beach volley venue as envisioned by the city's Olympic bid planners.

Yet if the physical landscape mirrored the wild one from earlier in the decade only with a lot fewer weeds, the social dynamic had entirely changed. The playfulness of the state's "in place" design had not been matched with an accordingly flexible or liberal administrative policy. State Parks' concerns about safety and liability and their own established protocols offered something vastly different from the make-your-own-environment dynamic that allowed skateboarders, marching bands, and Vietnam veterans to feel at home. Most of the activities that had pioneered the reclamation of BEDT, demonstrating that the waterfront was a safe and appropriate venue for leisure and other uses, were no longer allowed. Rules forbade fishing, swimming, beer drinking, dog walking, skateboarding, loud music, and feeding of wildlife. And with its close-at-dusk policy (as implemented, it was really close-*before*-dusk), it was impossible to watch the sunset. The eclectic and not-so-eclectic pursuers of these activities were forced to go elsewhere or not engage in them. Of course the homeless, the informal constituency that garnered the most ire from state officials, were also gone.

With the condominium towers rising just to south, where a decade earlier garbage had been sorted, and inland where thousands more residential units were rising in the form of infill construction, renovations, and loft conversions, a new constituency for the park was emerging. Unburdened by a memory of the accidental park that once existed at BEDT, these new arrivals would become some of the park's most frequent users. Likewise, they would experience no sense of loss of possibility or wildness, and the park might simply seem innovative or cool to them.

Yet even as the park's popularity grew, it also continued to generate dissatisfaction among some area residents, who by mid-2008 viewed the park policies in the context of the larger physical and social dynamic that was sweeping the waterfront and the neighborhood. Spurred by the 2005 rezoning and previously existing market demand, thousands of apartment units, nearly all market-rate, were under construction or recently completed, many of them going up along or nearby the waterfront.[10] "The only way to see a million-dollar sunset in Williamsburg is to own a million-dollar condo," quipped the *Brooklyn City Paper*. Community Board member Evan Thies noted that residents had more access to the terminal "when it was an abandoned lot." Unsympathetic to longstanding locally generated traditions, State Parks continued to cling to its regulations and conventions. "We have to close at dusk because of health and safety requirements," said Rachel Gordon.[11] (With the installation of lighting fixtures in 2011, State Parks extended the hours of the park until nine during the summer.)

Later in 2008, with budget cuts looming, State Parks proposed closing ERSP for the winter and not reopening until the following spring. Assemblyman Lentol called the action "outrageous" and complained that ERSP would be the only park in the entire state system to close entirely.[12] Given the park's modest size and lack of expensive facilities, he offered an alternative, outlining an agreement he had negotiated with the city police to open and close the park each day and regularly patrol it. But state officials declined and closed the park in January to save $40,000.[13] With continued pressure from Lentol and the Friends of ERSP, as well as their pledge to help with basic maintenance tasks, State Parks reopened ERSP on March 1, one month ahead of schedule.[14]

Waterfront Rock and Roll

Unfazed by complaints and not-so-flattering reviews in local papers and blogs, State Parks took pride in the volume of visitors and tried to be locally responsive in other ways, plugging into the area's arts and performance scene.[15] The long-anticipated reconstruction of the McCarren Park Pool, which was to begin in 2009, meant that the popular Jelly NYC Pool Parties had to find another venue. For three summers (2006–8), the free concert series had been held inside the repurposed, graffiti-covered WPA-era pool, which had been closed since 1983.[16] Looking for another venue, Jelly was connected to ERSP through the Open Space Alliance (OSA) for North Brooklyn, the not-for-profit that was created in 2003 to perform various fundraising, maintenance, and programming for city parks in Community District #1. Chip had already envisioned the Slab as an ideal venue for concerts, so when OSA approached him, it seemed like an ideal marriage. The *Times* hailed the arrangement, noting that that the park had an even greater capacity than the pool, allowing for 7,500 concertgoers and would "keep the indie and eclectic spirit of McCarren alive." Like the pool, it opined, the park and surrounding area were "emblematic of the area's cultural and economic revolution." Stephanie Thayer, executive director of OSA, told the *Times* that the concerts were "a way of seeing that music continues in our neighborhood, a neighborhood that's built in part by artists and other creative people."[17]

The 2009 series, which featured concerts by noted local and not-so-local rock bands such as Mission of Burma, the Dirty Projectors, and Grizzly Bear, attended by thousands and generally praised among younger residents in the neighborhood and city, provided some logistical challenges for State Parks and OSA. At one concert, heavy winds in advance of a storm blew down part of the stage framing. No one was hurt, but the band on stage earned the ire of State Parks when they did not immediately direct people to the exits at the first sign of lightning. Chip said that State Parks was also concerned about other operational issues that had not been fully addressed during the first run of concerts, including access for emergency vehicles and insurance policies.

In 2010, when State Parks' safety concerns threatened to derail the entire concert series just weeks before it was to begin, Senator Charles Schumer stepped in and convened a series of meetings with the conflicting parties.[18] While it was highly unusual for a U.S. senator to be involved in a local park dispute that lacked federal property or funding, at Schumer's urging OSA and State Parks worked out a new agreement with Jelly. For this second season, OSA also added a series of pay concerts, billed as "fundraisers," promoted and staged by the Los Angeles–based AEG Live. OSA and State Parks also bolstered safety and security measures, creating more space near the Slab for security vehicles and better segregating of what Chip called "the beer garden" on the second slab from the main viewing area on the first. They also moved the stage to the inland end of the Slab to better protect it from wind and storms.

But as the 2010 season moved ahead, conflict continued behind the scenes. By mid-August, OSA announced it was canceling the last two Jelly concerts for the season, citing unpaid bills, a charge that Jelly denied.[19] After more pressure

In 2009 and 2010, rock fans gathered on the Slab for free concerts staged by Jelly NYC (2009).

from Schumer and Lentol, the series was reinstated five days later when Jelly paid additional money toward what OSA claimed Jelly owed. The remaining balance was paid for by adjacent property owners; Douglaston Development, the builder of the Edge condominiums to the south (on the former USA Waste portion of the terminal); and the Brodsky

State Parks bolstered safety and security measures for concerts held at ERSP during the summer of 2010.

family, which owned the Citistorage warehouse to the north. (Douglaston had also sponsored a free evening movie series.) But the larger dynamic was fundamentally not reparable. The *Times* noted that Jelly had clashed with both State Parks and the city Parks Department, which had the larger operating agreement with OSA, over a range of issues including "safety regulations, sponsorship agreements and even the lyrics of bands booked for the shows."[20]

By 2011, a growing chorus of residents wanted the concerts to end. Responding to the barrage of complaints at an April general meeting, Community Board #1 had voted unanimously to ban the waterfront concert series at ERSP, even though it had no power to do so and there was no official item on the agenda that called for such a vote.[21] By the beginning of summer, Stephanie Thayer was on the defensive, suggesting that OSA was a victim of larger resident "frustrations about the neighborhood" and larger changes in which OSA had played no part. "People have gotten mixed up in their feelings about development and gentrification, and we make for a friendly target," she told the *Times*.[22] She also noted that the recently installed $260,000 solar lighting was paid for with revenue from the concert series.

The *Times* characterized the conflict as "competing ideas about who should determine the use of public lands" that pitted younger concertgoers against older, longer-tenured residents against a backdrop of rapid neighborhood gentrification. "You can't hear yourself think," sixty-seven-year-old Genya Wolowacz complained to the *Times*. Having lived in the same North 8th Street house since 1957, she said that she spoke for her family and neighbors who were fed up with the crowds, trash, noise, and use of "the street as a toilet" before and after these events.[23] Others complained that scheduling these events on prime Sunday afternoons and some weeknights was unfair to those residents who wanted to enjoy the park without attending a concert. Ironically, the park was open past sunset for the AEG evening concerts (Jelly's were in the afternoon) but only for those who paid admission (close to $50 for the concerts). It was also open in the evening to the general public (without charge) for the movie series and a handful of special events, but most nights the park was closed. Finally, there was the larger issue of who was making decisions about the park and how these decisions were being made. Sarah Porter, a local landscape architect who had been active in both NAG and the Friends over the preceding years, complained about the lack of transparency and accountability. "It's a public park, and they're closing it off and privatizing it for people to make money," she told the *Times*.[24]

Without the Jelly concerts, OSA moved forward in 2011 with the AEG-promoted series and other more locally targeted, quieter programming. Attempting to address some of the issues generated from the previous two summers, OSA included a greater variety of music and performers, some of which were geared to children and parents, leaving more July and August weekend afternoons and evenings unprogrammed and moving the start times of the evening series up so the concerts would end earlier. Yet tensions with residents continued throughout the season and crescendoed after a September 17 concert by the jam band Widespread Panic. The concert ended around 9:40 P.M. with attendees spilling out onto neighborhood streets where potentially dozens of people consumed balloons filled with nitrous oxide. One resident shared with the *Gothamist* blog a video and letter she later sent to OSA, recounting the scene as a "lawless drug nightmare" with concertgoers "walking around like zombies holding fists of balloons" while police were nowhere to be found.[25] *Gothamist* and other blogs suggested that the resident complaints about this concert were overblown and the concert itself had taken place without violence or rowdy behavior. When the police arrived on the scene, they made no arrests and found only three discarded, empty nitrous oxide canisters.[26] (My own perspective from attending three of the free and one of the paid concerts between 2009 and 2011 was that these were peaceful events that took place without major incident or destructive behavior among attendees.) In early October, Stephanie Thayer announced at a Community Board meeting that OSA was moving the concerts out of ERSP to a location farther up the waterfront, an asphalt-covered lot that will be part of Bushwick Inlet Park.[27]

Chip did not want to discuss the termination of State Parks' relationship with OSA and its concert series, or the public dispute with Jelly from the previous summer. He did acknowledge the volume of resident complaints but more generally reasoned that the concert series had "run its course." As the promoter, OSA had been the public face of the concert series and thus received the brunt of the criticism while State Parks was more insulated. Yet since the beginning Chip and other officials had been involved in almost every detail of the concerts. Earlier he had explained to me how some of the preparation and staging worked and the degree to which State Parks attended to public health, safety, and security concerns. During the first year, the concerts were put together more "on the fly," he said, and the state had no larger agreement with OSA and Jelly. Still, Jelly's own contract, insurance policy, security arrangements, "site plan," and every other aspect of their production needed to be approved by State Parks. (Jelly would reimburse OSA for security and setup.) By the second year, the agreement with OSA was more formal and the second series with AEG required a separate set of contracts, insurance documents, security, and site plans, as did Jelly's. Even as Chip steered the conversation away from specifics, I well imagined the great volume of paperwork, the numerous people

While generating a large volume of complaints from local residents, concerts staged at ESRP were generally peaceful events enjoyed by many (2010).

who needed to see and approve every aspect of these complicated events, and the amount of back-and-forth vetting they would generate.

When I interviewed Chip that October, he promised to facilitate the fulfillment of my stalled Freedom of Information Law request for documents related to the development of the park. When my request was finally fulfilled in December 2011, five months after I had filed it, there were no documents pertaining to the two concert series, even though I had explicitly requested them. But the 2010 cancellation and then reinstatement of the Jelly concert series, covered by the press, provides a window into how State Parks and OSA approached events at ERSP.

When OSA abruptly canceled the last two of the 2010 Jelly concerts, citing unpaid bills, Jelly fired back a 1,300-word press release rebutting all claims that they had failed to live up to the terms of their contract or had acted in bad faith:

> . . . OSA's cancellation of our final show of the season refers to "fees" that were not defined in our contract, and in addition had no contracted payment schedule of any kind. These fees include beverage-sampling fees, origination fees for filming, additional security above what was contracted, extra stagehands, an additional generator for sponsor activations, and [a] barricade to be used to segregate the state park on our show days. Pursuant to the terms of the contract, JELLY was to be held responsible for any additional production fees that were incurred by OSA for Pool Party dates, but again, no mention of payment terms, or schedules of any kind. Some of the fees made sense to us

due to the scope of our shows. Other fees, however, seemed arbitrary and we simply desired to come to a reasonable conclusion. It is important to mention that OSA laid out the first additional fees, which were significant to say the very least, less than 48 hours before our first show on July 11th. It is also important to mention that we have been consistently met with additional production costs/fees throughout the summer.[28]

It was a difficult and ultimately untenable three-way partnership. While state officials like Chip thought it would be nice to enjoy a concert on the Slab while taking in its spectacular vistas and unique postindustrial characteristics and Stephanie Thayer (and OSA board members) thought the concerts would preserve and nurture the area's considerable music community and raise needed money for local park maintenance; official protocols, legally required logistic preparation, and a social-professional climate that does not easily accommodate DIY practices doomed the Jelly series. When I asked Chip if the great security and safety apparatus assembled and deployed for each concert was perhaps excessive, he quickly reminded me that the state had an obligation to "protect the public safety."

Not without generating their own controversy, AEG's concerts lasted an additional year at ERSP and, in 2012, the company was given the opportunity to restage its series on an OSA-controlled asphalt lot up Kent Avenue purchased by New York City for inclusion in Bushwick Inlet Park. But large national (and international) corporate entities such as AEG and their expensive productions were always anathema to the spirit of the waterfront and the Greenpoint and Williamsburg art and music scenes. In fact, Jelly NYC was formed as an alternative to these sorts of corporate productions. "The Pool Parties have never made us money," Jelly said in its 2010 response to OSA. "[T]hey are a labor of love that we gladly do each year because they make both us and the community happy . . . not to mention we get to see some of our favorite artists in our own backyard, for free."[29]

When Jelly staged its events inside the empty McCarren Park Pool from 2006 to 2008, the novelty of playing in a co-opted architectural relic matched the DIY tenor of Jelly's events. At ERSP, state-administered protocols significantly diminished the social vibe, even though the park itself was also an architectural relic and the views were more spectacular. Chip explained to me that net revenue from the concerts was placed in two separate accounts—one was a city account that was directed toward the maintenance and improvement of OSA-controlled parks and the other was a state account dedicated to ERSP. OSA has frequently noted that the concerts were necessary for funding the development and maintenance of ERSP and all eighteen parks it manages in the community district. While staging concerts on the waterfront, OSA was never involved in the day-to-day administration of ERSP. "It was only the concerts," Chip explained. OSA's annual statement proclaims that it raised $200,000 for ERSP over the course of 2009 and 2010, which paid for the bulk of the solar lighting, thereby allowing park visits after sunset.[30] But lights were never needed for the informal performances that took place at BEDT a decade before, and, likewise, they were not required for Jelly's daytime concerts, both at ERSP and McCarren previously. OSA's vision of improvement and spectacle was something quite different from the more locally oriented vision of Jelly, or the more accidental setting prized by the Hungry March Band and fire spinners a decade earlier.

In 2011, I tried to speak with Stephanie Thayer, the executive director of OSA, about its vision for the North Brooklyn waterfront, its partnership with State Parks, and the concert series. But after I was initially invited to a concert I was not able to make it to, she declined to respond to any of my requests for interviews or comments. Still, it was clear that she had not entirely endeared herself to Greenpoint and Williamsburg residents. The concert controversy was not the only one involving OSA at this time, but it was the most prominent. Julie Lawrence, a local planning consultant and co-chair of the formed (and retitled) "Friends of ERSP," said that many residents appreciated and supported the concerts, particularly local businesses, many of whom had been active agents for change since the garbage conflict of the 1990s and had generously contributed to NAG, the development of the state park, and other neighborhood campaigns. However, she said, the consensus among residents was that OSA, in its zeal to promote the concerts, had neglected less glamorous responsibilities such as park maintenance.

I met Julie at a Bedford Avenue café in June 2011, to discuss not just the concerts but the evolution of the park and the larger transformation of the waterfront. A Williamsburg resident since 1989, Julie was chair of the Community Board #1 Waterfront Committee during the late 1990s and early 2000s, guiding the Williamsburg Waterfront 197-a plan to fruition. Her perspective on ERSP was tempered from her experience as a veteran of many local environmental and development conflicts, including the garbage transfer station and expansion plan, and later the power plant and rezoning battles. OSA had evolved out of the rezoning and was intended (along with the city's commitment to develop Bushwick Inlet Park) to provide an effective local stake in the transformation of the waterfront it would facilitate, she explained. Acknowledging the fractious politics in CD #1 and the myriad local advocacy groups that had been pushing their own vision for the waterfront or parts thereof, the organization was to provide a unifying voice. "In theory, the OSA represents everybody," Julie said, but in practice, it was "less than democratic."

The organization had been patterned after the Central Park Conservancy and the Prospect Park Alliance, the not-for-profits that, through contracts with the city's Parks Department, handle most of the planning, development, and programming of New York's two signature parks. At Central Park, the Conservancy also handles most of the park's maintenance and daily operations. Lacking not just the famed Olmsted landscapes but also larger commitments from the city and deep-pocketed benefactors, the public–private partnership model may not be well suited for CD #1's eighteen smaller and mostly utilitarian city parks.[31] But what particularly bothered Julie was OSA's failure to be inclusive in its decision making, even as it champions itself as an organization that "has grown from an idealistic local community vision."[32]

A sunny person by nature, Julie had recently given a presentation entitled "Why the Waterfront Rezoning Isn't as Bad as We Thought It Was" and said she was happy with the ongoing development of ERSP. However, she viewed the transformation of the waterfront not just in terms of outcomes—what areas are for public use and the rules and programs by which they are developed—but in terms of process and participation, how decisions are made and who is making them. OSA was "unraveling a more collaborative form of planning and advocacy in North Brooklyn," she complained. In its incorporation OSA was accountable to its board members, not the public at large, and it was doing little to promote a shared vision for the waterfront in the district that she and many others had worked to establish through the more open collective of local stakeholders working within the city's community board structure. Given CD #1's long history of conflict over the use and redevelopment of the waterfront, there were bound to be issues with OSA. Even Julie acknowledged that there was no way to please everyone.

The wealth of news stories and blog posts about ongoing development of the North Brooklyn waterfront and the respective roles played by OSA, State Parks, and the city Parks Department surely suggests a poor public dynamic. Some people have complained that too much of the revenue generated by OSA's concert series was invested back into ERSP instead of into other neighborhood parks, while others have suggested that Community District #1 would be better off without the concerts *and* OSA.[33] The organization itself admitted that it had not been doing an entirely good job at maintaining the parks under its jurisdiction, particularly at McCarren Park, the largest it controls.[34] In 2010, OSA's concert series brought in $1.7 million, yet its annual report shows that most of the money went into the concert productions themselves, generating only about $100,000 for the maintenance and upkeep of eighteen city parks (and about $200,000 for improvements at ERSP). Another issue raised by critics has been staffing costs. OSA's statement for 2010 notes more than $130,000 in personnel costs, with most of it going to support its two full-time employees, Stephanie Thayer and her assistant. Yet Thayer also holds a full-time position in the city's Department of Parks and Recreation as Administrator of North Brooklyn Parks, for which she is also paid a regular salary. OSA has defended the arrangement, noting that Thayer's dual position provides advocacy for obtaining scarce city money and that the city has "cut funding for parks almost every year since the 1977 financial crisis." It also touts the organization's role in facilitating an "unprecedented level of investment of park projects in Greenpoint/Williamsburg" and its "close relationship with elected officials."[35]

Even now that there are no longer any large concerts at ERSP and OSA is not involved in programming, local issues with its administration have not entirely subsided. Ironically, some residents have taken issue with the solar lighting fixtures that were installed to enable visitors to use the park after dusk. One resident implored the state to remove them, questioning their aesthetics and noting that they "ruin the city vista for photographers and filmmakers" and "bounce mirrored sunlight" into adjacent apartments.[36]

Unplanned Futures and Public Investments in Williamsburg Waterfront Parks

Other issues remain unresolved as the state and the city continue to develop their respective parks and public spaces along the Williamsburg waterfront. At ERSP, state allocations for capital improvements continue to be minimal. The resolution of other issues, including those concerning design, programming, and governance, are not entirely contingent on funding but are complicated by its absence. I asked Chip Place how ERSP would physically connect with Bushwick Inlet Park to the north and the esplanade to the south. He could say only that the state and city were planning to install three sets of gates that would allow for passage back and forth between the respective parks. As for the esplanade, he said that the presence of the subway tunnel ventilation shaft complicated that potential connection. State Parks had no plans to develop the esplanade within the park itself but would try to create a coherent linkage to it across North 7th Street.

At Brooklyn Bridge Park, the city and state worked together. The previously existing Empire–Fulton Ferry State Park was merged with properties to the south and north, purchases funded by both the city and the state, with significant land donations from the Port Authority of New York and New Jersey. The entire set of formerly noncontiguous spaces has been developed as one single park, managed by the Brooklyn Bridge Park Corporation on property owned by the city (though the *Times* reported that the state was "reluctant to give up bragging rights for the park").[37] Chip had worked on that project years earlier, obtaining environmental permits and working out property transfers and legal issues. Why should ERSP and Bushwick Inlet Park be separated by fences and managed by different entities? Why couldn't there be a similar cooperative arrangement and eventual merging of the parks in Williamsburg? When I asked Chip about it, he said there were no plans to do so. Given the slow pace of development north of ERSP, state officials seemed to feel that there is little immediate need to collaborate.

While the development of Bushwick Inlet Park has been slow, the city has not been penurious, at least not recently so. It has already invested more than $143 million in the purchase of three of the six parcels (totaling sixteen of the twenty-eight acres) that will constitute the park. The Bloomberg administration has budgeted another $60 million for the remaining three parcels (twelve acres) but will likely need much more. In attempting to keep its commitment (made at the time of the 2005 rezoning) to build thirty acres of waterfront parks, the city took by eminent domain in 2007 two of the parcels it now owns. But lawsuits by the affected owners forced the city to pay a whopping $96.4 million for the block between North 9th and North 10th streets—one of the four blocks that Norman Brodsky had purchased as in late 1999 for $5 million total. (My own conservative, "back of the envelope" calculation suggests that the city paid more than sixty times what the initial Brodsky–Silverman ownership entity had paid for it.) The second parcel represents the inland half of the block

As part of the 2005 waterfront rezoning, the city agreed to develop thirty acres of waterfront parkland in CD #1. The development of Bushwick Inlet Park has been slowed by escalating property acquisition costs (2012).

The recreation pier developed by the city Department of Parks and Recreation at North 5th Street along with its connecting esplanade have become popular leisure sites that attract a range of Brooklyn residents (2010).

between North 11th and 12th streets, for which the city was forced to pay $28.7 million. In court, the city had argued that these properties were worth $13.6 million and $6.4 million, respectively. But its assessments were based on the value of these parcels as zoned for industrial use. This argument was rejected by the court, which ruled that the value should be tied to the parcels' current and more valuable residential zoning. In 2011, the city paid $18 million for the third property—the wedge-shape Bayside Oil fuel terminal north of North 12th Street. None of these prices are inclusive of the clearance and environmental remediation costs associated with these longtime industrial properties.[38]

The city's own rezoning forced it to pay many times more for these properties than was necessary. Had the Bloomberg administration negotiated these property sales or conducted the eminent domain proceedings prior to their rezoning, it would have likely paid a fraction of the cost. Had it simply followed the recommendations of the 197-a plan that it had approved in 2001, before it had announced the rezoning initiative in 2003 that stoked the waterfront's real property market, it would have paid even less. The city's poor acquisition strategies make the state's seven-acre, $8.3 million purchase of the land for ERSP a relative bargain.

While the operating budget for ERSP comes from general state funds—increases to which have enabled State Parks to hire a full-time superintendent, improve the park's maintenance, occasionally renourish its beach with sand, and keep it open throughout the year, day and evening—the city's strategy for the Inlet will rely on its partnership with OSA, which will have to generate much of its operating budget through revenue-generating programs and events and private donations. The "park pays for itself" model has run into problems at Hudson River Park and Brooklyn Bridge Park, where initially projected revenue streams have not been enough to cover ongoing development and maintenance costs. Fourteen years after development began, Hudson River Park is only 70 percent complete, and the cost of maintaining the pier pilings and structures built at or over the water's edge greatly exceeds its $15 million yearly maintenance budget.[39] Brooklyn Bridge Park's finances are stronger and the development is proceeding at a quicker pace, but both development corporations are working with the city and state to better leverage their respective assets and develop new streams of revenue, including market-rate housing and hotel and retail development.[40] In a less prominent location and smaller donor base, OSA will be even more challenged to make Bushwick Inlet Park pay for itself.

As this book goes to press, the soccer field between North 9th and 10th streets is the only portion of the Inlet assemblage that has been developed as park. A second parcel, a paved lot hemmed in by active warehouses on two sides, was the site of the 2012 concert series. The city has admitted to having no timetable for completing the property purchases and will look to sell the air rights from these parcels to adjacent property owners to defray purchase costs.[41] NAG members and other residents are again frustrated, as it might be another decade before the park is complete.[42] The city's more immediate but modest investment in the waterfront esplanade to the south of ERSP, which includes a new recreation pier at North 5th Street and a smaller ferry pier at North 6th Street, is almost complete, with a large portion of the development and maintenance costs' having been borne by the developers of the condominiums adjacent to it.

These spaces are already well used, even by those who do not live in the adjacent condominium towers, and the ferry service has proved to be popular, exceeding the city's initial ridership projections.[43]

In 2011, I discussed the continuing evolution of ERSP as well as public investments in and the larger redevelopment of the waterfront with Peter Gillespie, who still works for NAG and remains a tireless champion of local environmental causes. NAG now stands for Neighbors Allied for Good Growth, which reflects the larger transformation of Greenpoint and Williamsburg. The district's environmental issues related to its industrial past and hazardous uses persist, but the issues that garner the greatest amount of public concern are related to redevelopment, including gentrification, displacement, and affordability.

By the mid-2000s, Peter and other NAG veterans were satisfied with the plan to build a state park on part of the terminal. With the battle against the waste carters won, NAG could focus on advocating for creating more park spaces across the entire Greenpoint–Williamsburg waterfront, much of which was still up for grabs. Like many who fought for "the community" in the battle for the North Brooklyn waterfront, he had not anticipated the rise of interests that would ultimately usurp his coalition of local advocates and their democratic principles. "We were trying to control the destiny of the waterfront," Peter explained. "We thought that it was going to be our place, we'd control it and define it," he said of the terminal. "We were very naïve in a way." Peter was always a fighter for a better waterfront, one that was more public and safely accessible to local residents. Yet now that this waterfront was taking shape, he recalled the previous waterfront, which was uncertain and unsafe. He thought about the offbeat practices and events held on the "Brooklyn Riviera," including NAG's spirited protests, festivals, and waterfront cleanups. "There was an openness and possibility" that no longer exists today ". . . even though we have the park," he observed.

The informal park to which Peter referred never had a chance under state ownership. Yet the vision of a community park with shared, locally based governance that advocates had been championing for almost two decades has not fared much better. Perhaps now that the state has no major partners, it can refocus its efforts toward something closer to truly collaborative planning. At the same time, local efforts may facilitate more democratic practices for the city-owned Bushwick Inlet Park as it is developed. Even if these parks and their administrators do not allow for collaboration and shared decision making, few residents of Williamsburg would argue that they are not better off with these parks than the previous garbage transfer facility and its planned expansion that was almost realized in the late 1990s, and the power plant proposed for the Inlet in the early 2000s.

CHAPTER 9

PLANNING FOR THE UNPLANNED

Play can occur only in a condition of freedom, because it is above all doing what you want to do, when and where you want to do it.

Richard Dattner, *Design for Play*[1]

HANGING OUT WITH the Hungry March Band one afternoon in 2001, I asked one of the saxophone players, Emily, how she felt about letting her nine-year-old son, Sam, run around BEDT as they practiced. Was she worried about broken glass, rusty or sharp edges, hard surfaces, or something more unsavory lurking in the margins? "You must think that I am a terrible mom," she replied, somewhat defensively. After thinking about it some more she said, "I'm concerned about rats—I've never seen them but I know they are there." As with many vacant places in the city, particularly those along the waterfront, there were a few rats at BEDT, though not nearly as many as when the warehouses still stood. "Once, a dog scared him," she remembered.

Sam had been at nearly every rehearsal I attended that year. No one could fault Emily if she could not find an affordable babysitter; New York is an expensive place to raise children. He was a friendly, inquisitive kid and had lots of energy but was never really too wild and usually stayed close to the band. He was also very interested in the music and was developing an aptitude for the drums, another incentive for him to stay close by. Little more needed to be said and I thought Emily was through explaining, but my question had provoked some deeper reflection:

> The reason I bring him down here is because it's one of the only places where he can run around and be himself. He can draw big things and when the skateboarders were here, it was fun for him to watch what they were doing and do all the jumps on his bike and things like that. Once he used all the scrap metal and all the crazy stuff out here to make a supercomputer. He spent a long time—he picked [up] bricks and nails and paint fragments—you could say that he handled a lot of broken glass. It was fun for him. I think it's nice to come out here and not feel you're being watched—and for a kid too—it's like a place that you can really be yourself.

While Emily was worried about Sam's physical, intellectual, and creative development, those responsible for building and maintaining places for children in the city have long held a different set of concerns. Municipal parks and recreation departments have stressed safety and security above all else, creating play environments that keep children away from objects, people, or situations that can potentially cause them harm.[2] Unlike the concrete of the Slab, most of New York's playgrounds feature padded surfaces, play equipment rigorously tested for safety, and few loose objects that can be swallowed or pierce the skin. Most New York playgrounds are also enclosed by a fence, keeping them socially removed from the city around them. Rules posted at the gates of city-owned playgrounds prohibit adults without children from entering. It is hard to argue with the logic that adults who are not attending to children have no business in a playground. Yet child abductions have always been a sensational but rare occurrence in New York and elsewhere, even when the city was less safe.[3] Fear of harmful objects, surfaces and structures, and potentially dangerous strangers may isolate children from some of the richer physical and social experiences of the city. Surely the homeless men who sometimes kicked a soccer ball around with Sam while his mother practiced would not meet the litmus test of the secure playground.

There was a time when many designers, developmental psychologists, and scholars argued for something quite different from the safe playground of today. Born in the urban aftermath of World War II, the adventure playground movement advocated for play environments that offered children the freedom, the challenges, and the physical and social dynamics found in both natural and urban settings.[4] The movement purportedly began when a Danish architect noticed children in Copenhagen happily playing on vacant lots and construction sites with the tools and materials they had found lying about, rather than in the organized playgrounds nearby.[5] (William H. Whyte would make a similar discovery on the streets of Harlem, New York City, in the 1970s.[6]) The movement's champions came to believe that play sites should mimic the sorts of adventure, inquiry, and unpredictability found in these unbuilt environments.[7] The resulting playgrounds, called "workyards" in the United Kingdom, were messy places where children created through the uninhibited manipulation of "found materials"—including discarded lumber, bricks, auto tires, assorted junk, and sometimes tools like hammers and nails—made their own designs.[8] A workyard was both a constructive and destructive environment and was accordingly socially unpredictable; children were largely responsible for working out their own differences and conflicts.

While the movement in its most adventurous (and messy) form never entirely caught on in the United States, several adventure playgrounds were built in New

People of all ages need opportunities for adventure and environmental engagement (2000).

York City during the 1960s and 1970s, and it did have an impact on American playground design. New York's adventure playgrounds were more formal in nature than their looser European counterparts but still provided children with a range of physical challenges and varied opportunities to appropriate space or manipulate loose materials that mimicked both natural and urban realms.[9] But perceived risk of injury pushed these designs out of favor along with a broader range of play equipment of that era which encouraged physical exertion, exploration, and assessing risk. By the 1990s, safe playgrounds had entirely supplanted their more adventurous predecessors in New York and other American cities.[10]

Recently there has been a revival of the adventure playground ideal. With new research finding that the safe playground does little to encourage the physical, social, and cognitive development of children, designers are working toward creating more challenging play spaces.[11] This countermovement, still in its formative stages, can be seen in David Rockwell's designs for playgrounds at the South Street Seaport and in Brownsville, Brooklyn, which feature numerous fabricated plastic "loose parts" for constructive play.[12] While the playgrounds' expensive finishes and rigorous safety standards betray the more anarchic ideal of the workyard, they do retain some of its sense of unplanned possibility and may inspire more radical designs.

But the recent revival of the adventure playground ideal raises a question: Why should challenging play environments be just for children? Don't adults have the same needs for discovery, experimentation, and opportunities for both constructive and destructive acts in their leisure environments? Couldn't people of all ages benefit from unstructured and uninhibited play? This is not a radical idea; traditional urbanists such as William H. Whyte, Kevin Lynch, and Jane Jacobs have all argued for some form of this in their writings about cities and public spaces.[13] This was also, of course, what BEDT offered and why so many people found it compelling. The recreators of the North Brooklyn waterfront, young and old, were seeking this unconstrained experience, a playground for adventure, environmental engagement, and creative expression. They wanted something different from a city park where social limitation was cloaked in naturalness, grandiosity, or sustainability. They desired the "unpark" or what a range of scholars have called loose, heterotopic, insurgent, everyday, or vernacular or other space.[14]

In many respects that part of BEDT that is now East River State Park is physically similar to its vernacular predecessor, formally retaining some of its otherness and potential for adventure. Even if driven only by budgetary considerations and the collapse of partnerships, state officials eventually embraced the accidental landscape of the terminal. Rather than rebuild, they created a park by leaving it in a more or less "as is" condition, what the *Times* hailed as an "industrial era ruin" that was "half green and half concrete."[15] But the state's governance of this waterfront restructured its social dynamic and eliminated those qualities that made BEDT "other." As documented in the previous chapter, the

East River State Park is popular and retains some of the physical elements of the undesigned leisure space that preceded it (2011).

adventure playground philosophy—recreation as re-creation, creative anarchy, and unconstrained social, artistic, or political expression—is not part of State Parks' calculus.

While formally different, the park is in fact much like most other designated spaces of leisure in the city. Socially controlled, the experience of ERSP (and that of the city's esplanade to the south) is also consistent with the perspective of many commentators who have argued that commodification, privatization, globalization, simulation, and surveillance have severely constrained our endeavors and expressions within American public spaces.[16] Williamsburg waterfront recreators sought to subvert these pervasive spatial practices. Most did not view their actions as a form of rebellion but did consider BEDT as a sort of refuge: a space where these forces were suspended rather than canceled entirely.

Perhaps it was inevitable that more powerful interests would reclaim the terminal: Cities are dynamic, conditions on the ground are always subject to competing uses, and marginal conditions are usually temporary. Additionally, I have long acknowledged the contradictions of planning the unplanned, designing for the undesigned, and legitimizing the practices of people who have little desire to be legitimate.[17] Even if the undesigned social conditions of BEDT a decade ago could have been "preserved" and given legitimacy by city and state governments and made to fit within their legal umbrellas of spatial practices, leisure on this waterfront would still have been quite different. Outsider experiences come from being *outside* of the laws, protocols, or conventions of professional development and governance. As the artist Ür described, the waterfront was a place to enjoy the "disturbance to the established order of things."

So if the undesigned is mostly accidental and an anathema to accepted forms of urban governance and development, how do we plan for it? The answer is we don't—at least not in the conventional sense of planning and urban design. But the undesigned can be incorporated into a number of practices that subvert conventional ways of building and maintaining urban space. In cities like New York, such subversions will almost always be time-based, existing for a little while, maybe just moments, before being co-opted by some more powerful force.

Yet this vernacular ideal has the potential to more broadly impact urban building practices, and not just those intended for leisure. Few involved in the creation of East River State Park—including those in state and city governments and those allied in partnership—understood the accidental landscape they inherited when the state purchased part of the BEDT site. Fostering an understanding of and appreciation for the undesigned among professional and other audiences is a beginning. It is my hope that these narratives will inspire planners, designers, advocates, scholars, students, and citizens to learn from and not hastily destroy unplanned spaces and the experiences they engender. In the sections that follow, I provide some guidance on where or under what circumstances these connections to the undesigned may occur.

DIY and the Production of Space in the City

While the undesigned and unplanned have been rejected even by those who now control the Williamsburg waterfront and most public spaces in New York, do-it-yourself is quietly transforming the fabric and culture of the city. The experiments are many: design and craft collectives; skill shares; DIY concerts, parties, and nightlife; art and performance encounters in co-opted public space; critical mass bike rides; pop-up restaurants and mobile food vending; guerrilla gardens and agriculture; improvised leisure environments; and other surprising forms of adult learning, sharing, consuming, and play.[18] On any given day, thousands of New Yorkers are involved in an activity or a business that circumvents professionalism, traditional notions of commodity and profit, and, in many cases, city permits or time-honored conventions of building and exchange. For two decades, North Brooklyn has been a haven for these sorts of activities, and now with its gentrification some of the action has moved east to Bushwick and to Ridgewood, Queens.[19]

In her seminal book on "design-it-yourself" crafts and graphic and digital arts, Ellen Lupton has argued that people engage in do-it-yourself for "practical and political motivations" and "the pleasure that comes from developing an idea, making it physically real, and sharing it with other people."[20] Similarly, BEDT provided time and space for an environmental DIY. This is not at all unique to New York; I have seen many sympathetic practices, collectives, and experiments in cities across North America and elsewhere. As a concept for public space and city design, DIY practices have been neither embraced nor understood by urban leadership or practitioners. While the architecture and planning establishments promote digital design, post-urbanism, landscape urbanism, new urbanism, and sustainability, there is little call for undesigned or "incomplete" design that would allow end users to exercise spatial discretion. The great investments in the city's new leisure spaces, including those at and away from the waters' edge, including Brooklyn Bridge Park, Hudson River Park, and the High Line, make them ill suited for DIY practices. Accordingly, the unplanned will continue to exist and thrive in the margins and outside existing conventions of urban development.

A happier medium between the designed and undesigned may exist in many European cities, including Amsterdam, Copenhagen, and Berlin, where looser, make-your-own-experience practices are allowed time and space by creative policy, willful neglect, or creative circumvention of standard municipal land development and regulation practices.[21] New York, by contrast, while a tolerant and urbane city, provides a more constrained regulatory environment. The city is also not the live-and-let-live place it was decades earlier, and in the decade after September 11, it has been even less so. As a growing number of its citizens are involved in ever more creative endeavors in urban space, the practices of city government and allied development interests emphasize spatial order, safety, and control even as they promote New York as the ultimate creative city. Even in those European cities I cite, freer spatial practices are far from conflict-free. As informal places like Christiania Island in Copenhagen demonstrate, the boundaries between the professional and informal cities are constantly in flux, being renegotiated and fought over by disparate stakeholders who often see little room for compromise.[22] In cities where people want to be, there will always be spatial conflict, and outsider activities will always sit uneasily next to the conventional city.

But still it is hard for those who were a party to the experiences that I document in this book not to see the stark contrast between BEDT a decade ago and the state park that is there today. The accidental place that was destroyed—replaced by a pleasant waterfront park with some of its old, crumbling landscape still "intact"—was unique, vital, and entirely fitting the constantly promoted ideal of Brooklyn as a creative, diverse, and provocative urban center.

Can urban leadership, planning, and design professionals and advocates make unplanned or DIY practices more common and less exceptional, or better exploit opportunities to create "otherly" spaces? Doing so will surely be a challenge. In the years since I first began thinking about the unplanned and documenting the Williamsburg waterfront, I have received both encouragement and dismissal from my peers. When I showed my photographs to and talked about the terminal with planners, architects, academics, artists, activists, and students, they often became quite excited and sometimes countered with their own stories of sites where the undesigned occurs. It was easy for them to recognize that these informal sites were compelling, and I rarely had to belabor or argue the point. At the same time, planners and designers, and many students training to be so, were unwilling or unable to connect these ideas directly to their own practices. When I casually showed some photos to one of my former colleagues at the Department of City Planning, he replied, "Dan, this is great but we live in the real world here. We can't base city policy on this," and made reference to environmental and public-safety issues. Others similarly noted that free spaces cannot exist in New York and elsewhere because of "insurance and liability."

I am sympathetic to this point of view. Urban planners and designers (particularly those who work in the public sector for major cities) have little choice but to follow the directives of their supervisors, many of whom are political appointees and arc not even trained in the urban arts. Given that those who are outside municipal government and serve as advocates for progressive urban practices have been largely preoccupied with sustainability and more traditional notions of equity, it is unlikely that the "unpark" will be championed anytime soon by these city builders, policymakers, and advocates. So if there is a rallying cry for revolution here, it is with urban citizens. I hope that those who have even the slightest insurgent impulse will be inspired by the narratives I have documented. Take to the streets, the sidewalks, the waterfront, the vacant lots, and residual spaces—even official city parks. Subvert, co-opt, occupy, and colonize. As the Occupy Wall Street movement showed during 2011, even those spaces that are well trafficked and are of high value can be reclaimed temporarily or in a moment by insurgent protagonists. And do not wait. The undesigned does not take place in the meeting room or in cyberspace; it is firmly rooted in on-the-ground action. And do not wait for permission; seize the moment and savor the moment when you have it.

Yet those who have the ability to affect the form and practices of city should also act. Planners and designers should find opportunities to introduce insurgent aspects to normally staid projects—however small or temporary—and use their considerable communication skills to share, promote, and create a context for the undesigned and unplanned to whatever extent possible. I strongly believe that the formal and informal, the professional and the DIY, the official and the underground can have a robust dialogue, one that may lead to more vital urban development practices. The accidental playground is not merely an ideal but a tactic, a way to think and operate.[23] The transformation will *not* come from professionals who attempt to create ever more novel designs to mimic or compete with DIY practices. It will instead come from those who facilitate the designs, programs, whims, and accidents of others. Professionals need to develop a comfort with and eventually embrace indeterminacy, incompleteness, and the unknown. They also need to use their discretion to determine when *not* to plan or design. Urban spaces filled with permanent objects, landscaping, or programs are more difficult to loosen from the practices and governing protocols that inhibit the undesigned.

Rethinking Marginality in a Creative City

The allied design and development professions have long viewed vacant or underutilized lots as something to be "assembled" into larger plots of land ready for urban development. These "assemblages" represent the future, but it is often a latent future contingent upon finding investors, making complicated property purchases and partnership agreements, and obtaining regulatory approvals such as changes in zoning or urban renewal plans. As the Williamsburg waterfront demonstrates, it can take decades. Vacant sites have great potential, but professionally determined marginality, blight, or underutilization misses local co-options, colonizations, and regenerative acts, which frequently make these places less than vacant for those who live nearby. Marginality has always been relative: One person's derelict lot is another's oasis. Not merely an undercapitalized asset or building block for some eventual revitalization plan, vacant spaces need to be considered within a greatly expanded set of meanings and possibilities that enable immediate practices and can evolve into de facto (and sometimes permanent) public spaces with vital civic functions.

The relationship between vacant and nonvacant sites is also an issue that requires reconsideration. In Williamsburg, as in SoHo and the East Village before it, creative practices flourished in part because there was an abundance of low and no-cost space available for creative endeavors. We typically think of creative colonizations in urban space as occurring in private, indoor spaces—the loft buildings, factories, warehouses, and commercial structures—where artists, designers, and musicians have the opportunity to cheaply rent or occupy space to live, work, practice, perform, and host events. Yet public (or publicly accessible) outdoor spaces are also essential to these communities. Insurgent and de facto public space practices were vital to Williamsburg's creative scene and its broader prosperity, just as the Hudson River piers were to the downtown scene in the 1970s. We now recognize this earlier art scene, which spilled from the raw lofts of lower Manhattan onto the piers, vacant lots, and the Battery Park City landfill, as being particularly vital. These marginal spaces became the sculptural, conceptual, performance, and environmental art experiments of now-lionized artists—Gordon Matta Clark, Dan Graham, Richard Serra, Vito Acconci, Laurie Anderson, and Trisha Brown, among others—and helped New York maintain its place as the art capital of the postwar world at a time when most mainstream indicators of urban health showed the city in serious decline.[24] The Williamsburg scene that began in the mid-1980s and flourished through the 1990s and early 2000s may never be as important to art critics and historians, but the scene was surely vital and continues in the 2010s even as it has been marginalized by gentrification and pushed farther east to Bushwick and elsewhere. Williamsburg's diaspora continues, and creative communities may eventually be pushed out of Bushwick as well. Already the lack of marginal space has sent New York–based artists farther afield to Philadelphia, Baltimore, Buffalo, Newark, and Paterson.[25]

Creative spatial practices are by no means limited to those people whom we typically label as creative. Gestures that alter the landscape, whether in the form of environmental art or an improvised club house, will always be anathema in Central or Prospect parks or other public spaces in which millions have been invested. Traditional urban parks, large and small, cannot possibly be all things to all constituencies. This is indeed the value of marginal public space.

Rethinking Urban Aesthetics and Nature

The same marginal conditions that are desirable for creative exploitation also form an intriguing aesthetic that challenges traditional notions of landscape harmony, beauty, and order. While there is a long cultural tradition that values these conditions for varied aesthetic pleasures, few urban development practices exploit conditions of vacancy, decay, and ruin in conception or design.[26] Some described BEDT a decade ago as an "eyesore," but others found it inspiring, relaxing, contemplative, or beautiful. Not every park or public space needs an Olmstedian design of rolling meadows, serpentine paths, meandering streams, and planting schemes that aim to be more natural than nature itself. Likewise, smaller public spaces need not be consistent with the symmetry, hierarchy, and monumentality as imagined by Daniel Burnham, the great designer and promoter of the city beautiful. Olmsted's great parks and the Beaux Arts, Burnham-esque plans of City Hall Park, Union Square, Brooklyn's Grand Army Plaza, and many smaller parks in the city, however beautiful or functional, offer only two respective ideals for the design of public spaces.

Even on cold days, people came to BEDT to experience and engage nature (2001).

A new aesthetic is emerging in the postindustrial or "landscape urbanism" designs for reclaimed sites across the United States and elsewhere.[27] In New York, these new public spaces prominently include Brooklyn Bridge Park, the High Line, and Fresh Kills Park, being built on the former Fresh Kills landfill in Staten Island. The architects and landscape architects of these projects—Michael Van Balkenburg Associates (Brooklyn Bridge Park), Diller-Scoffidio-Renfro (High Line), and James Corner Field Operations (High Line, Fresh Kills)—have embraced and creatively altered these landscapes in a way that both disturbs and builds upon Olmstedian and "city beautiful" traditions. These parks are compelling reclamations of urban land to serve the needs of the contemporary city. Their perfected execution, however, does not allow for the messy aesthetics generated by undesigned agents and anarchic experiments in the use, occupation, and alteration of urban space. Additionally, their great expense makes the sort of design and administrative strategies unreplicable for all but the wealthiest public clients. The 85-acre Brooklyn Bridge Park, developed atop a 1.3-mile stretch of piers and former port properties, cost an estimated $350 million to develop and costs another $16 million a year to operate and maintain.[28] The estimated development cost for the High Line, a 1.5-mile linear park built atop a vacant elevated train viaduct, is more than $242 million.[29] The property purchases alone for less than 60 percent of the future Bushwick Inlet Park have cost New York city more than $143 million. Achieving balance between the designed and the undesigned in perhaps a hybrid form of public space has the potential to provide more cost-effective options than the expensive parks that are now championed by urban leadership, advocates, and designers. It will also enable a range of projects in cities where there is little or no money to build or maintain new parks.

Like conventional conceptions of beauty, how we think about nature in urban settings has been limited to a narrow set of ideals. Derived from the Olmstedian ideal of natural-looking landscapes seemingly devoid of significant human influence, nature in urban parks is something to appreciate rather than to use. A walk through the more wooded areas of Central or Prospect Park will surely confirm this: "Restoration areas" are plentiful; you can look but you can't touch and you must stay on the path.[30] We can admire and enjoy nature only from trails, walkways, park drives, and designated areas of recreation; untrammeled nature is always the best kind.

The issue of nature *in* and *of* the city has long been a topic for scholarship, and we have somewhat begrudgingly begun to accept cities as a whole as "natural."[31] Yet the way many urban parks are designed and maintained still separates city and nature as if they are mutually incompatible. Thus far I have attributed much of this unhealthy legacy to Olmsted, but it is perhaps part of a longer, culturally rooted mistrust of cities in America and the seeming incompatibility of the urban endeavor with "natural," traditional, or preindustrial landscapes.[32] In designing the great American urban park, Olmsted was reacting to the often horrific environmental and social conditions of the nineteenth-century city. He envisioned parks as a respite from city life, believing that the salubrious effects derived from the insertion of pastoral landscapes within cities could lift urban dwellers physically, socially, and spiritually and foster a more democratic and prosperous society.[33]

A century and a half after Olmsted and Calvert Vaux designed Central Park, New York and American cities on the whole could not be more different. Noxious industry is mostly gone, and most U.S. cities have never been more green. Yet we still seem to think of nature in parks in some ideally imagined state of purity where natural ecologies must play out devoid of human presence. The appeal of the untrammeled landscape, the forest primeval or the Garden of Eden, has surely helped foster a sense of responsibility and conservation that we see in the creation of large urban parks as well as in the American National Park system and other federal conservation programs. But systems designed with this romantic vision of nature, however powerful or culturally ingrained, are not entirely realistic or compatible with urban life and limit creative impulses. Urban nature must respond to a broader set of needs and be inclusive of a greater variety of human actors.

Even as we now realize the need for sustainability and reimagine parks as vital components of larger infrastructural and social systems, pliability is limited to park professionals.[34] Only the designers, engineers, horticulturalists, or park managers can change the form of urban parks. Such creative play is limited for everyone else, who are to appreciate these systems for their aesthetic properties, as settings for recreational activities, or for the satisfaction gained knowing they support larger communal goods, such as energy efficiency, the use of recycled materials, or local biodiversity. The dazzling array of plantings atop the High Line, many selected for their ability to withstand and thrive in difficult growing conditions as well as for their visual juxtaposition to their intensely urban context, is something to enjoy and savor. However, these plantings have been selected *for us*, and the activity of planting itself and most other aspects of its design, even those that are changing or evolving, is off-limits to visitors. The sheer cost (in both its development and upkeep) of the High Line and the city's other new postindustrial parks provides a strong incentive for management policies that limit or prohibit alterations by park visitors.

The concept of nature held by BEDT recreators was less perfectly imagined, more fungible, and relative to point of view. Like the adventure playground, nature was also pliable: It allowed for immediate rearrangement, construction, and destruction. Creators and recreators found the terminal's pliability not just desirable but also exhilarating or personally regenerative. In a sense, it was a revision of the Olmstedian notion of the healthful effects of "rural" landscapes on the human spirit. Far more than scenery and fresh air, actual rural places are messy and often unstable—places where the landscape is continually altered to serve human needs, whether it is the rotation of crops and harvest practices, the adaptation of natural drainage features, or the construction of provisional buildings.[35] Likewise, contemporary urban life demands opportunities for recreation as "re-creation," and nearly all people desire some opportunity to exercise, improve, and grow through intimate interaction with and alteration of natural (or built) environments.

Those who live in a house with a yard already have these opportunities for this form of play, as do those who are members of community gardens programs. But in a crowded, competitive, and expensive city such as New York, few have either of these opportunities, and those who enjoy them hold on to them zealously. New York's community gardens, which number in the hundreds, do not come close to meeting the demand for garden space. And even today as such gardens are accepted and celebrated by city leaders, the status of many lots is still tenuous and they could eventually be redeveloped.[36] The rules and functions of individual gardens also vary widely. While creative activity within community gardens need not be limited to growing plants, these gardens cannot possibly serve all needs and few would allow for serendipitous constructions by nonmembers. Cities need the nature of community gardens, but they also need another form of nature that is more flexible, pliable, open, and available on a more ad hoc basis.

Adventure and Risk on the Waterfront and in the City

Like those who wanted to alter the landscape, many came to the Brooklyn waterfront to experience a mix of urban and natural conditions, without mediation or supervision. They were seeking a site for exploration and escape, and a place to engage their bodies and imaginations where no one would monitor or supervise their actions. As I have noted, they were seeking *other* space—a contradictory mix of utopian and dystopian ideals: outsider space, wild space, edge space, heterotopia, the badlands.[37]

For centuries the urban waterfront has functioned as a form of *other* space. We now recognize the unique biological and physical ecology of the place where land meets water and attempt to live in harmony with these earthly systems. But less understood is the waterfront's social ecology. As the city's point of entry and exit for people and goods from close and distant lands, the waterfront has always been associated with excitement, adventure, and danger. We popularly imagine and celebrate this setting and the outsider characters who have populated it: sea captains, sailors, fishermen, stevedores, gangsters, pirates, thieves, bootleggers, rum runners, stowaways, prostitutes, immigrants, schemers, and

Recreators were titillated by the sensation of being in urban space that existed *outside* of the regulations and conventions of urban development (2001).

PLANNING FOR THE UNPLANNED

dreamers. In New York, it's a milieu that has been celebrated by Walt Whitman, Joseph Mitchell, Arthur Miller, Elia Kazan, and Hubert Selby Jr., among dozens of prominent writers, artists, and filmmakers.[38] As the country's largest and most storied shipping port by almost any measure for most of the past two centuries, it's a larger-than-life place with characters and events to match. Yet the extraordinary characters and their stories sit side-by-side with smaller ones: the stories of everyday people, work and play.

Even as the activities that defined the meta-narrative of the city's waterfront since the seventeenth century (fishing, shipping, manufacturing, refining, warehousing, transit, and long-distance travel) rapidly declined in the post–World War II period, the *otherness* of that waterfront remained and was appropriated by a new set of characters—some larger than life and others not so much so. Recreators had, in fact, been appropriating the waterfront all along. Even at the zenith of freight and passenger travel and waterside industry, people have always swum, fished, and enjoyed the pleasure of being in or near the water (and even when the water quality was far worse than it is today). But as port movement and industry receded, informal leisure became, in many locations, the most culturally meaningful use to those who lived nearby.

Like the Hudson River piers decades earlier, the Williamsburg waterfront as it was used in the 1990s and early 2000s may have been one of the more spectacular waterfront sites for insurgent activity, but there were many others. For decades, city residents appropriated and colonized declining waterfronts in all five boroughs: on the piers of Red Hook and Sunset Park in Brooklyn; in the area that evolved into Socrates Sculpture Park in Queens, along the north shore of Staten Island; on former industrial and waste sites on the East River in the South Bronx; and on hundreds of waterfront parking lots, rail yards, street ends, and vacant sites.[39] With the success of the city's waterfront revitalization programs, these spaces are rapidly being replaced by residential towers, big-box stores, tourist and entertainment facilities, infrastructure, and formally planned parks.[40]

New York's great density has long been a facilitator of informal activity, not just encouraging concentrated or clustered insurgent activities along its waterfront but also greatly expanding the social possibility of such endeavors. But this *other* experience is not at all limited to New York. My own survey of Philadelphia's Delaware Riverfront as well as observations in many other American cities and emerging research and documentation from elsewhere suggest that "make your own urban experience" exists somewhere along a river or on the waterfront of every port city.[41]

(*Top*) Decaying piers allowed for intimate dialogue with the water, making them ideal for many common leisure practices (2001). (*Bottom*) The esplanade built along the edge of the former garbage transfer station enables safe enjoyment of the waterfront (2011).

While the water's edge seems to be a particularly special setting for heterotopic activity, these appropriations can happen anywhere. As a vacant site, BEDT was exceptional in many ways, but its underlying nature as an open, available, and nearby space that can be claimed by a great variety of actors is common in cities. There is a long tradition of vacant lots' serving as play sites for children and young adults, and many people I talked to within and beyond the context of this project fondly recalled childhood adventures on the vacant lots and streets of the city.[42] As Whyte and Lynch have noted, the appropriation of urban space for play creates its own vitality and occurs in the absence or presence of formal parks or playgrounds.[43] For many, the North Brooklyn waterfront was *not* about "making do" until the real parks were built. Recreators came not in spite of but *because* of the conditions that others, usually far removed from the water's edge, had deemed unfit for human leisure or other uses.

Vernacular recreators needed little of the expensive infrastructure and physical and social maintenance systems usually planned for waterfront and other urban parks. They were well aware of and thrived in the conditions around them: discomfort, danger, uncertainty, and impermanence. Many were unbothered or even titillated by perceived or real risks, environmental or social, even those whose actions were not particularly risky. Fishing, sunbathing, picnicking, walking dogs, and taking photos of the skyline, among other common activities, far outnumbered more purely thrilling or eclectic practices. I do not want to romanticize activity at the terminal as "splendor amid the ruins," "life on the edge," or "gritty" or "ghetto" conditions. These clichés cannot adequately describe the complexity of this place or the perspectives of those who inhabited it. It was certainly not an experience that everyone wanted, nor was it an Eden where all cool things always happened without friction, incident, or injury. The conditions of the undesigned are inherently unstable.

Larger sociocultural shifts have also affected these places. The longer social history of the Williamsburg waterfront, like that of the Hudson River Piers before it, shows a great range of creative and destructive activities—with predatory, wanton, or criminal behavior also occupying prominent parts of this longer narrative. The great decline in crime in Greenpoint, Williamsburg, and the city as a whole during the 1990s and early 2000s was surely a condition that brought more people to its decaying waterfront, even as the same general trends also accelerated its demise and its reconnection with established conventions, practices and regulations.

Larger concerns about social safety were only one part of a more complicated calculus of each individual recreator. The risky physical and social conditions generated by vacant, decaying space did create a milieu that many desired even if it was only to watch the sunset. As for assessing risk, many were unconcerned or simply shrugged it off. Activities such as skateboarding and playing with fire already generate certain levels of risk, regardless of where they occur, and those seeking places to do them are often unfazed by locations deemed risky by society at large. People need places within the city to experience, experiment with, and push against risk or apparent danger. For some, testing their limits is their passion and identity, whereas for others, perceived environmental risk adds stimulation and excitement to ordinary activities. There is also a political component. More than a few felt that their presence in a place where others had implicitly or explicitly told them not to go was a modest form of rebellion against the more dominant interests that govern the development and use of urban space. Others used BEDT as an explicit civic forum to express dissent or ideas outside the mainstream.

A commonsense argument about risk in public places also needs to be made. It is taken almost as an article of faith that liability concerns trump all others, and the perceived threat of a lawsuit eliminates the possibility of most unusual and many very common activities in public space. Nearly anyone who has been involved in a public space

Rules at ERSP and on the esplanade to the south (pictured) prevent many of the common and eclectic leisure practices that once took place in these respective spaces (2010).

project can attest to a public meeting in which someone said, "What if someone gets hurt?" Or, "We can't do that because of the insurance." It is beyond the scope of this book to develop policies that treat risk in public spaces sensibly, but it is well worth asking if liability or the mere chance of a lawsuit has become a reflexive crutch for saying no to things.

My experience during the planning of ERSP was that few if anyone who made statements concerning insurance and liability could explain the legal considerations involved in risk assessment and municipal and state liability as they were applied to this project. Liability was sometimes invoked as a blanket reason to keep the park site closed while state government came up with a plan, worked out funding issues, or developed administrative partnerships. State officials' vague assertions that informal activity at BEDT exposed the state to unacceptable risk were never formally substantiated. Conversely, Shantytown skateboarders argued that risk and the potential for injury were solely the responsibility of those involved. They told me that no one in the United States had ever sued anyone as a result of an injury suffered while skateboarding. It seemed like a preposterous claim, but why should it be the responsibility of local citizens possessing no specialized knowledge of the law to prove to government officials that their activities are indeed within the bounds of reasonable risk when those activities are so commonplace in cities? Perhaps the demolition of the skatepark at BEDT was justifiable, but State Parks' lack of transparency in describing its role and rationale surely does not inspire confidence that any real risk analysis was ever performed.

Other aspects of municipal liability may also benefit from reform. Urban dwellers routinely travel 20, 50, or 500 miles not merely to be away from the city but also to be *away from the rules that govern the city* and freely engage in their favorite sports and pastimes. Even as city leadership in New York and elsewhere encourages residents to plan a "staycation" or make the most of the recreational activities within the city, only some of the activities people routinely engage in while on vacation are allowed in the public space of the city. And it's not just rock climbing, bungee jumping, or other forms of thrill seeking. As New York City has aggressively seized opportunities to remake its once maritime and industrial waterfront for leisure, nearly every foot of esplanade or recreation pier it has built or rebuilt secures recreators well behind railings that keep them from getting too close to the water. The railings themselves are often covered with a grille to keep people from dangling their feet over the edge of the pier or presumably to keep children from falling off. To be close to the water, to touch or be *in* the water, is why city residents take trips to Long Island and New Jersey beaches, bays, and sounds. While the new piers that New York City has built on the southern end of the former BEDT yard are well fortified, there is hardly a pier in all the Great South Bay of Long Island that offers similar "protection" from the water.

Any number of outdoor pastimes and indulgences seem to be needlessly forbidden or restricted in New York and elsewhere. The long list of prohibitions that greets visitors to ERSP (and is posted on the esplanade and piers to the south) is emblematic of the secure protocols that govern parks and public spaces within the city. The lack of tolerance for risk also makes informal or temporary development difficult, and the apparent danger of being near the water complicates governmental liability concerns.

The city beach movement in Europe perhaps offers American cities some direction about risk and informal development. Hundreds of temporary, inexpensively developed outdoor "beaches" operated by private sector entrepreneurs on underutilized, residual, or soon-to-be developed plots of land (many but not all on urban waterfronts) have been set up across northern Europe with more than one hundred in the city of Berlin alone. As Quentin Stevens notes, the planning for these establishments bypasses the normally rigorous permitting required for conventional urban development, including those concerning franchising of public property, public access, building construction, liquor licensing, and insurance coverage. In Berlin, laws have also been modified to enable "one-stop" permitting to facilitate quick development.[44] No years of waiting for the public amenities or parks promised by large-scale development. The culture of European cities seems to be more tolerant of informal spatial practices, and such laws that enable city beaches, temporary uses in appropriated space, and, in some instances, squatting may not be easily adapted for American systems of municipal or state governance. However, sensible development policies and building codes do not treat temporary development the same as large-scale urban renewal projects.

Community-based Planning and the Unplanned

Community-based advocacy and planning has a mixed record on the Williamsburg waterfront. Led by NAG, resident advocates were able to defeat the Mayor Giuliani–backed coalition of trash-transfer interests in the 1990s and succeeded in keeping their waterfront from becoming a walled-off garbage dump. Later, local advocates defeated a proposal for a gas-fired electric and steam power plant for the Bushwick Inlet. However, when not in an entirely defensive mode, advocates were less successful. As they fought to win back their waterfront, a community-based planning process worked in parallel to generate alternative visions for that same waterfront. This process and the community-based visions it generated eventually became the 197-a plan that was approved by the city in 2001. This more modestly scaled vision of the waterfront, with ample space for industry, affordable housing, and parks, was undone four years later by the city's own rezoning initiative, which encouraged high-rise residential development with few urban design controls and less park space than residents had envisioned.

The Bloomberg administration's 160-block waterfront rezoning, passed by the City Council in 2005 with little modification, is largely the catalyst for the residential building boom that began shortly after. NAG and numerous other local advocacy groups first fought against and then attempted to negotiate with the administration to wrest some concessions. The compromise that was ultimately struck was contingent upon the provision of affordable housing and park development, with a city commitment to develop 30 acres of park space along the waterfront in Greenpoint and Williamsburg. Eight years after the measure was passed, several towers and many smaller buildings hold thousands of new residents, yet the city has yet to fulfill its commitment on building parks. As this book goes to press, the city has spent more than $143 million on property acquisitions, but only a soccer field is regularly open for use—and the eventual completion of Bushwick Inlet Park is many years away.[45] The soccer field notwithstanding, ERSP is the only full park on the Williamsburg waterfront that has been constructed and opened since 2005 (and was not a part of the thirty-acre city commitment).[46] It represents to date the most tangible success of two decades of waterfront advocacy and planning in the community district. Yet the park itself is less than 50 percent of the size envisioned in the late 1990s, and, as I have documented, local conflicts over its design, use, and programming continue to occur.

The partnership park plan that evolved during the late 1990s and early 2000s occurred at the same time the accidental playground flourished at BEDT. Yet there was a disconnect between the appropriation of informal recreators and the advocacy and community planning occurring simultaneously in the name of building a park at the terminal. While I have gone to some lengths to show how these two processes were distinct and unfolded independently of each other, there is little reason why they should have been so separated. Planning, architecture, and landscape architecture have long viewed their respective professions as a means to progressive change. Many of these practitioners have dedicated their careers to empowerment, shared decision making, and equitable practices. Yet in highly contested public environments in cities like New York, democratic ideals often disappear in negotiations and compromises in which more powerful interests have already established the terms of the debate and determined who will be allowed at the negotiating table. A decade ago, most BEDT recreators simply shrugged when I told them about the community design meetings for the planned state park. Their indifference turned out to be justified in a sense: The planning process and partnership with New York University eventually collapsed.

On the Williamsburg waterfront, the politics of appropriation was different from the politics of coordinated community action being undertaken to save that same waterfront. Accidental, incremental, and unpredictable—the "people's park," as a few dubbed it, was the continually accumulating sum of many diverse actors working independently rather than working together toward a common goal. The degree to which the stories of individual constituent groups were independent of one another made BEDT less of a "people's park" or coordinated rebellion against the dominant producers of urban space. The experience had some similar qualities to and may have eventually evolved into something like People's Park in Berkeley, but political expression was largely uncoordinated and diffuse. Whereas in Berkeley, the reclamation of the park by its owner, the University of California, provoked outrage and protest among the informal park's patrons and local advocates, there were no similar actions on the Brooklyn waterfront.[47] The park plan was embraced by local residents and there was no countermovement or "save our park" campaign to keep BEDT from being developed as a conventional state park. Likewise, most informal recreators had little inclination to fight the powers who were poised to transform the terminal.

Imperfect conditions once defined the Williamsburg waterfront (2002).

Yet the evolution of unplanned and uncoordinated activity into larger social action was occurring at BEDT, as successful informal uses formalized over time. The practices of the skateboarders and the Hungry March band were in their own way becoming part of the "institution" of the waterfront a decade ago. If these constituencies had been able to maintain their tenure at the terminal, new alliances and forms of alliance might have been possible. Both groups demonstrated a willingness to be a part of the larger politics of the waterfront: The skateboarders participated in the community design meetings of 2002, and the Hungry March Band, whose members practiced at the terminal long after other informal constituencies had left, played at several protests and occupations in connection with the larger waterfront rezoning.

Community planning on the Williamsburg waterfront and elsewhere can surely benefit from stronger connections to on-the-ground insurgent practices. Planners and advocates can better achieve their own agendas in alliance with these more activist or fringe individuals, groups, and ideas. Such connections, while fraught with contradictions and uncertainty, may also be valuable in securing a larger local stake in controversial redevelopment projects. Additionally, such alliances may incite more responsive urban or landscape designs and novel governance strategies, something far different from the top-down approach of State Parks' stewardship of ERSP and the privatized planning and management of the city parks in Community District #1 through the OSA partnership.

Valuing the Present, Living in the Moment

In contrast to urban space produced through conventional planning and design, the accidental playground that evolved on the North Brooklyn waterfront generated vitality through immediate and largely unmediated action. The waterfront was there for the claiming, and people went out and did just that without asking for permission, holding meetings, or making plans. They valued and exploited the present city as opposed to a more perfectly imagined, fairer, more prosperous or ecologically sensitive city of the future. While some dreamed, discussed, argued, developed alliances, raised money, and lobbied their elected officials, other New Yorkers just took to the waterfront to pursue their common or eclectic leisure and creative practices, or to fulfill more pressing needs. BEDT worked in the immediate present and possessed many desirable qualities that needed little enhancement. It was in a sense an adventure playground for all ages—an accidental playground where incompleteness was part of its allure. Professionals need to understand and appreciate the present as well as they can plan for or redraw the future.

As the advocates and residents of North Brooklyn continue to fight for their waterfront and must endure untold number of years before Bushwick Inlet Park is fully developed, the immediacy of the accidental could not be more striking. In this respect, New York is not tremendously different from many North American cities; traditional urban development is uncertain and takes a long time. Additionally, large-scale projects, when entirely completed, often produce very different parks, public spaces, or amenities from what was initially planned or locally promised. Why should local residents be this patient? In many cases they have no choice. But the models for public development now championed by planners and designers, whether they stress sustainability, novelty, artistry, economic prosperity, or traditional notions of equity, take years of planning and pursuit of investors, funders, land purchases, partnerships, and permits. There is only so much capital, particularly in the present era of squeezed municipal budgets and a dearth of federal money for urban development. Why not start with a different strategy that emphasizes, where appropriate, what can be accomplished in the immediate short term and make the most of local conditions and resources that are already on the ground—whether in New York City or elsewhere? It takes not just a shift in policy but a different kind of thinking among those trusted to build and maintain cities.

NOTES

Prologue

1. New York State, Office of the Governor, Press Release (June 13, 2000).
2. The oil spill, which accumulated over many decades from refining and storage facilities located along the Newtown Creek, contaminated more than fifty-two acres of Greenpoint and has greatly contributed to the contamination of the creek. See U.S. Environmental Protection Agency, "Newtown Creek/Greenpoint Oil Spill Study Brooklyn, New York" (2007).
3. NYC Department of City Planning, *Williamsburg Waterfront 197-a Plan* (approved by the City Planning Commission, December 2001; adopted by the City Council and published, 2002), p. 50.
4. The Parks Council (of New York City), *Creating Public Access to the New York Waterfront* (1990); Hunter College Graduate Urban Planning Studio, *Bridges: Greenpoint–Williamsburg Waterfront Plan* (1995); NYC Department of City Planning, *Williamsburg Waterfront 197-a Plan* (2001). See also Trust for Public Land, *New Parkland for New Yorkers* (1995).
5. A more formal opening and ribbon-cutting ceremony was held at the park on July 3, 2007.
6. NYC Department of City Planning, *Williamsburg Waterfront 197-a Plan* (2001).
7. See John Logan and Harvey Moltoch, *Urban Fortunes: The Political Economy of Place* (Berkeley, Los Angeles and London: University of California Press, 1987); Susan Fainstein, *The City Builders: Property Development in New York and London, 1980–2000* (2nd ed.) (Lawrence: University Press of Kansas, 2001); Laura Wolf-Powers, "Up-Zoning New York City's Mixed Use Neighborhoods: Property-Led Economic Development and the Anatomy of a Planning Dilemma," *Jnl. of Planning Education and Research* 24–4 (2005), pp. 379–93.
8. See Paul Davidoff, "Advocacy and Pluralism in Planning," *Jnl. of the American Institute of Planners* 31 (November 1965), pp. 331–38; Tom Angotti, *New York for Sale: Community Planning Confronts Global Real Estate* (Cambridge, Mass.: MIT Press, 2008).

1. Discovering and Engaging a Vacated Waterfront

1. Daniel Campo, "Brooklyn's Vernacular Waterfront," *Jnl. of Urban Design* 7–2 (2002); Daniel Campo, *On the Waterfront: Vernacular Recreation at Brooklyn Eastern District Terminal* (University of Pennsylvania dissertation, 2004).

2. This definition of the vernacular is adapted from James Brinkerhoff Jackson's *Discovering the Vernacular Landscape* (New Haven, Conn.: Yale University Press, 1985).

3. John Callahan, "Diesel Replaces Last Iron Horse," *N.Y. Times* (October 26, 1963), p. 54; Jay Bendersky, *Brooklyn's Waterfront Railways* (Mineola, N.Y.: Weekend Chief Publishing, 1988); Flagg, *New York Harbor Railroads*.

4. Edward Burks, "Rail-Car Floating: A Chancy Business," *N.Y. Times* (November 9, 1976); Flagg, *New York Harbor Railroads*, p. 10.

5. Thomas Flagg, *New York Harbor Railroads in Color, Volume I* (Kutztown, Pa.: Morning Sun Books, 2000).

6. Alfred Eichner, *The Emergence of the Oligopoly: Sugar Refining as a Case-Study* (Baltimore: Johns Hopkins University Press, 1966).

7. "New Flour Center Built in Brooklyn," *N.Y. Times* (March 24, 1964); Bendersky, *Brooklyn's Waterfront Railways*; Flagg, *New York Harbr Railroads*; BEDT web site maintained by Philip Goldstein (accessed March 2013).

8. See BEDT web site maintained by Philip Goldstein (http://members.trainweb.com/bedt/BEDT.html) (accessed March 2013).

9. NYC Department of City Planning, *New York City Comprehensive Waterfront Plan: Reclaiming the Edge* (1992).

10. Campo, "Brooklyn's Vernacular Waterfront."

11. An esplanade typically places people well·above and separated from the water's edge by a low fence. The Battery Park City Esplanade along the Hudson River in lower Manhattan, developed during the 1980s and 1990s, exemplifies the approach and has served as a model for subsequent waterfront projects in the city. The south side of the redeveloped BEDT site—between North 4th and North 7th streets—features a similarly designed esplanade, though one executed with different materials.

12. Campo, "Brooklyn's Vernacular Waterfront."

13. Richard Perez-Pena, "Reeling in Many a Meal on the East River, and Maybe a Risky Mess of PCBs," *N.Y. Times* (June 29, 2003). New York State Department of Health guidelines suggest that blue crabs caught in the East River be consumed only at the maximum rate of six per a week for men. For women under fifty and children under fifteen, guidelines recommend avoiding these crabs entirely. New York State Department of Health web site, "New York City Region Fish Advisories" (http://www.health.ny.gov/environmental/outdoors/fish) (accessed July 2012).

14. Galen Cranz, *The Politics of Park Design: A History of Urban Parks in America* (Cambridge, Mass.: MIT Press, 1982).

15. Michel Foucault, "Of Other Spaces," *Diacritics* 14–1 (1986), pp. 22–27.

16. *Village Voice*, Best of New York (2000), http://www.villagevoice.com/bestof/2000/award/best-vacant-lot-493785 (accessed December 2011).

17. My very abbreviated list of critiques of contemporary urban development practices with a particular focus on public spaces includes David Harvey, *The Condition of Postmodernity* (London and Cambridge, Mass.: Blackwell, 1989); Mike Davis, *City of Quartz: Excavating the Future of Los Angeles* (London: Verso, 1990); Michael Sorkin, ed., *Variations on a Theme Park: The New American City and the End of Public Space* (New York: Hill and Wang, 1992); Setha Low, Neil Smith, and Suzanne Scheld, *Rethinking Urban Parks* (Austin: University of Texas Press, 2005); Setha Low and Neil Smith, eds., *The Politics of Public Space* (New York and London: Routledge, 2006).

18. Karen Franck and Quentin Stevens, *Loose Space: Possibility and Diversity in Urban Life* (London and New York: Routledge, 2006), pp. 2–3.

19. Jeffrey Hou, ed., *Insurgent Public Space: Guerrilla Urbanism and the Remaking of Contemporary Cities* (London and New York: Routledge, 2010), pp. 1–2.

20. Margaret Crawford, "Introduction," in John Leighton Chase, Margaret Crawford, and John Kaliski, eds., *Everyday Urbanism, Expanded Edition* (New York: Monacelli, 2008), p. 6. Also note an emerging variant, "tactical urbanism"; see Mike Lydon, ed., *Tactical Urbanism: Short Term Action, Long Term Change, Volume I* (Street Plans Collaborative, 2011).

21. Campo, "Brooklyn's Vernacular Waterfront."

22. See Michel de Certeau, *The Practice of Everyday Life* (Berkeley: University of California Press, 1984).

23. de Certeau, *The Practice of Everyday Life*; Henri Lefebvre, *The Production of Space* (Oxford and Cambridge, Mass.: Blackwell, 1991); Chase et al., *Everyday Urbanism*; Franck and Stevens, *Loose Space*.

24. The connection between public space and democracy, collective action, and resistance is well explored by Don Mitchell, *The Right to the City: Social Justice and the Fight for Public Space* (New York: Guilford, 2003). See also Low and Smith, *The Politics of Public Space*; and David Harvey, *Rebel Cities: From the Right to the City to the Urban Revolution* (London and Brooklyn: Verso, 2012).

25. My improvisational methods were in part inspired by the urban ethnographer Elijah Anderson's intimate profile of life on a corner of Chicago's south side in *A Place on the Corner* (Chicago: University of Chicago Press, 1978).

2. The Rise and Fall of Shantytown Skatepark

1. See Jocko Weyland, *The Answer Is Never: A Skateboarder's History of the Universe* (New York: Grove Press, 2002), p. 6.

2. See Iain Borden, *Skateboarding, Space and the City* (Oxford and New York: Berg, 2001).

3. Ocean Howell, "The Politics of Security: Skateboarding, Urban Design, and the New Public Space," *Urban Action* 2001; Jeremy Nemeth, "Conflict, Exclusion, Relocation: Skateboarding and Public Space," *Jnl. of Urban Design* 11-3 (2006); Chihsin Chiu, "Contestation and Conformity: Street and Park Skateboarding in New York City Public Space," *Space and Culture* 12-1 (2009).

4. Interview by Ted Barrow of Steve Rodriguez, September 2, 2006, as published in Quartersnacks blog, July 17, 2010, http://quartersnacks.com/2010/07/brooklyn-banks-week-steve-rodriguez-interview/ (accessed July 2010).

5. Justin Porter, "Under a Bridge and Top of the World," *N.Y. Times* (June 24, 2005); Barrow interview of Steve Rodriguez (2006); John Branch, "To Fix Bridge, Skateboard Mecca May Be Lost," *N.Y. Times* (May 13, 2010).

6. Branch, "To Fix Bridge."

7. Burnside Park in Portland was featured and renamed "Paranoid Park" in Gus Van Sant's 2007 dramatic film of the same name. For FDR Skatepark see the official web site of FDR Skatepark in Philadelphia (www.fdrskatepark.org). There are also many videos and blog entries on the Internet; for a sampling see the park's Flickr pool (http://www.flickr.com/groups/394243@N21).

8. Bryan Karl Lathrop, "Skateboarders from our first nation's capital give us a lesson on rebellion: FDR, not 'Phillyside,'" *Transworld Skateboarding* 19-5 (April 2001); The Burnside History Project (www.burnsideproject.blogspot.com) (accessed August 2012).

9. See Skateboarders for Public Skateparks (www.skatepark.org).

10. *Close Encounters of the Third Kind*, Steven Spielberg, writer and director; Julia Phillips and Michael Phillips, producers, Columbia Pictures (1977).

11. Jocko Weyland, "Skankytown Requiem," *Thrasher* 251 (December 2001), pp. 47–48.

12. Barrow interview of Steve Rodriguez (2006).

13. See Sean Cronan, "The Seven Day War," *Transworld Skateboarding; Skateborder* 11-3 (November–December 2001), p. 56; *SLAP*, November 2001; Weyland, "Skankytown Requiem."

14. In addition to magazine and Internet coverage, a full-page photo of a skater on Shantytown's first quarter-pipe appears on page 1 of *Full Bleed: New York City Skateboard Photography*, ed. Alex Corporan, Andre Razo, and Ivory Serra (New York: Power House Books, 2010).

15. Skateboarding's Southern California origins are well covered by Borden, *Skateboarding, Space and the City.*

16. William Thompson, "A Good Thrashing: A Landscape Architect's Perspective on Skateparks," *Landscape Architecture* 88-3 (1998); John Nessen, "Want a Great Skatepark? Put the Experts to Work!" *Parks and Recreation* 36-8 (August 2001); Peter Whitley et al., *Public Skatepark Development Guide: A Handbook for Skatepark Advancement*, 2nd ed. (Portland, Ore.: Skaters for Public Skateparks, 2009).

17. Weyland, *The Answer Is Never*, p. 6.

18. Jane Jacobs, *The Death and Life of Great American Cities* (New York: Random House, 1961).

19. Weyland, *The Answer Is Never*, pp. 2, 7.

20. Patrick O'Dell, "Prime Cuts: Owl's Head Park," *Thrasher* 253 (January 2002).

21. City of New York, Department of Parks and Recreation (www.nycgovparks.org) (accessed June 2011).

22. O'Dell, "Prime Cuts."

23. See the 2006 and 2007 interviews of famed Brooklyn Banks skaters conducted by Ted Barrow. Posted as "Brooklyn Banks Week" on www.quartersnacks.com, July 12–18, 2010 (accessed June 2011).

24. The city police department does not have statistics on the BEDT site itself, but the drop in crime and violent crime in the two area police precincts—much like the larger experience of the entire city—has been dramatic. According to NYPD CompStat, the 94th Precinct, covering Greenpoint and Northside (including the BEDT site), by 2001 total violent crime had been reduced to only 28 percent of its 1990 total (for 2010, it was 27 percent of 1990). For the nearby 90th Precinct, covering the Southside and South and East Williamsburg, violent crime in 2001 was 37 percent of 1990, and 32 percent of 1990 in 2010. Data from CompStat, Vol. 18, #23, 2011, accessed from the NYPD web site, June 2011.

25. Borden, *Skateboarding, Space and the City*, pp. 174–75.

26. Thompson, "A Good Thrashing"; also see Ocean Howell, "Skatepark as Neoliberal Playground: Urban Governance, Recreation Space, and the Cultivation of Personal Responsibility," *Space and Culture* 11-4 (November 2008).

27. Matt Rankin and Tim Payne, "We're Going to Build What? City-run Skateparks Are not a Recipe for Disaster," *Parks and Recreation* 32-7 (July 1997).

28. *Transworld Skateboarding* web site blog post, July 23, 2001 (http://skateboarding.transworld.net/) (accessed May 2002).

29. The building was in a manufacturing zoning district that did not permit residential use. See Chapter 7 for more details.

30. Weyland, "Skankytown Requiem."

31. See New York State Consolidated Laws, General Obligation Law, Article 9, Title 1 (1–103), "Conditions on Real Property."

32. Site "cleanup" undertaken by an unidentified city agency in coordination with State Parks (e-mail from Cathleen Breen, Friends of BEDT Park, July 25, 2002). State Parks representative Warren Holliday noted that the cleanup was necessary to open "sight lines" for "police patrols." He also noted the presence of homeless people and "crack parties" occurring on the site (e-mail from Warren Holliday, New York Office of Parks, Recreation and Historic Preservation, July 25, 2002).

33. At least hundreds of spectators watched the demolition of the twin 400-foot-tall "Maspeth Holders" on the morning of Sunday, July 15, 2001. Among the most prominent structures for many miles east of the East River, they "defined the landscape of northern Brooklyn for decades." Brought down by their owners, then Key Span Energy, they were both loved and hated by local residents and were the largest structures of their kind in the world. See Andy Newman's 2001 coverage in the *N.Y. Times*: "Last Days for Brooklyn's Giants" (July 9) and "Memories Rise as Tanks Fall in Brooklyn" (July 16).

34. Brooklyn Historical Society, "Neighborhood History Guide: Greenpoint" (2005), pp. 34–35; Colin Moynihan, "Hidden Populace Mourns Fiery Loss of 'Forgotten City,'" *N.Y. Times* (May 12, 2006).

35. Julia Boorstin, "The Pill Whose Name Goes Unspoken: How do you sell painkillers to an entire generation of consumers hooked on body piercing and extreme sports?" *Fortune* (September 20, 2004) (http://money.cnn.com/magazines/fortune/fortune_archive/2004/09/20/381167/index.htm) (accessed July 2010).

36. Moynihan, "Hidden Populace Mourns Fiery Loss."

37. "Autumn Bowl Update—Closed November 1 (2010)" and related stories posted to www.nyskateboarding.com (accessed October 2012).

38. See the Autumn Bowl web site (http://theautumnbowl.com) (accessed October 2012).

39. See City of New York, Department of Parks and Recreation (http://www.nycgovparks.org/) (accessed June 2012).

40. Branch, "To Fix Bridge."

41. Barrow interview of Steve Rodriguez (2006).

42. See City of New York, Press Release #183-05 (2005) (www.nyc.gov); Diane Cardwell, "City Backs Makeoever for Decaying Brooklyn Waterfront," *N.Y. Times* (May 3, 2005).

43. Martha Sutro (Trust for Public Land), "Taking Back the Waterfront" *Land & People* (Spring 2001); *N.Y. Times*, "Reclaiming New York's Waterfront," editorial (August 17, 2002).

3. March and Burn

1. My use of the word "triangulation" is a variant on that used by William H. Whyte, who defined it in the context of public space as "some external stimulus [that] provides a linkage between people and prompts strangers to talk to each other. . . ." Whyte, *City: Rediscovering the Center* (New York: Doubleday, 1988), p. 154.

2. *Village Voice*, "Best of New York City" issue, 2004. Also see Andy Newman, "Playing Oompah in the Key of Whatever: A Brooklyn Band Marches to a Different Sousaphone," *N.Y. Times* (June 29, 2000) and Caryn Ganz, "Blood on the Sousaphone,"*Spin* (February 2006).

3. Ben Sisario, "The Rise of the Gypsy Punkers," *N.Y. Times* (July 2, 2005).

4. See Rude Mechanical Orchestra web site (http://rudemechanicalorchestra.org/) (accessed October 2011).

5. Hungry March Band web site (http://www.hungrymarchband.com) (accessed February 2011).

6. Mathew Warren, "Need a Party Livened Up? Try a Fire Eater or Two," *N.Y. Times* (September 18, 2008).

7. As described by their long-defunct web site, accessed in 2003. In 2011, the Collective revived the site (http://spacegypsy303.com/index.php) as a memorial to one of their members, Charles Battenhausen (aka Chuck), who passed away in late 2010.

8. Anya Kamenetz, "Fire, Fire Burning Bright: NYC Outsider Artists to Perform Dante's Eighth Circle of Hell," *Village Voice* (June 4, 2002).

9. Warren, "Need a Party Livened Up?"

10. This rezoning initiative was unpopular with African American and Hispanic communities, as well as small manufacturers who felt they were being pushed out of the area by the city's initiative in favor of the Hasidic community and unidentified developers who stood to profit from building housing for them. See Kit Roane, "New Neighbors Pushing at the Edge," *N.Y. Times* (July 17, 1999); Bob Liff, "Rezone Sparks Bias Blast Hasidic: Developers' Plan Called Segregated Housing," *N.Y. Daily News* (March 30, 2001).

11. The rezoning covering fifteen blocks was passed by New York City Council in May 2001; see application number C000109 ZMK in the LUCATS database at the Department of City Planning web site (www.nyc.gov/html/dcp/) (accessed July 2011).

12. Richard Sennett, *The Uses of Disorder* (New York: Random House, 1970); Colin Ward, *Anarchy in Action* (London: George Allen & Unwin, Ltd., 1973); Ward, *The Child in the City* (New York: Pantheon Books, 1978).

13. Norm Bolotin and C. Laing, *The World's Columbian Exposition: The Chicago World's Fair of 1893* (Urbana: University of Illinois Press, 2002); Carl Smith, ed., *The Plan of Chicago: Daniel Burnham and the Remaking of the American City* (Chicago: University of Chicago Press, 2006).

14. Site "cleanup," as it was referred to in an e-mail I received from State Parks, was undertaken by an unidentified city agency in coordination with State Parks in July 2002 (e-mail from Cathleen Breen, Friends of BEDT Park, July 25, 2002). See Chapter 7.

15. New York State Regional Parks Director Jim Moogan repeatedly referred to the planned ball fields as "state of the art" at the November 1, 2001 site walkthrough and during the community planning meetings the following spring. See Chapter 7.

16. The Amstar (aka Domino) Sugar Plant closed in 2004. As of 2012, a 2,200-unit residential complex is planned for the vacant waterfront sugar refining complex. Plans include the retention and rehabilitation of the landmarked 1883 Havemeyer sugar factory building, but all other buildings on the 11.5-acre site will be demolished. See Charles Bagli, "Big Plans for Old Sugar Refinery Faces Review," *N.Y. Times* (January 4, 2010) and Jason Sheftell, "Domino Site Could Go for $160 Million," *N.Y. Daily News* (June 10, 2012).

17. The Lunatarium was shut down by New York City in 2002 for multiple violations, including not having alcohol and public assembly permits and for fire safety. It was sporadically used for specific events over the next two years but eventually closed for good and is now office space. See Nonsense NYC, "Lunatarium Lunacy" (February 1, 2002) (http://www.nonsensenyc.com/features/dumboluna.html) and Dumbo Beat, "10 Jay Street's storied past, and a solid argument for renter's insurance" (January 25, 2008) (http://801a.info/blog/archives/363) (accessed July 2011).

18. Michael Saab was profiled in Warren, "Need a Party Livened Up?" Other information comes from his Linkedin web site (www.linkedin.com) (accessed October 2011).

19. See Karen Franck and Lynn Paxson, "Transforming Public Space into Sites of Mourning and Free Expression" in Franck and Stevens, eds., *Loose Space* (New York and London: Routledge, 2007), pp. 132–53.

20. Amid the many ideas for rebuilding the World Trade Center site and the city as a whole (both in its physical sense and its collective psyche), there were numerous calls for reexamination of the public or civic experience in the city and the spaces in which they occur. See Michael Sorkin and Sharon Zukin, eds. *After the World Trade Center: Rethinking New York City* (London: Psychology

Press, 2002); Setha Low and Neil Smith, *The Politics of Public Space* (New York: Routledge, 2006), pp. 1–16; Lawrence Vale and Thomas Campenella, eds., *The Resilient City: How Modern Cities Recover from Disaster* (New York: Oxford University Press, 2005).

4. Outside Art

1. See Neil Smith, *The New Urban Frontier: Gentrification and the Revanchist City* (New York: Routledge, 1996).
2. Daniel Campo, "Brooklyn's Vernacular Waterfront," *Jnl. of Urban Design* 7-2 (2002).
3. NYC Department of City Planning, *New York City Comprehensive Waterfront Plan: Reclaiming the Edge* (1992). Also see the Department's updated waterfront plan, *Vision 2020: New York City Comprehensive Waterfront Plan* (2011).
4. See the photographs of Shelley Seccombe in her volume *Lost Waterfront: The Decline and Rebirth of Manhattan's Western Shore* (New York: Fordham University Press, 2007); see also the photographs of Harry Skunk and János Kender in "Projects: Pier 18" and the essay by Douglas Crimp, "Action Around the Edges," in Lynne Cooke et al., eds., *Mixed Use, Manhattan* (Cambridge, Mass.: MIT Press, 2011), pp. 65–118; and Elisabeth Sussman, ed., *Gordon Matta-Clark: You Are the Measure* (New Haven, Conn.: Yale University Press, 2007) and Lydia Yee et al., *Laurie Anderson, Trisha Brown, Gordon Matta-Clark: Pioneers of the Downtown Scene, New York 1970s* (Munich, London, and New York: Prestel, 2011), pp. 116–17.
5. Contemporary street art media and styles are documented and contrasted with the graffiti or earlier eras in Tristan Manco's *Street Logos* (New York: Thames & Hudson, 2004).
6. *Laws of Gravity* (Cineplex Odeon Films, 1992) Nick Gomez, director; Bob Gosse and Larry Meistrich, producers; *Hurricane Streets* (Giv'en Films, 1997), Morgan Freeman, director; L. M. Kit Carson et al., producers.
7. David Rohde, *N.Y. Times* (June 22, 1997).
8. The provocative power of the waterfront, abandoned places, and urban ruins is explored in my previous works: "Brooklyn's Vernacular Waterfront" (2002) and "In the Footsteps of the Federal Writers' Project: Revisiting the Workshop of the World," *Landscape Journal* 29-2 (2010). Also see Kevin Lynch, *Wasting Away* (San Francisco: Sierra Club Books, 1990); C. J. Vergara's *American Ruins* (New York: Monacelli, 1999); and Timothy Edensor's *Industrial Ruins: Space, Aesthetics and Materiality* (Oxford and New York: Berg, 2005).
9. *On the Waterfront* (Columbia Pictures, 1954), Elia Kazan, director; Sam Spiegel, producer; Budd Schulberg, screenplay (based on a story by Malcolm Johnson); Arthur Miller, "A View from the Bridge," original Broadway production, 1955, book publication (New York: Viking Press, 1955); Hubert Selby Jr., *Last Exit to Brooklyn* (New York: Grove Press, 1964). For nonfiction accounts see Joseph Mitchell, *The Bottom of the Harbor* (Boston and Toronto: Little, Brown, 1959); Nathan Ward, *Dark Harbor* (New York: Farrar, Straus & Giroux, 2010).
10. See Karen Franck and Lynn Paxson, "Transforming Public Space into Sites of Mourning and Free Expression" in Franck and Stevens, eds., *Loose Space: Possibility and Diversity in Urban Life* (London and New York: Routledge, 2006), pp. 132–53.
11. Campo, "Brooklyn's Vernacular Waterfront," p. 193; Julia Nevarez, "Central Park, the Aesthetics of Order and the Appearance of Looseness" in Franck and Stevens, eds., *Loose Space*, pp. 154–69.
12. Carol Vogel, "Work Begins on Colossal Artwork-in-the-Park," *N.Y. Times* (January 4, 2005).

13. Raymond Gastil, *Beyond the Edge: New York's New Waterfront* (New York: Princeton Architectural Press, 2002), pp. 40–41; and Socrates's web site (www.socratessculpturepark.org).

14. Campo, "Brooklyn's Vernacular Waterfront," p. 196.

15. These themes are well explored in the literature of public spaces; see David Harvey, *The Condition of Postmodernity* (Cambridge, Mass. and Oxford, U.K: Blackwell, 1989); Mike Davis, *City of Quartz* (London and New York: Verso, 1990); and Michael Sorkin, ed., *Variations on a Theme Park: The New American City and the End of Public Space* (New York: Hill and Wang, 1992) for seminal discussions. For discussion of such conditions on the waterfront and in the public spaces of New York City, see Christine Boyer, "City for Sale," in Sorkin, *Variations on a Theme Park*; Smith, *The New Urban Frontier*; and Jerold Kayden et al., *Privately-Owned Public Space: The New York Experience* (New York: Wiley, 2000).

16. The Cave Gallery is located at 58 Grand Street in Williamsburg, one block from the waterfront and several blocks south of the BEDT site (http://www.cavegallery.com).

17. The New York State Parks Office was never forthcoming about their policy concerning interim use. Over the preceding two years, State Parks representatives rebuffed my own attempts for answers as to what might be considered lawful interim use and when and under what circumstances. See Chapter 8.

18. Brad Grooch, "The New Bohemia: Over the Bridge to Williamsburg," *New York* (June 22, 1992) and Sharon Zukin, *Naked City: The Death and Life of Authentic Urban Places* (New York: Oxford University Press, 2010), pp. 35–61.

19. Ür maintains a French-language web site that describes with flair his various exploits and shares a bit of his colorful history (http://www.thefamousfrenchartist.com) (accessed June 2011). Its home page features a partial photograph of the Pirate and the New York skyline.

20. See Suzaan Boettger, *Earthworks: Art and the Landscape of the Sixties* (Berkeley, Los Angeles and London: University of California Press, 2002); and John Beardsley, *Earthworks and Beyond: Environmental Art in the Landscape*, 4th ed. (New York and London: Abbeville Press, 2006).

21. See Jack Flam, *Robert Smithson: The Collected Writings* (Berkeley, Los Angeles and London: University of California Press, 1996), pp. xiii–xv; Beardsley, *Earthworks and Beyond*, pp. 7–8.

22. See Flam, *Robert Smithson*, pp. xvii–xx; and reclamation projects described by Boettger, *Earthworks*, pp. 44–69, 231–32.

23. Flam, *Robert Smithson*, p. xiii.

24. Robert Smithson, "Frederick Law Olmsted and the Dialectical Landscape," in Flam, *Robert Smithson*, p. 160.

25. Ann Buttenwiesser, *Manhattan Waterbound: Manhattan's Waterfront from the Seventeenth Century to the Present*, 2nd ed. (Syracuse, N.Y.: Syracuse University Press, 1999), p. 23.

26. More than 150 years of landfill practices along the North Brooklyn waterfront yielded a significantly larger landmass. Comparing the shorelines of historic maps, my rough calculation is that more than half the east–west extent of BEDT as it existed from the mid–twentieth century until the mid-1990s (when the bulkhead was still mostly intact) is landfill. See *Perris Atlas of the City of Brooklyn* (1855), Sections 6, 7; *Drips Atlas of Brooklyn* (1869), Plate 8; *Bromley Atlas of the City of Brooklyn* (1880), Section 22; *Hyde's Atlas of New York* (1898), Volume 1, Plates 31 and 33; *Bromley Atlas of Brooklyn* (1908), Volume 1, Sections 10 and 11; *Hyde's Atlas of the City of New York, Borough of Brooklyn* (1929), Volume 2, Plates 11, 15, 23; Sanborn Map Company, *Brooklyn Property Atlas* (1999), Vol. 4.

27. David Herszenhorn, "Pest Is Eating at City's Edges," *N.Y. Times* (July 28, 1999); Lisa Foderaro, "Cleaner Harbor Has a Downside: Pests that Plague Park Construction," *N.Y. Times* (August 24, 2011).

28. The complicated laws governing waterfront development in the city involve regulation from all three levels of government (federal, state, city), most prominently the federal Clean Water Act of 1972 (see Betsy McCully, *City at the Water's Edge: A Natural History of New York* (New Brunswick, N.J. and London: Rivergate Books, 2007, p. 92). Some explanation concerning regulations covering landfill, a fairly common urban development practice until the 1970s, can be found in the New York City Department of City Planning's *Comprehensive Waterfront Plan: Reclaiming the Edge* (1992) and on the department's web site (www.nyc.gov/html/dcp/).

29. In 2010, the U.S. Environmental Protection Agency designated the Newtown Creek as a "superfund" site on the National Priorities List (EPA ID#: NYN000206282; see http://epa.gov/region02 (accessed February 2013). Also see U.S. EPA, "Newtown Creek/Greenpoint Oil Spill Study Brooklyn, New York" (2007).

30. Crimp, "Action Around the Edges," in Cooke et al., eds., *Mixed Use, Manhattan*, p. 104.

31. See Roberta Smith, "Cascades, Sing the Body Energetic," *N.Y. Times* (June 27, 2008) and Nick Paumgarten, "Useless Beauty," *New Yorker* (August 31, 2009).

5. Local Tales

1. Jay Bendersky, *Brooklyn's Waterfront Railways* (Mineola, N.Y.: Weekend Chief Publishing, 1988), p. 46; Thomas Flagg, *New York Harbor Railroads in Color, Volume I* (Kutztown, Pa.: Morning Sun Books, 2000), p. 103.

2. "New Flour Center Built in Brooklyn," *N.Y. Times* (March 24, 1964); Thomas Flagg, e-mail message (February 10, 2003).

3. Brooklyn Eastern District Terminal Property Map (1962), courtesy of Thomas Flagg; Sanborn Map Company, *Brooklyn Property Atlas*, Vol. 4 (1988).

4. *Billy Bathgate* (Touchstone Pictures, 1991), Robert Benton, director; Tom Stoppard, screenplay (based on a novel by E. L. Doctorow).

5. The city police department does not have statistics on the BEDT site itself, but the drop in crime and violent crime in the two area police precincts—much like the larger experience of the entire city—has been dramatic. According to NYPD CompStat, the 94th Precinct, covering Greenpoint and Northside (including the BEDT site), by 2001 total violent crime had been reduced to only 28 percent of its 1990 total (for 2010, it was 27 percent of 1990). For the nearby 90th Precinct, covering the Southside and South and East Williamsburg, violent crime in 2001 was 37 percent of 1990, and 32 percent of 1990 in 2010. Data from CompStat, Vol. 18, #23, 2011, accessed from the NYPD web site, June 2011.

6. *Soylent Green* (Metro-Goldwyn-Mayer, 1973), Richard Fleischer, director; Stanley Greenberg, screenplay (based on a novel by Henry Harrison).

7. Joseph Balkoski, *Beyond the Beachhead: The 29th Infantry Division in Normandy* (Harrisburg, Pa.: Stackpole Books, 1989).

8. Rachel and Steve Kaplan, *The Experience of Nature: A Psychological Perspective* (New York: Cambridge University Press, 1989), pp. 150–60; Kevin Lynch, *Wasting Away* (San Francisco: Sierra Club Books, 1990), p. 112.

9. The National Park Service calls the ailanthus tree an "ecological threat," a "fast growing and a prolific seeder that can take over sites and replace native plants" and "form dense thickets." It says that the tree is common in "disturbed urban areas, where it sprouts up just about anywhere including alleys, sidewalks, parking lots and streets" and "has been known to cause damage to sewers and foundations." NPS Fact Sheet, Plant Conservation Alliance (2009) (www.nps.gov/plants/alien/fact/aial1.htm) (accessed June 2011).

10. Much like the ailanthus, the phragmite is also considered an "ecological threat" by the National Park Service. See NPS Fact Sheet, Plant Conservation Alliance (2005) (www.nps.gov/plants/alien/fact/phau1.htm) (accessed June 2011).

11. William Yardley, "The Last Grain Falls at a Sugar Factory," *N.Y. Times* (January 31, 2004).

12. Henry Reed Stiles, *History of the City of Brooklyn Including the Old Town and Village of Brooklyn, the Town of Bushwick, and the Village and City of Williamsburgh, Volume II* (Brooklyn: Published by subscription, 1869).

13. Ibid.

14. Alfred Eichner, *The Emergence of the Oligopoly: Sugar Refining as a Case-Study* (Baltimore: Johns Hopkins University Press, 1966).

15. Mark Francis, Lisa Cashdan, and Lynn Paxson, *Community Open Spaces* (Washington: Island Press, 1984), p. 100.

16. Stephen Carr, Mark Francis, Leanne Rivlin, and Andrew Stone, *Public Space* (New York: Cambridge University Press, 1992), pp. 116–17; Francis et al., *Community Open Spaces*, pp. 99–109.

17. Carr et al., *Public Space*.

18. NYC Department of City Planning, *Williamsburg Waterfront 197-a Plan* (approved by the City Planning Commission, December 2001; adopted by the City Council and published, 2002), p. 6; Daniel Campo, "Brooklyn's Vernacular Waterfront," *Jnl. of Urban Design* 7-2 (2002).

19. New York City Department of Parks and Recreation web site (www.nycgovparks.org/parks/B401/history) (accessed June 2011).

20. Tom Gogola, "Activism on the Waterfront," *New York* (December 7, 1998).

21. In November 2002, New York was designated by the U.S. Olympic Committee as the U.S. candidate for hosting the 2012 Summer Olympic Games. In 2005, the International Olympic Committee selected London over New York and Madrid as the host city. Local waterfront implications for Olympic development were discussed by Phoebe Nobles, "Pie in the Sky or Oven in the Baking? The 2012 Olympics at Williamsburg," *The Brooklyn Rail* (February 2002); also see Raymond Gastil, *Beyond the Edge: New York's New Waterfront* (New York: Princeton Architectural Press, 2002), pp. 156–60.

6. Residential Life

1. Homeless encampments and conflicts at Tompkins Square Park and the Hill have been well documented by a variety of sources; see Neil Smith's *The New Urban Frontier: Gentrification and the Revanchist City* (New York: Routledge, 1996) and Diana Balmori and Margaret Morton's *Transitory Gardens, Uprooted Lives* (New Haven and London: Yale University Press, 1993), pp. 122–42.

2. John Kifner and Jayson Blair, "Construction Worker Dies in Brooklyn Building Collapse," *N.Y. Times* (November 24, 1999).

3. Christopher Drew and Jayson Blair, "Builders' Self Policing Failed Before Brooklyn Floor Did," *N.Y. Times* (February 21, 2000).

4. Juan Forero, "Immigrant Laborers Say They Knew of Job Risks," *N.Y. Times* (November 24, 1999).

7. Neighbors Against Garbage

1. NYC Department of City Planning, "Environmental Assessment Statement," Greenpoint-Williamsburg Rezoning (Reference #04DCP003K), August 1, 2003.

2. The Parks Council (of New York City), *Creating Public Access to the New York Waterfront* (1990); NYC Department of City Planning, *Williamsburg Waterfront 197-a Plan* (Approved by the City Planning Commission, December 2001; adopted by the City Council and published, 2002); Benjamin Miller, *Fat of the Land* (New York: Four Walls Eight Windows, 2000).

3. The Parks Council, *Creating Public Access to the New York Waterfront*; "Brooklyn Community Board No. 1 Statement of Community District Needs" (pp. 14–34) in NYC Department of City Planning, *Community District Needs Statement, Fiscal Year 2000* and *Williamsburg Waterfront 197-a Plan* (2002); see also Tom Angotti, *New York for Sale: Community Planning Confronts Global Real Estate* (Cambridge, Mass. and London: MIT Press, 2008).

4. Among the NYC Department of City Planning's many plans that aimed to stimulate development on underutilized land in M-zones were *New York City Comprehensive Waterfront Plan: Reclaiming the Edge* (1992) and "Comprehensive Retail Strategy for New York City" (1995).

5. Brian Cudahy, *Box Boats: How Shipping Containers Changed the World* (New York: Fordham University Press, 2006).

6. NYC Department of City Planning, *Comprehensive Waterfront Plan* and NYC Department of City Planning, *Plan for the Brooklyn Waterfront* (1994).

7. The city's garbage crisis reached its public nadir in the summer of 1987 when a barge laden with 3,200 tons of city and Long Island commercial waste sat moored in New York's Lower Bay for months after a 6,000-mile odyssey in which the barge had been formally refused by six states and at least three foreign countries. The garbage was ultimately burned in a southwest Brooklyn incinerator, which closed shortly after. See Miller, *Fat of the Land*, pp. 1–14.

8. Douglas Martin, "Boroughs Battle over Trash as Last Landfill Nears Close," *N.Y. Times* (November 16, 1998); Kirk Johnson, "Council Approves Long-Term Plan for City Garbage," *N.Y. Times* (November 30, 2000); Miller, *Fat of the Land*, p. 282–84.

9. New York City Department of City Planning, *Williamsburg 197-a Plan*.

10. Andy Van Kluenen, "Nekboh Watch," *WaterfrontWeek* 4–24 (December 1–14, 1994).

11. Laura Williams, "Group NAG Gets Results," *N.Y. Daily News* (October 29, 1995).

12. Ibid.

13. Joe Sexton, "Monitors to Oversee Finance of Indicated Trash Haulers," *N.Y. Times* (September 17, 1995).

14. Tom Robbins, "Trashed by New Charge Hauler Accused of Assault," *N.Y. Daily News* (October 5, 1995); Laura Williams, "Recycle Biz Put Out of It," *N.Y. Daily News* (October 6, 1995); and "Neighborhood Report: Brooklyn Update," *N.Y. Times* (October 22, 1995).

15. "Neighborhood Report: Brooklyn Update."

16. Robbins, "The Kings of Trash," *N.Y. Daily News* (December 17, 1995).

17. Laura Williams, "Garbage Out, Garbage In," *N.Y. Daily News* (January 23, 1996).

18. Marc Francis Cohen, "Neighborhood Report: Williamsburg/Greenpoint; for Nekboh, New Owner, New Fight," *N.Y. Times* (May 26, 1996).

19. Jim Yardley, "Dump Site Could Clash with Park Plans," *N.Y. Times* (April 22, 1998).

20. Miller, *Fat of the Land*, pp. 282–84.

21. Like the waste transfer facility planned for BEDT, the Giuliani administration's plans for the Linden, New Jersey, site became mired in charges of corruption and thus the city never entered into contract for it. See Barbara Stewart, "Seeing Garbage, Smelling Money," *N.Y. Times* (June 25, 2000); Michael Cooper, "Garbage Plan Ignites Tensions," *N.Y. Times* (August 1, 2001).

22. "State Commits to Creating Open Space On the Northside Waterfront," *Nag Rag* Vol. 5-1 (May 2000).

23. "Community Appeals to City Hall," *Nag Rag* Vol. 4–2 (September 1999).

24. Jim Yardley, "At Hearing in Brooklyn, Crowd Jeers Proposal for Trash Station," *N.Y. Times* (April 30, 1998).

25. New York City Department of City Planning, *Williamsburg Waterfront 197-a Plan*, pp. 35, 42; New York City Department of Finance, Automated City Register Information System (ACRIS) (accessed July 2012).

26. Douglas Martin, "Settlement Allows Trash Companies to Merge after Divesting," *N.Y. Times* (July 17, 1998).

27. See "How Brooklyn Became Cool," in Sharon Zukin, *Naked City: The Death and Life of Authentic Places* (New York: Oxford University Press, 2010), pp. 35–61.

28. NYC Department of City Planning web site (www.nyc.gov/html/dcp/html/community_planning/197a.shtml) (accessed October 2011). See also Eve Baron, "The Long Struggle of Community-Based Planning in New York City," *Progressive Planning* 184 (Summer 2010), pp. 30–32.

29. NYC Department of City Planning, *Williamsburg Waterfront 197-a Plan*, p. 12.

30. NYC Department of City Planning, *Plan for the Brooklyn Waterfront*, p. 97.

31. See Empire State Development Corporation, "Hunters Point (Queens West) Waterfront Development Land Use Improvement Project: Modified and Restated General Project Plan" (March 17, 2009).

32. Lisa Foderaro, "A Metamorphosis for Old Williamsburg," *N.Y. Times* (July 19, 1987); Trust for Public Land, *New Parks for New Yorkers* (1995), p. 21.

33. Trust for Public Land, *New Parks for New Yorkers*; New York City Department of Finance, Automated City Register Information System (ACRIS) (accessed July 2012).

34. NYC Department of City Planning, *Williamsburg Waterfront 197-a Plan*, pp. 35, 42.

35. NYC Department of City Planning, "Comprehensive Retail Strategy."

36. Rachel Newman, "What's to Become of Our Waterfront," *Waterfront Week* 9–12 (June 17, 1999); Bob Liff, "Sanit Cops Grab Truck, 'Dozer after River Dump," *N.Y. Daily News* (August 4, 1999).

37. Yardley, "Dump Site Could Clash with Park Plans."

38. "Waterfront Open Space Threatened: Community Outbid for the Northside Site," *Nag Rag* Vol. 4–3 (December 1999).

39. New York City Department of Finance, Automated City Register Information System (ACRIS) (accessed July 2012).

40. "State Commits to Creating Open Space on the Northside Waterfront," *Nag Rag* Vol. 5–1 (May 2000).

41. New York State, Office of the Governor, Press Release (June 13, 2000).

42. New York State Office of Parks, Recreation and Historic Preservation property deed (January 25, 2001).

43. Trust for Public Land (1995).

44. A 2001 amendment to state law was also needed to empower the Commissioner of Parks, Recreation and Historic Preservation to enter into a long-term leasing agreement with NYU at the park site. See New York State Parks, Recreation and Historic Preservation Law, Section 3.09 (2e) and Christopher Rizzo, "Enhancing the Protection of Parkland in New York," *Environmental Law in New York* 15–6 (June 2004).

45. New York State, Office of the Governor, Press Release (June 13, 2000); "It's a Park!" *Nag Rag* 5–1 (September 2000); "Reclaiming New York's Waterfront," *N.Y. Times* editorial (May 27, 2002).

46. Susan Clark, Trust for Public Land. E-mail posting to CYBERPARK Listserv (August 22, 2000).

47. New York State Office of the Governor, Press Release (June 13, 2000).

48. Martha Sutro, "Taking Back the Waterfront," *Land and People* (April 2001).

49. "It's a Park!" *Nag Rag*.

50. NYC Department of City Planning, *Williamsburg Waterfront 197-a Plan*.

51. Friends of Brooklyn Eastern District Terminal Park, Fact Sheet, 2002.

52. The residential apartments contained by the "in-holding" property (at 110 Kent Avenue) were illegal because the M-zoning did not permit residential use *and* because the residential use of the property was established after the zoning was instituted in 1961. The property had also not been granted a variance (an exception to zoning) or listed on the city's "Interim Multiple Dwelling" list, which provides for legal residential occupancy in industrial buildings in manufacturing zones that have long-established residential or live-work uses. The property was omitted from the 2005 rezoning area for fear that the owner would attempt to build a tall structure that would tower over the park. In 2013, it contained offices (including the NAG office), a photography studio, and the quasi-legal apartment of the building superintendent.

53. Friends of BEDT Park Design Committee, *Form and Matter* (2002). Document design by Avigail Thompson.

54. Friends of BEDT Park meeting minutes (September 27, 2002).

55. See Raymond Gastil, *Beyond the Edge: New York's New Waterfront* (New York: Princeton Architectural Press, 2002), pp. 156–60.

56. Roger Toman, "Pulling for 2012: NYU Supports Olympic Bid," *Washington Square News* (April 17, 2003), http://nyunews.com/2003/04/17/47/ (accessed December 2010).

57. E-mail message from Cathleen Breen to Friends of BEDT Park members (November 21, 2003).

58. Ibid.

59. New York State Office of the Governor, Press Release (June 13, 2000).

60. Andrew Revkin, "Pataki to Commit $100 Million Share to a Hudson Park," *N.Y. Times* (April 3, 1997); "Memorandum of Understanding between the State of New York and the City of New York Regarding Brooklyn Bridge Park" (May 2, 2002).

8. Unplanned Postscript

1. Robert Caro, *The Power Broker: Robert Moses and the Fall of New York* (New York: Knopf, 1974).

2. East River State Park project description, New York State Office of Parks, Recreation and Historic Preservation, internal document (June 28, 2007).

3. With funding from a J. M. Kaplan fund grant, the Friends of BEDT State Park and Brooklyn Architects Collective sponsored a design competition that generated a few submissions. The Friends and BAC ultimately asked the various submitters to collaborate on a single plan. The resulting plan, "East River State Park: From Public Process to Public Space," completed in 2006, was sustainability-themed and won an American Society of Landscape Architects New York Chapter award for unbuilt projects in 2010. Serving more as an inspiration, the fanciful and likely expensive plan was never fully championed by its sponsors and not embraced by State Parks.

4. Anthony Ramirez, "In Brooklyn, Modest Space, But It Does Have a View," *N.Y. Times* (May 27, 2007).

5. Elizabeth Hays, "New W'burg park panned: Too many rules, too few hours!" *N.Y. Daily News* (July 31, 2007).

6. Julana Bunim, "Park yourself here," *Brooklyn City Paper* (July 21, 2007).

7. Ibid.

8. Ramirez, "In Brooklyn, Modest Space."

9. New York State Office of Parks, Recreation and Historic Preservation press release, "Playground at East River State Park Opens" (April 29, 2010).

10. Anna Bahney, "Williamsburg Reinvented," *N.Y. Times* (March 20, 2005); David Amsden, "The Billyburg Bust," *New York* (July 12, 2009).

11. Ben Muessig, "Kicked out of Eden," *Brooklyn City Paper* (June 14, 2008).

12. Ben Muessig, "State park to close," *Brooklyn City Paper* (November 13, 2008).

13. Ben Muessig, "Pol: Why can't cops run the park?" *Brooklyn City Paper* (November 19, 2008).

14. Ben Muessig, "W'burg park reopens!" *Brooklyn City Paper* (March 3, 2009).

15. State Parks' estimated attendance for 2009 as shared in previously noted State Parks press release (April 24, 2010) was "nearly 240,000." Attendance for other years was not available.

16. Themis Chronopoulos, "The Politics of Race and Class and the Changing Spatial Fortunes of the McCarren Pool in Brooklyn, New York, 1936–2010," *Space and Culture* 16 (2013), pp. 104–22.

17. Ben Sisario, "Keep the Music, Add the Views," *N.Y. Times* (July 3, 2009).

18. Ben Sisario, "Free Brooklyn Concert Series Finds a Big Fan in the U.S. Senate," *N.Y. Times* (June 5, 2010).

19. Ben Sisario, "Abrupt End for Concert Series in Brooklyn," *N.Y. Times* (August 19, 2010).

20. Ben Sisario, "Canceled Brooklyn Concert Reinstated," *N.Y. Times* (August 23, 2010).

21. Brooklyn 11211, "Williamsburg Bans Music" (April 12, 2011, http://brooklyn11211.com/2011/04/top-the-music/) (accessed November 2011).

22. John Leland, "Rocked Hard: The Battle of Williamsburg," *N.Y. Times* (May 29. 2011).

23. Ibid.

24. Ibid.

25. Jen Carlson, "Video: Nitrous Oxide–Fueled Fans Terrorize Williamsburg Locals" Gothamist (September 21, 2011; http://gothamist.com/2011/09/21/video_nitrous_oxide_fueled_fans_ter.php) (accessed November 2011).

26. Aaron Short, "No Laughing Matter," *The Brooklyn Paper* 34–38 (September 23–29, 2011).

27. Brownstoner, "Following Complaints OSA Moving Concerts out of the Park" Gothamist (October 6, 2011; http://www.brownstoner.com/blog/2011/10/following-complaints-osa-moving-concerts-out-of-park/) (accessed November 2011).

28. Jelly NYC press release (August 18, 2010) as posted on the Brooklyn Vegan (http://www.brooklynvegan.com/archives/2010/08/jelly_resonds_t.html) (accessed December 2010).

29. Ibid.

30. "The 2010 Report of the Open Space Alliance for North Brooklyn," draft version [accessed from the Open Space Alliance's web site (http://osanb.org) June 2011].

31. Central Park Conservancy's "Annual Report 2011" notes that it generates 85 percent of its annual operating budget through donations, sponsorship, programming, franchising, and related revenue streams. While the Prospect Park Alliance generates approximately 92 percent of its operating budget from a similar mix of revenues (see its "Annual Report 2011"), this figure is not directly comparable to the Conservancy's, as the city's Parks Department still plays a significant role in the administration of Prospect Park.

32. "The 2010 Report of the Open Space Alliance for North Brooklyn," draft version.

33. See "Community Board One: OSA defends Its Relevance," May 11, 2011, posting of "A Short Story" (http://aaronshortstory .blogspot.com/2011/05/community-board-1-osa-defends-its.html) (accessed November 2011).

34. Open Space Alliance for North Brooklyn, Steering Group of Community Committee meeting minutes (August 17, 2009).

35. "The 2010 Report of the Open Space Alliance for North Brooklyn," draft version.

36. "Remove the East River State Park Lights Petition" (http://www.ipetitions.com/petition/parks-matter/) (accessed November 2011).

37. Diane Cardwell, "State Agrees to Let the City Finish Brooklyn Bridge Park," *N.Y. Times* (March 9, 2010).

38. Yolanne Almanzar, "Did city miscalculation sideline North Brooklyn's new waterfront park?" *The New York World* (December 11, 2011) (accessed from the *World*'s web site, September 2012); Friends of Bushwick Inlet Park (web site accessed September 2012); NYC ACRIS On Line Property Register (accessed September 2012).

39. Charles Bagli and Lisa Foderaro, "Times and Tides Weigh on Hudson River Park," *N.Y. Times* (January 27, 2012).

40. New York State Urban Development Corporation et al., "Brooklyn Bridge Park Civic and Land Use Improvement Project: Modified General Project Plan" (Adopted July 2005, Modified December 2006); Lisa Foderaro, "Housing Deal Ensures Park in Brooklyn Will Expand," *N.Y. Times* (August 1, 2011); Lisa Foderaro, "Deal Allows Development in Brooklyn Bridge Park," *N.Y. Times* (May 22, 2012); "A Pier to Pay for a Park," *N.Y. Times*, Editorial (September 17, 2012).

41. Meredith Hoffman, "City Attempts to Develop Long Stalled Greenpoint Park" (August 8, 2012) and "City Admits It Has No Concrete Plan for Promised Waterfront Space" (June 14, 2012), DNAinfo.com (accessed September 2012).

42. See Erin Durkin and David Ospino, "Residents, Pols Irked That Only 1 Park Has Been Built on the Williamsburg Waterfront," *N.Y. Daily News* (June 6, 2012).

43. Patrick McGeehan, "Pleased by Ridership, City Looks for Bids to Bolster East River Ferry Success," *N.Y. Times* (December 19, 2012).

9. Planning for the Unplanned

1. Richard Dattner, *Design for Play* (New York: Van Nostrand Reinhold, 1969), p. 7.

2. John Tierney, "Grasping Risk in Life's Classroom," *N.Y. Times* (July 17, 2011).

3. Paula Fass, *Kidnapped: Child Abduction in America* (New York: Oxford University Press, 1997); Barry Glassner, *The Culture of Fear* (New York: Basic Books, 1999); Kristen Zgoba, "Spin Doctors and Moral Crusaders: The Moral Panic Behind Child Safety Legislation," *Criminal Justice Studies* 17-4 (2004).

4. M. Paul Friedberg, *Playgrounds for City Children* (Washington: Association for Childhood Education International, 1969); Nancy Rudolph, *Workyards: Playgrounds Planned for Adventure* (New York: Teachers College Press, 1974).

5. Colin Ward, *The Child in the City* (New York: Pantheon, 1978), p. 90; Aase Eriksen, *Playground Design* (New York: Van Nostrand Reinhold, 1985), p. 20.

6. William H. Whyte, *The Social Life of Small Urban Spaces* (Washington: The Conservation Foundation, 1980), pp. 10–12.

7. Friedberg, *Playgrounds for City Children*.

8. Rudolph, *Workyards*, pp. 8–10.

9. Richard Dattner, a champion of the movement in the United States, designed many of New York's adventure playgrounds, the most of prominent of which was built in Central Park. See Dattner, *Design for Play*.

10. Susan Solomon, *American Playgrounds: Revitalizing Community Space* (Hanover, N.H.: University Press of New England, 2005); Tierney, "Grasping Risk in Life's Classroom."

11. Solomon, *American Playgrounds*; Ellen Sandseter, "Children's Expressions of Exhilaration and Fear in Risky Play," *Contemporary Issues in Early Childhood* 10-2 (2009), pp. 92–106 (http://dx.doi.org/10.2304/ciec.2009.10.2.92) (accessed October 2011); Shirley Wyver, Anita Bundy, Geraldine Naughton, Paul Tranter, Jo Ragen, and Ellen Sandseter, "Safe Outdoor Play for Young Children: Paradoxes and Consequences," Australian Association for Research in Education, International Education Research Conference, Melbourne (2010), (http://www.aare.edu.au/10pap/2071WyverBundyNaughtonTranterSandseterRagen.pdf) (accessed October 2011); Rebecca Mead, "State of Play," *The New Yorker* (July 5, 2010).

12. Imagination Playground, Play Associates (http://imaginationplayground.com/parks/) (accessed October 2011); Javier Hernandez, "A Playground Where Creativity Can Run Wild," *N.Y. Times* (July 14, 2008); Laurel Graeber, "Science and Secrets in New York City Playgrounds," *N.Y. Times* (April 14, 2011).

13. Jane Jacobs, *The Death and Life of Great American Cities* (New York: Random House, 1961); William H. Whyte, *City: Rediscovering the Center* (New York: Doubleday, 1988); Kevin Lynch, *Wasting Away* (San Francisco: Sierra Club Books, 1990).

14. Michel Foucault, "Of Other Spaces," *Diacritics* 16-1 (1986), pp. 22–26; Karen Franck and Quentin Stevens, *Loose Space: Possibility and Diversity in Urban Life* (London and New York: Routledge, 2007); Jeffrey Hou, ed., *Insurgent Public Space: Guerrilla Urbanism and the Remaking of Contemporary Cities* (London and New York: Routledge, 2010); John Chase, Margaret Crawford, and John Kalisky, eds., *Everyday Urbanism*, expanded ed. (New York: Monacelli Press, 2008); Daniel Campo, "Brooklyn's Vernacular Waterfront," *Jnl. of Urban Design* 7-2 (2002). Also see Reyner Banham, *Scenes in America Deserta* (Salt Lake City: Gibbs M. Smith, Inc., 1982).

15. Ben Sisario, "Keep the Music, Add the Views," *N.Y. Times* (July 3, 2009).

16. David Harvey, *The Condition of Postmodernity* (Cambridge, Mass. and Oxford, U.K.: Blackwell, 1989); Mike Davis, *City of Quartz* (London and New York: Verso, 1990); Michael Sorkin, ed., *Variations on a Theme Park: The New American City and the End of Public Space* (New York: Hill and Wang, 1992); M. Christine Boyer, *The City of Collective Memory: Its Historical Imagery and Architectural Entertainments* (Cambridge, Mass.: MIT Press, 1994); Sophie Watson and Katherine Gibson, *Postmodern Cities and Public Spaces* (Cambridge, Mass.: Blackwell, 1995); Neil Smith, *The New Urban Frontier: Gentrification and the Revanchist City* (New York and London: Routledge, 1996); Jerold Kayden et al., *Privately-Owned Public Space: The New York Experience* (New York: Wiley, 2000); Setha Low and Neil Smith, *The Politics of Public Space* (New York and London: Routledge, 2006).

17. Campo, "Brooklyn's Vernacular Waterfront"; Daniel Campo, *On the Waterfront: Vernacular Recreation at Brooklyn Eastern District Terminal* (University of Pennsylvania dissertation, 2004).

18. New York's DIY scene has been well documented and celebrated by the city's cultural media. For artisan collectives, see coverage of the Bushwick-based Third Ward, including Melissa Ryzick, "Urban Artisans: A Collective Thrives in Brooklyn," *N.Y. Times* (July 3, 2010); for concerts, nightlife, and parties, see Ryzick, "Off the Beaten Path," *N.Y. Times* (May 11, 2007); Annie Fischer, "A Place to Impress Strangers," *Village Voice* (April 30, 2008); Erica Orden and Candace Taylor, "New York Is Underground," *Timeout New York* (November 6–12, 2008); for appropriated leisure environments, see Ryzick, "Forget the Trash Bag, Bring a Towel," *N.Y. Times* (July 20, 2009) and "A Smashing Idea: Eco-Friendly Aggression," *N.Y. Times* (May 12, 2010); for occupations and co-options

of public space, see Dan Avery, "Street Fighters," *Timeout New York* (August 9–15, 2007); Anthony Ramirez, "An Outdoor Party Where Dancers Supply, but Don't Share, the Music," *N.Y. Times* (April 20, 2008); for critical-mass bike rides, see Lydia Polgreen, "The Bike Helmet as Riot Gear," *N.Y. Times* (November 11, 2004); for urban farming, see Catherine Price, "A Chicken on Every Plot, a Coop in Every Backyard," *N.Y. Times* (September 19, 2007).

19. Mathew Warren, "Need a Party Livened Up? Try a Fire Eater or Two," *N.Y. Times* (September 18, 2008); James McKinley Jr., "Underground Musicians Lose a Haven," *N.Y. Times* (September 12, 2011); also see Bushwick's Third Ward (www.3rdward.com) (accessed September 2011).

20. Ellen Lupton, *D.I.Y.: Design-it-Yourself* (New York: Princeton Architectural Press, 2006), p.18.

21. See Senatsverwaltung für Stadtentwicklung, *Urban Pioneers: Berlin: Stadtentwicklung durch Zwischennutzung* (translation: "Temporary Use and Urban Development in Berlin" (Berlin: Jovis, 2007) (http://tiny.cc/urban-pioneers); Quentin Stevens, "The German 'City Beach' as a New Approach to Waterfront Development," in Gene Desfor et al., eds., *Transforming Urban Waterfronts: Fixity and Flow* (New York and London: Routledge, 2012); Tracy Metz, *Fun! Leisure and Landscape* (Rotterdam: NAi Publishers, 2002).

22. Christa Amouroux, "Normalizing Christiania: Project Clean Sweep and the Normalization Plan in Copenhagen," *City & Society* 21–1 (2009).

23. See Michel de Certeau, *The Practice of Everyday Life* (Berkeley: University of California Press, 1984).

24. Michael Kimmelman, "The Greatest Generation," *N.Y. Times Magazine* (April 6, 2003); Lynne Cooke et al., eds., *Mixed Use, Manhattan* (Cambridge, Mass.: MIT Press, 2011); Barbican Centre et al., *Laurie Anderson, Trisha Brown, Gordon Matta-Clarke: Pioneers of the Downtown Scene, New York 1970s* (Munich, London, and New York: Prestel, 2011).

25. The net flow of creative people from New York to Philadelphia over the past decade is particularly striking. See Jessica Pressler, "Philadelphia Story: The Next Borough," *N.Y. Times* (August 14, 2005). For broader analysis of net migration between the two cities, see the Pew Charitable Trusts' "Destination Philadelphia: Tracking the City's Migration Trends" (October 2010).

26. For a sample of works that celebrate the power of ruins, see Bernard Rudofsky, *Architecture Without Architects* (Garden City, N.Y.: Doubleday, 1964); J. B. Jackson, *The Necessity for Ruins and Other Topics* (Amherst: University of Massachusetts Press, 1980); Camilo José Vergara, *American Ruins* (New York: Monacelli Press, 1999).

27. See Charles Waldheim, ed., *The Landscape Urbanism Reader* (New York: Princeton Architectural Press, 2006).

28. Brooklyn Bridge Park, "Brooklyn Bridge Park Financial Plan" (2009) (www.brooklynbridgepark.org/) (accessed August 2012).

29. Kate Taylor, "After High Line's Success, Other Cities Look Up," *N.Y. Times* (July 14, 2010); Lisa Foderaro, "Record $20 Million Gift to Help Finish the High Line Park," *N.Y. Times* (October 26, 2011).

30. The Prospect Park Alliance is presently undertaking a twenty-five-year "Woodlands Campaign" that seeks to restore the park's "natural ecology" while staying true to the park's historic Olmsted design. See Setha Low, Dana Taplin, and Suzanne Scheld, *Rethinking Urban Parks: Public Space and Cultural Diversity* (Austin: University of Texas Press, 2005), pp. 48, 199–201.

31. Anne Spirn, *The Granite Garden: Urban Nature and Human Design* (New York: Basic Books, 1984).

32. Many historians and cultural scholars have argued that the United States has never fully embraced dense city life. The American rural, natural, and later suburban traditions have been advanced by some of the most quintessentially American thinkers, including Jefferson, Thoreau, and Olmsted. For a representative sample of this scholarship, see Leo Marx, *The Machine in the Garden: Technology and the Pastoral Ideal of America* (New York: Oxford University Press, 1964); Sam Bass Warner Jr., *The Urban Wilderness: A History of the American City* (Berkeley and Los Angeles: University of California Press, 1972); Kenneth Jackson,

Crabgrass Frontier: The Suburbanization of the United States (New York: Oxford University Press, 1985); David Schuyler, *The New Urban Landscape: The Redefinition of City in Nineteenth-Century Urban America* (Baltimore: Johns Hopkins University Press, 1986); Robert Bruegmann, *Sprawl: A Compact History* (Chicago: University of Chicago Press, 2006).

33. Frederick Law Olmsted, *Public Parks and the Enlargement of Towns* (1870) in S. B. Sutton, ed., *Civilizing American Cities: A Selection of Frederick Law Olmsted's Writings on City Landscapes* (Cambridge, Mass. and London: MIT Press, 1971); Galen Cranz, *The Politics of Park Design: A History of Urban Parks in America* (Cambridge, Mass.: MIT Press, 1982); Schuyler, *The New Urban Landscape*; Roy Rosenzweig and Elizabeth Blackmar, *Parks and People: A History of Central Park* (Ithaca, N.Y.: Cornell University Press, 1992); Vitold Rybczynski, *A Clearing in the Distance* (New York: Simon & Schuster, 2000).

34. Low, Taplin, and Scheld, *Urban Parks*, pp. 199–200, note the prominent exceptions of Van Cortlandt Park and Pelham Bay Park in the Bronx, where, not operating "under the burden of historic [Olmsted] designs," park managers have been more flexible in accommodating user appropriations and alterations to the landscape.

35. J. B. Jackson, *Discovering the Vernacular Landscape* (New Haven, Conn. and London: Yale University Press, 1984).

36. The legal standing of community gardens in New York has frequently been contested and has never comfortably sat within the city's regulatory framework for governing land use and development. See *N.Y. Times* coverage including C. J. Chivers, "Stepping up Turf Battle, City Seizes Garden and Arrests 31" (February 16, 2000); Brette Taylor, "Where Does Your Garden Grow?" (September 22, 2002); and Colin Moynihan, "New Rules Being Drafted for Community Gardens" (July 7, 2010).

37. Foucault, "Of Other Spaces"; Benjamin Genocchio, "Discourse, Discontinuity, Difference: The Question of Other Spaces," in Watson and Gibson, *Postmodern Cities and Public Spaces*; Campo, "Brooklyn's Vernacular Waterfront."

38. See Walt Whitman's "Crossing Brooklyn Ferry" in his famed volume of poetry *Leaves of Grass* (maritime depictions and metaphors also figure prominently in several other poems in the various versions of this volume). And Henry Christman, ed., *Walt Whitman's New York: From Montauk to Manhattan* (1963; New York: New Amsterdam Books, first paperback edition, 1989). See also *Arthur Miller, A View From the Bridge: Two One-act Plays* (New York: Viking, 1955); Joseph Mitchell, *The Bottom of the Harbor* (Boston and Toronto: Little, Brown, 1959); Elia Kazan, director, *On the Waterfront* (Columbia Pictures, 1954), Sam Spiegel, producer; Budd Schulberg, screenplay (based on a story by Malcolm Johnson) and Hubert Selby Jr., *Last Exit to Brooklyn* (New York: Grove Press, 1964).

39. For a survey and contemplation of vernacular waterfront sites in Brooklyn as they existed in the early 2000s, see Campo, "Brooklyn's Vernacular Waterfront."

40. NYC Department of City Planning, *New York City Comprehensive Waterfront Plan: Reclaiming the Edge* (1992); NYC Department of City Planning, *Vision 2020: New York Comprehensive Waterfront Plan* (2011).

41. A portion of my several Philadelphia waterfront field experiences is described in my paper "In the Footsteps of the Federal Writers' Project: Revisiting the Workshop of the World," *Landscape Journal* 29–2 (2010). Emerging research and documentation for make-your-own-experience sites in Los Angeles and Albany, California include John Arroyo, "Culture in Concrete: Art and the Re-imagination of the Los Angeles River as Civic Space," M.I.T. Master's Thesis in Urban Planning (2010) and Gabe Crain, "Life on the Bulb: What Happens When Everybody Wants a Piece of the Last Good Place on Earth?" (2007), Center for Programs in Contemporary Writing, University of Pennsylvania (http://writing.upenn.edu) (accessed February 2013).

42. See Amanda Dargan and Steve Zeitlin, *City Play* (New Brunswick, N.J.: Rutgers University Press, 1990).

43. Whyte, *The Social Life of Small Urban Spaces*; Lynch, *Wasting Away*.

44. Stevens, "The German 'City Beach' as a New Approach to Waterfront Development"; see also Senatsverwaltung für Stadtentwicklung, *Urban Pioneers*.

45. Yolanne Almanzar, "Did City Miscalculation Sideline North Brooklyn's New Waterfront Park?" *The New York World* (December 11, 2011) (accessed from the *World*'s web site September 2012); Meredith Hoffman, "City Admits It Has No Concrete Plan for Promised Waterfront Space," dnainfo.com (June 14, 2012) (accessed August 2012); Friends of Bushwick Inlet Park web site (http://www.bushwickinletpark.org) (accessed September 2012); NYC ACRIS On Line Property Register (http://www.nyc.gov/dof) (accessed September 2012).

46. In August 2012, the city opened the long-anticipated 1.6-acre WNYC Transmitter Park on the site of the former WNYC transmission tower on the Greenpoint waterfront three-quarters of a mile north of ERSP.

47. Don Mitchell, *The Right to the City: Social Justice and the Fight for Public Space* (New York: Guilford Press, 2003).

ACKNOWLEDGMENTS

This book was a long and complicated undertaking. It would have been impossible without the contributions of so many people. Foremost, I thank Anne Leonard, whose love, patience, and enthusiasm sustained this project. She also read an untold number of drafts, provided companionship on numerous trips to the waterfront, and kept my my logistics in order. I also thank my parents, Seena and Vincent Campo, who supported and encouraged me in countless ways. They took utter delight in this work, and I enjoyed sharing it with them. Just as I began final corrections in June 2012, my mother passed away. This book is dedicated to her memory and to my father.

My editor, Fred Nachbaur, championed this different and sometimes difficult book when few others were willing to take a chance and then did a fantastic job of shepherding it through to print. It was a joy to work with him; Eric Newman, who patiently guided me through the editorial process; and the staff at Fordham University Press, including William Cerbone, Kathleen Sweeney, Kathleen O'Brien-Nicholson, Loomis Mayer, and Mark Lerner. Also thanks to Jeremy Wang-Iverson and his colleagues at Oxford University Press. Special thanks to Karen Franck, whose detailed review of the manuscript guided my final revisions. Also thanks to those who reviewed or provided feedback on all or part of the manuscript, including Setha Low, Margaret Crawford, Robert Lockhart, Michael McGandy, and Marissa Walsh. Many of the ideas that would form the basis of the "undesigned and unplanned" were tested in dialogue with Brent Ryan. He was (and still is) a tireless advocate for this work. My longtime friend Brian Dworkin assisted me in field studies, along with Brandon Beck and Dan Wallenstein. My brother, Marc Campo, and friends Alton Robertson, Evan Salan, Shampa Chanda, and V. S. Mani also helped me through the fieldwork phase. Joanna Oliver edited and proofed earlier versions of this work.

At the University of Pennsylvania, I received excellent guidance from Seymour Mandelbaum, Eugenie Birch, and David De Long. Other Penn contributors include Christa Wilmanns-Wells, Paul Buck, and Raymond Gastil. (My exploration of the undesigned and unplanned began when I was a student in Ray's landscape architecture seminar on the urban waterfront.) At Morgan State University, I have been supported by my colleagues Mary Anne Akers, Siddhartha Sen, Joyce Pressley, and Sidney Wong and my research assistant, Megan Griffith. Salimah Hashim and Julie Alexander provided excellent administrative support.

In Brooklyn, my research was facilitated by current and former members of Neighbors Allied for Good Growth (NAG), including Julie Lawrence, Peter Gillespie, Michelle and Jim Rodecker, Ryan Kuonen, and Cathleen Breen. Also thanks to Chip Place of the New York State Office of Parks, Recreation and Historic Preservation; Erik Kulleseid at the Alliance for New York State Parks; Andy Stone and Christina Kelly at the Trust for Public Land; and Sasha Sumner, Thomas Flagg, Steve Rodriguez, Nevitt Steele III, Jen Colasuonno, Shige Moriya, Adam Louie, and Kathryn Madden. If I've missed anyone, the error is surely mine.

I benefited from the generous financial support of the National Endowment for the Humanities, which provided me with a faculty research award. (Special thanks to Jim Turner at the Endowment.) I also received funding from the Smart Family Foundation (and thanks in particular to Mary Smart). I received prior funding from a University of Pennsylvania fellowship and a grant from the Grosser Research Foundation. At Morgan State, I also benefited from a U.S. Department of Education Title III summer grant.

INDEX

communal life, residents of waterfront, 170–78

community gardens, 253

community use of sports fields, 205

community-based planning, 260–63

community's waterfront, 214–15

concert series, 228–36

contradictions in BEDT, 26

cooking, residents, 174–76

Crawford, Margaret, everyday space, 28

day labor, residents and, 165–70

Delaware Riverfront (Philadelphia), 255

derelict assessment by state, 212

designing: landscape urbanism, 251–52; public spaces, 27–29; vacant spaces and, 250–51

Diller-Scoffidio-Renfro, 251

diversity, 148–50

DIY (do-it-yourself) practices, 246–49

dogs: BEDT, 20–21; ERSP and, 224

Environmental Protection Fund, 1

Erasto (resident), 162; events bringing him to waterfront, 168

erosion: gribbles, 127; phragmites and, 152; shipworms, 127

ERSP (East River State Park): access decrease, 227; building foundations and, 225; Bushwick Inlet Park connection, 236; complaints, 224; constructed landscape compared to vernacular, 226; development problems, 4; dog ban, 224; erosion problems, 5; esplanade connection, 236; opening, 4, 223–24; planning problems, 29; playfulness loss, 226–27; playground, 224–25; site purchase, 5; sunset watching, 227; winter closing proposal, 227

esplanade completion, 219; connection to ERSP, 236

everyday space, 28. *See also* appropriated spaces; insurgent public spaces

fashion shoots, 107–8

ferry landing completion, 219

FGH Realty, 197–98

fire spinners, 19, 31, 68–69, 80; as agents of change, 86–87; area upkeep, 90–92; Burning Man Festival and, 81; community planning and, 93–96; demise, 96; Lunatarium, 96; members, 82–83; party performance, 87–88; police and, 89; safety, 85–86; shared space, 90–92; Slab use, 83–84; visitors, 83

fishing, Department of Health guidelines, 24

float bridge, 15

Franck, Karen, loose space, 28

freedom: loss with ERSP, 226–27; traditional parks and, 129–30; unpark and, 130–32; workyards and, 244–46

Fresh Kills Landfill, 188

Friends of BEDT park, 201–2; community's waterfront, 214–15; general public use, 206; informal use and, 213–14; in-holding parcel and, 205, 208–9; reclaiming land from erosion, 204–5

garbage. *See* solid waste plans

gardens, community, 253

The Gates (Christo and Jeanne-Claude), 110

George (resident), 161–62; cooking, 174–76; events bringing him to waterfront, 168; requests for money, 173–74

George (the locals), 135

Gillespic, Peter, 188–91

Giuliani, Rudolph: solid waste transfer point, 3; waterfront re-zoning, 27

governing, public spaces, 27–29

grafitti, 106

Grand Ferry Park. *See* Grand Street

Grand Street, 153–54; renovation, 155

greenery: phragmites, 152; replanting native species, 152; trees, 152

health status of residents, 172

HMB. *See* Hungry March Band

Holliday, Warren, 206–7

homeless persons, 159. *See also* residents of waterfront; the Hill, 160; Tompkins Square Park, 160

58; skateboarding Internet sites, 42–43; skateboarding magazines, 42–43; Slab cleanup, 33–34; *SLAP*, 58; social aspect, 42; street skating, 35–36; *Thrasher*, 41; *Transworld Skateboarding*, 42, 58; the Volcano, 34, 38–40

shared space: fire spinners, 90–92; Hungry March Band, 90–92

site cleanup, 17–18

skateboarding: self-risk sport, 57–8; as way of life, 54

skateparks, 31; Owl's Head, 49; sports fields plans and, 203–4

skatespots, 35–36

Slab, the: fire spinners, 83–84; performers, 67–68. *See also* Shantytown Skatepark

soccer field completion, 219

social ecology of waterfront, 254–55

social groups, 31

Socrates Sculpture Park, 110

solid waste plans: Fresh Kills Landfill, 188; Nekboh Recycling, 3, 188–90; transfer stations, 188–89; USA Waste Corporation, 192–93

Soylent Green references, 146–47

spatial conflict, 247–48

spinners. *See* fire spinners

Spiral Jetty, 126, 127

sports fields plans, 198–210

state parks, site cleanup, 17–18

Steven, Quentin, loose space, 28

street skating, 35–36; East Coast style, 49

successional landscape, invasive species, 24–25

sunset watching, 227

surface water absorption, opening plans and, 222–23

surprises, 16–18

Thrasher, 41, 42

tolerance, 148–50

transfer station problems, 188–89; Barretti Carting Corporation of Hoboken, 188–89; USA Waste Corporation, 192–93

Transworld Skateboarding, 42, 58

trees: ailanthus, 152; self-seeding in ERSP, 226

Trust for Public Land, 1–2

undesigned areas, 244–46; city policy argument, 248

undesigned practices, 28–29

unpark, 130–32; workyards and, 244–45

unplanned practices, 28–29; narratives overview, 30–31

Ür, 112–21

urban land reclamation, 251–52

urban nature, 22–26; contemporary, 252–53

urban waterfront as other space, 254–55

U.S. Olympic Committee, 156

USA Waste Corporation, 192–93; merger with Waste Management, Inc., 194–95

vacant spaces: design and, 250–1; marginality and, 249–50; traditions, 256

vandalism, reverse vandalism, 112–22

veterans, 148–49

Village Voice: 1337 Collective, 82; "Best Anarchist Parade Group," 70; "Best Vacant Lot," 26

Waste Management Inc., merger with USA Waste Corp., 194–95

waste reclamation, art installations, 123–29

waterfront residents. *See* residents of waterfront

weed trees, 152

Weyland, Jocko, 41–42

Williamsburg, residents' reactions, 2–3

Williamsburg Waterfront 197-a Plan, 196

Williamsburg Waterfront Park, 221

winter closing proposal, 227

winter for residents, 178–81

wooden balls art installation, 106–7

work status of residents, 165–70

workyards, 243

World Trade Center: attacks (*See* September 11 attacks); memorials, 109–10